EASTER WITNESS

From Broken Dream To A New Vision For Ireland

by
Michael D. Greaney
*with eye witness statement
by Patrick Caldwell of the Irish Volunteers,
Kimmage Garrison, 1916*

Economic Justice Media
Center for Economic and Social Justice
April 24, 2016

Center for Economic and Social Justice
Arlington, Virginia, U.S.A.
Economic Justice Media

Published by Economic Justice Media, an imprint of the
Center for Economic and Social Justice
P. O. Box 40711, Washington, D.C. 20016 U.S.A.
(Tel) 703-243-5155 • (Fax) 703-243-5935
(Eml) publications@cesj.org • (Web) www.cesj.org

© Center for Economic and Social Justice
   April 24, 2016

All rights reserved. No part of this edition may be reproduced, stored in a retrieval system, or transmitted, in any form, or by any means, electronic, mechanical, photocopying, recording or otherwise, without the prior written permission of the Center for Economic and Social Justice, except for brief excerpts for fair use and in reviews.

International Standard Book Number: 978-0-944997-12-3

Library of Congress Control Number: 2016905331

Cover design by Rowland L. Brohawn

Acknowledgements

The interfaith Center for Economic and Social Justice (CESJ) and the Ancient Order of Hibernians Colonel John Fitzgerald Division Number 1, Arlington, Virginia, U.S.A., would like to thank Mr. Peter Butler for a copy of the Statement By Witness of his father-in-law, Patrick Caldwell, from the archives of the Irish Bureau of Military History, which provided the inspiration for this project.

We would also like to thank Dr. Norman G. Kurland, president of CESJ and leading proponent of the Just Third Way, for his review of those portions of the manuscript dealing with economic and social justice, and Dawn K. Brohawn, CESJ's Director of Communications, for her overall review of the manuscript and input on Justice-Based Management.

The encouragement and guidance of Father Edward Krause, Jr., C.S.C., Ph.D., CESJ Counselor, former professor of social ethics at Gannon University in Erie, Pennsylvania, and now in residence at the University of Notre Dame du Lac in South Bend, Indiana, was invaluable, particularly in the understanding and application of the principles of Catholic social teaching.

A number of issues could not have been resolved without the cooperation of the staff at the Monsignor Field Archives and Special Collections Center, Walsh Library of Seton Hall University and their help in obtaining a copy of Archbishop Michael A. Corrigan's personal record of the Father Edward McGlynn case. Much of the material was corroborated by the Bishop Bernard McQuaid/Corrigan correspondence in the archives at the University of Notre Dame.

Special thanks are due to the volunteer staff of the Parish Office of the Church of Mary Immaculate Refuge of Sinners, Rathmines, and the Diocesan Archivist of the Archdiocese of Dublin, who supplied information on Father Francis O'Loughlin, Curate of the Rathmines Catholic Church during the Rising.

The Irish Bureau of Military History (Buro Staire Mileata) 1913-21 was especially valuable for the many first-hand accounts and newspaper articles in their archives, which clarified a number of otherwise obscure points and revealed previously undisclosed facts. Specific Statements By Witnesses cited are listed in the Bibliography.

Acronyms in Text

CESJ: Center for Economic and Social Justice

CLNRB: Citizens Land and Natural Resources Bank.

EDA: Economic Democracy Act.

ESOP: Employee Stock Ownership Plan.

GAA: Gaelic Athletic Association.

GPO: General Post Office in Dublin.

ICA: Irish Citizen Army (IGWTU militia).

IGWTU: Irish General Workers and Transport Union.

IRA: Irish Republican Army, often referred to as the "Old IRA."

IRB: Irish Republican Brotherhood.

IWFL: Irish Women's Franchise League.

POA: Personal Ownership Account

RIC: Royal Irish Constabulary.

UVF: Ulster Volunteer Force.

Note: For convenience, cites to Statements By Witnesses given to the Bureau of Military History (Buro Staire Mileata) 1913-21 in the 1940s and 1950s are in the format "(Name of Witness), W.S. (Number of Document), (Page Number)," *e.g.*, "Patrick Caldwell, W.S. 638, 25."

Table of Contents

Chapter 1: A Poets' Dream	1
Chapter 2: A Terrible Beauty	25
Chapter 3: From the Jaws of Victory	53
Chapter 4: Back to the Beginning	83
Chapter 5: Down by the Glenside	111
Chapter 6: The Irish Question	135
Chapter 7: Home Rule All Round	159
Chapter 8: Caldwell's Statement	191
Chapter 9: Ireland's Future, the Just Third Way	217
Bibliography	243
Index	253

IRISHMEN AND IRISHWOMEN

In the name of God and of the dead generations from which she receives her old tradition of nationhood, Ireland, through us, summons her children to her flag and strikes for her freedom. . . . We declare the right of the people of Ireland to the ownership of Ireland and to the unfettered control of Irish destinies, to be sovereign and indefeasible. . . . The Republic guarantees religious and civil liberty, equal rights and equal opportunities to all its citizens, and declares its resolve to pursue the happiness and prosperity of the whole nation and of all its parts, cherishing all of the children of the nation equally, . . . We place the cause of the Irish Republic under the protection of the Most High God, . . . In this supreme hour the Irish nation must, by its valour and discipline, and by the readiness of its children to sacrifice themselves for the common good, prove itself worthy of the august destiny to which it is called.

— Easter Proclamation, April 24, 1916

Chapter 1: A Poets' Dream

The Irish have a saying that other people would do well to remember: "Neither make nor break a tradition." This is wise, for custom and tradition are types of social habits or institutions, those "social tools" by means of which each human person — every child, woman, and man — develops in a manner consistent with a common vision for all, both as an individual and as a member of society within the framework of the common good. This is true whether we refer to the common good of the Family as the basic unit of society, a village, a city, a nation, or the whole of humanity.

Institutions, while distinct from the human person, are social tools created by people, for people, and have no independent existence. Institutions exist to recognize and protect fundamental religious and civil liberties, equal rights, and the equal opportunity of every member of society.

Any institution, up to and including the State, that does not maintain equality of opportunity for each person, or that goes contrary to human nature, must be reformed. Each human person must be able to control his or her own destiny through the exercise of inherent rights in a manner consistent with the natural law written in the heart of every human being, while at the same time respecting the right of all others to do the same.

Institutions cannot legitimately be imposed by force and maintained by coercion, especially for the benefit of others. Nor can change be imposed by some on members of an institution from the outside "for their own good."

The principle of subsidiarity — a key component of social justice — demands that change come from within an institution and be in conformity with human nature. Thus, institutions must develop naturally out of the wants and needs of each person in free association with others. When institutions no longer serve the needs of every person, people must organize and take action to correct the problem. . . .

Easter Monday 1916, About Noon
We are not ones to break tradition needlessly. That being the case, we begin our account of the Easter Rising (as is cus-

tomary) with the Irish Volunteers and the Irish Citizen Army (ICA) marching up what was then Sackville (now O'Connell) Street to the General Post Office (GPO) in Dublin around noon on Monday, April 24, 1916, occupying the building, and coming out to read the Proclamation that claimed to establish a provisional government for an Irish Republic.

Spectators, in keeping with the incomprehensible nature of the event, were amused, baffled, annoyed, exasperated, outraged, or simply ignored the whole thing. The damned "Shinners" (Sinn Féin) were out again, making more trouble, just as they had been doing for months . . . no, make that years past. As the playwright Seán O'Casey (who was an eyewitness) wrote in the third volume of his memoirs, *Drums Under the Windows* (1945), an old man muttered, "half to himself and half to an elderly, thin lady beside him," "What th' hell are th' up to now?"[1]

Nor was the old man being particularly obtuse in not realizing what we take for granted with a century of hindsight. Considering the level of chaos and confusion even among the leadership of the Volunteers (to say nothing of the rank and file) it's no wonder no one knew what was going on.

This was not a turning point in world history, the beginning of the end of the British Empire. No, this was just a gang of ruffians and blackguards disrupting things — *again* — probably in an effort to try and force parliament's hand to implement the recent, hard-won Home Rule bill despite the emergency of the war in Europe and the controversy over the bill in the United Kingdom. As O'Casey's old man said, "Somethin' brewin'? Ma'am, there's always somethin' brewin'. I'm seventy, an' I've never known an hour that I didn't hear tell of somethin' brewin'."[2]

The Situation

As far as anyone knew (and that wasn't very far), the occupation of the GPO appeared to be some kind of protest to demand "Home Rule" for Ireland. Home Rule was a vague term that meant pretty much what someone wanted it to mean. For some it meant full independence, for others au-

---

[1] Sean O'Casey, *Autobiography, Volume 3, Drums Under the Windows*. London: Pan Books, Ltd., 1972, 272.
[2] *Ibid.*

tonomy in local matters with everything else handled by the British Imperial Parliament in London. For still others, it meant the end of the British Empire.

In reality, the latest Home Rule Bill — the third since 1886 — was, all things considered, nothing to get excited about. Introduced by Prime Minister Herbert Henry Asquith (1852-1928) in 1912, the Government of Ireland Act, signed into law on September 17, 1914 (and immediately suspended for the duration of World War I), granted nothing substantive. The Irish parliament was to be reestablished after its abolition by the 1800 Act of Union, but it would be given no real power. The "Irish Question" — trying to figure out how Ireland related to the rest of the United Kingdom and the British Empire — remained unresolved.

Despite the fact that the latest Home Rule Act was essentially meaningless, there had been demonstrations, riots, and people arming on both sides of the issue since before the war began in Europe in July 1914. Some, the "Unionists," threatened a civil war if the Act was implemented, others, the "Nationalists," vowed to fight if it wasn't. Some demanded that the country be partitioned, others that it remain a single political entity.

Irish women had taken the lead in the protests, acting almost as soon as Asquith introduced the bill. The Irish Women's Franchise League staged a "military campaign" on Thursday, June 13, 1912, to protest the exclusion of women from the bill. Eight members of the IWFL carried out the campaign. These included Johanna Mary "Hanna" Sheehy-Skeffington (1877-1946), later an important political figure and the wife of Francis Joseph Christopher "Skeffy" Sheehy-Skeffington (1878-1916), "one of those great characters Ireland produces from time to time."[3] He was —

> . . . a man bulging with goodness but full of eccentricity and an understanding of human frailties. With voice and pen "Skeffy" fought for the underdog, any sort of underdog. In sympathy with Sinn Féin ideals, as he was with the suffragette movement — there were startling parallels between the

---

[3] Calton Younger, *Ireland's Civil War*. Glasgow, UK: William Collins & Sons, Ltd., 1979, 39.

two groups struggling for their respective freedoms — he was no believer in violence.[4]

Hanna and her sister suffragettes attacked the General Post Office, Custom House, the Police Barracks, and the Land Commission Office[5] with sticks and stones. They broke no bones, but shattered about fifty windows. They were arrested and sentenced to a month to six months in prison. They garnered little sympathy, even when they went on a hunger strike.

Ulster Volunteer Force

Some of those opposed to Home Rule for Ireland, especially in the northern province of Ulster, had been drilling and marching informally since 1912 out of fear that the bill might be enacted this time around. The House of Lords had blocked both the 1886 and 1893 bills, but a reform of parliament in 1911 made it impossible for the Lords to impose a permanent veto as they had done in the past. The 1912 bill, especially considering the fact that it really granted nothing, stood a good chance of passing.

In response, in January 1913 Sir Edward Henry Carson (1854-1935), later Baron Carson, a Unionist politician, organized the Ulster Volunteer Force (UVF). Nominally under the command of a retired Indian Army officer, General Sir George Richardson (1847-1931), the UVF was actually the private army of Carson, or (more accurately) that of Carson's aide, James Craig (1871-1940), First Viscount Craigavon. There is some doubt whether Carson was the leader of the inner circle, or its hostage.[6]

It seems incredible that the British government would permit the formation and continued existence of such a potentially hostile and numerically powerful force on British — or Irish — soil, particularly one that had publicly announced it was prepared to go to war with Great Britain if its de-

---

[4] *Ibid*.
[5] Most accounts add Dublin Castle, but the Castle was not mentioned in the report published in *Votes for Women*, a suffragette journal, on June 21, 1912, page 622.
[6] George Dangerfield, *The Damnable Question: A Study in Anglo-Irish Relations*. Boston, Massachusetts: Little, Brown and Co., 1976, 70.

mands were not met. Yet that is precisely what happened. As Calton Younger summarized the prevailing attitude in his book on the Irish Civil War of 1922-1923,

> Supporting [the UVF] was no less a person than Bonar Law, leader of the Conservative Party, who could "imagine no length of resistance to which Ulster will go in which I shall not be ready to support them", a minatory utterance which not only bespoke the ferocity of the Irish question engendered in the political arena of the day but postulated that treason was excusable if a view were strongly enough held. The lesson was noted by those who held strong views in the South, but when the leaders of the Easter Rising were tried, and Roger Casement prosecuted, the length of *their* resistance found few supporters at Westminster.[7]

A hundred thousand strong, the UVF recruited mostly from the Protestant Orange Lodges. The only organized counter to the Orange Lodges, the Ancient Order of Hibernians under the control of Joseph "Wee Joe" Devlin (1871-1934), the Catholic political boss of West Belfast, lacked the numbers and economic and political strength of the Orange associations.[8]

Making the situation even worse was the fact that the Unionists had already arranged to finance a provisional government of Ireland under Carson, once it had been established by force of arms if there was an attempt to implement Home Rule — in other words, the Unionists planned to establish Home Rule to prevent Home Rule. Beginning in March 1913, Alfred Milner, First Viscount Milner (1854-1925), solicited sizable contributions from wealthy sympathizers in London.

Irish Volunteers

On November 25, 1913, Eoin MacNeill (1867-1945), an important member of the Gaelic League founded in 1893 to promote the preservation of the native Irish language, decided there needed to be a Nationalist response to the UVF. During a mass meeting held at the Rotunda in Dublin, MacNeill proposed forming a volunteer organization "to secure

---

[7] Younger, *Ireland's Civil War, op. cit.*, 21.
[8] Dangerfield, *The Damnable Question, op. cit.*, 72.

and maintain the rights and liberties common to all the people of Ireland."

The Irish National Volunteers were established ("National" quickly dropped out of the name) and put under the nominal command of John Edward Redmond (1856-1918), Irish parliamentary leader and acknowledged head of the Home Rule movement. Redmond, who had devoted his entire political career to achieving Home Rule by peaceful means, had no prior knowledge of the meeting, nor of his embarrassing appointment as commander-in-chief.

MacNeill himself was unaware that in forming the Volunteers he had been manipulated to some extent by the Irish Republican Brotherhood (IRB),[9] an organization that skirted the Catholic Church's prohibition against membership in "secret societies." The IRB was organized in "Circles." The head of a Circle was called the "Center."

Behind the IRB was the old Fenian, Thomas Clarke (1858-1916), alias "Henry Wilson." Clarke had revived the IRB on his return from America, where he had been living after serving fifteen and a half years in English prisons for an attempt in 1883 to blow up London Bridge.

Clarke reorganized the IRB, having been sent back to Ireland from America by John Devoy (1842-1928), John Daly (1845-1916), and Clan na Gael for that purpose. Devoy was one of the few people to play a leading role in the Fenian Uprising of 1867, the Easter Rising, and the War of Independence. Daly was a Fenian living in exile in New York, the uncle of Clarke's wife, Kathleen Daly Clarke (1878-1972). Clan na Gael was an Irish republican organization in the United States. It survives today, although much fragmented.

The Dublin Strike and Lockout

The Home Rule issue also got entangled in the labor movement. The Marxist-socialist labor leader James Connol-

---

[9] "I had a very shrewd idea that there was some body of the kind behind the origin of the Volunteers; I subsequently found out that nearly all the officers of the Volunteer[s] were already members of the I.R.B. before they were elected officers." Judge Fionan Lynch, W.S. 192, 4.

ly[10] (1868-1916), especially, was convinced that only in an Ireland free of British imperialism could the Irish workers and farmers ever become part of a truly free people.

The demand that Irish industry, agriculture, and commerce be run for the (collective) benefit of the Irish people led to the great Dublin strike and lockout of August 26, 1913 to January 18, 1914. This was the most serious labor dispute in the history of Ireland, involving approximately 20,000 workers and three hundred companies.

Connolly and James Larkin (1876-1947), founders of the socialist Irish Transport and General Workers' Union (ITGWU), organized the strike. Two hundred or so policemen were injured, while hundreds of strikers were injured and two were killed. In the end, neither the capitalists nor the union got everything they wanted, so (naturally), both claimed victory.

In response, Connolly and Larkin organized the Irish Citizen Army (ICA). The ICA had the goals of an independent, socialist Ireland, destruction of the capitalist system, and protection of the people and the workers from the brutality of the British Army, the police, the bosses, and the capitalists.

The war in Europe had not forced the ITGWU to abandon its goals or its tactics. At first, Liberty Hall in Dublin (the headquarters of the ITGWU) had displayed a large banner reading, WE SERVE NEITHER KING NOR KAISER, BUT IRELAND! British authorities removed the banner on December 19, 1914,[11] but not before photographs could be taken and circulated. From October 27, 1915 to on or about April 15, 1916, the very eve of the Rising, Connolly carried on a strike in support of forty casual laborers demanding a sixpence increase in their daily wage[12] — about eleven cents in 1916.[13]

Curragh: The Turning Point

Some important factors contributed to the confusing situation and increased the tension between Unionists and Na-

---

[10] The Irish Times' *Sinn Féin Rebellion Handbook*, Dublin, Éire: The Irish Times, Ltd., 1917, 262, gives Thomas as Connolly's middle name.
[11] Dangerfield, *The Damnable Question: op. cit.*, 153.
[12] *Ibid.*, 154.
[13] In 1916, £1 = $4.77.

tionalists. First, the numbers enrolled in the UVF were impressive. These were, however, matched by those signing up under the Nationalist banner.

There was also the threat of armed force. The UVF had been importing arms and ammunition in quantity since early 1913. This was technically legal, albeit difficult, since the lapse of the Peace Preservation Act of 1814 of Sir Robert Peel (1788-1850), which had eventually led to the establishment the Royal Irish Constabulary. In December 1913, however, Asquith re-imposed the arms embargo by Royal Proclamation.[14]

At first the gunrunning by Unionist forces was carried out in semi-secrecy. Retired British senior officers, however, were openly sympathetic. Even King George V, with his unquestioned affection for Ireland, pressured the Prime Minister to exclude Ulster from the Home Rule bill in order to prevent a civil war from breaking out in Ireland. As the king said, "The government is drifting and taking me with it," and complained constantly that his own ministers were not keeping him informed of the situation.

What really put the UVF into a position of power, however, was the miscalled "Curragh Mutiny." This was not a mutiny at all, but another symptom of the confused state of affairs. As Sir Francis Fletcher Vane (1861-1934) described the situation in his autobiography, *Agin the Governments* (1929),

> It must be borne in mind that the Irish National Volunteers had only come into being after the enrolment of the Ulster Volunteers, whose object — good or bad — was definitely to oppose the Act of Parliament which had given self-government to Ireland. These Volunteers had come to the Colours in fact — as all things are somewhat topsy-turvy in Ireland, to defend an Act passed by the British Legislature, against their Northern brethren, who were out to oppose it by force.[15]

In March 1914, Carson and other Unionists in the government were on the verge of being arrested for their plans to oppose Home Rule and set up a provisional government; a

---

[14] Dangerfield, *The Damnable Question, op. cit.*, 83.
[15] Sir Francis Fletcher Vane, Bt., *Agin the Governments*. London: Sampson Low, Marston & Co., Ltd. (1929), 251-251.

"motion of censure" was scheduled for March 19. The authorities expected to issue bench warrants within a few hours.

Carson got out of London and went to Craigavon, the UDF's fortified headquarters in County Armagh, a few hours ahead of the police, as he believed. He wrote to Andrew Bonar Law (1858-1923) in terms suggesting that he had found the threat of rebellion and the establishment of a provisional government more useful than the fact.[16]

At this point, the British military Commander-in-Chief in Ireland, Sir Arthur Henry Fitzroy Paget (1851-1928), in a confused and confusing declaration, demanded the resignation of any officer who was not willing to act against the UVF if it went into rebellion. Paget, of course, was fully aware that many of his senior officers were in sympathy with the Unionists, as the anti-Home Rule faction was called, if not Unionists themselves. He evidently believed, however, that putting things on the line would remind them of their sworn oaths as King's Officers, and where their duty and loyalty lay.

The effort backfired. Nearly sixty of Paget's officer corps, including Brigadier General Sir Hubert de la Poer Gough (1870-1963), tendered their resignations. British officialdom decided that turning a blind eye to Unionist threats was the best way to maintain order — and incidentally cut the ground out from under the Nationalists and other supporters of Home Rule.

What even Carson believed by this time to be empty and possibly treasonous threats had worked. He was once again a power in the land. There would be no Home Rule for Ireland that included Ulster.

Consequently, when the UVF openly unloaded a massive illegal arms and munitions shipment from Germany at Larne Harbor, County Antrim, on April 24, 1914, the police stood by and watched, taking no action then or afterwards. Instead, even the UVF members reported that the police acted like "benevolent spectators," and were possibly amused instead of outraged or worried at such open flouting of the law

---

[16] Dangerfield, *The Damnable Question, op. cit.*, 89.

and threats to the King's Peace. The UVF suffered one casualty: a messenger who died of heart failure.[17]

Gunrunning

In response, the Volunteers, too, began importing arms and ammunition. Lacking the financial, political, military, and even royal support (however reluctant) accorded the UVF, this was in much smaller quantities and of lower quality.

This deficiency was remedied in part when a committee in London, chaired by Mrs. Alice Stopford Green (1847-1929), purchased a consignment of weapons and ammunition in Germany for the Volunteers. The shipment was transferred off the coast of Belgium from the German tug *Gladiator* out of Hamburg to two private yachts, the *Asgard*, belonging to soldier-statesman-novelist Robert Erskine Childers (1870-1922), and the *Kelpie*, belonging to Edward Conor Marshall O'Brien (1880-1952). The *Kelpie's* cargo was transshipped again off the coast of Wales to the schooner *Chotah*, belonging to a prominent surgeon, Sir Thomas Myles (1857-1937). Mary Alden Osgood Childers (1875-1964) — Childers's American wife — and Mary Ellen Spring Rice (1880-1924), daughter of Thomas Spring Rice, Second Baron Mounteagle of Brandon, crewed the *Asgard*.

The *Asgard* and the *Chotah* unloaded their cargoes at Howth, County Dublin, and Kilcoole, County Wicklow, respectively, on Sunday, July 26, 1914. This was not something British officialdom could tolerate. Police and British soldiers, "the King's Own Scottish Borderers," attempted to stop the Volunteers and confiscate the newly acquired weapons as they marched away, rifles shouldered . . . unloaded, as the unusable ammunition supplied was not issued. Only the day before the UVF had paraded openly with their arms in Belfast while the police and the military looked the other way.

The police and military were largely unsuccessful in the endeavor, and the police quickly and prudently departed. The Scottish Borderers ended up marching back to their barracks after capturing only nineteen of the nine hundred rifles landed at Howth, and none of the six hundred landed at Kilcoole. Unfortunately, a large crowd decided to follow them,

---

[17] *Ibid.*, 121.

loudly mocking them for their ineptitude and the obvious double standard being employed by the government.

Some people in the crowd decided that catcalls and insults were insufficient and, as the soldiers marched along Bachelor's Walk, a street and quay in Dublin on the north side of the Liffy, began throwing rocks. Unable to tolerate the heckling and being pelted with stones, the soldiers began firing into the crowd. They killed four people (three on the spot, one dying later of wounds) and wounded thirty-seven. Francis Sheehy-Skeffington called this "the Irish Zabern" (Saverne),[18] after the 1913 incident in Alsace-Lorraine in which Prussian troops attacked a group of civilians, one of whom a German officer sabered for laughing at him.

The Outcome of the Mutiny

The Curragh Mutiny may thus, in a sense, be regarded as a turning point in history, the bend in the road of destiny that led to the Rising. Had Asquith's government not given in, Carson's arrest and the official censure of the other Unionist leaders was a foregone conclusion — a blow from which the Unionist cause would not have recovered in time to prevent Home Rule being implemented on schedule and without partition.

After Curragh, no one in Ireland believed that Home Rule could be implemented without partition. A significant number were convinced that Home Rule would not be implemented at all; it was another British trick. It also taught both Unionists and Nationalists that threats of armed violence were effective.

Curragh, with its clear message that the British government could be blackmailed, dealt a fatal blow to Redmond's legislative strategy. At the same time, it confirmed many in their opinion that violence and threats were all the British understood.[19]

In September 1914, after King George V signed Home Rule into law, 218,206 men and 228,991 women (or so it was

---

[18] Francis Sheehy-Skeffington, *A Forgotten Small Nationality: Ireland and the War*. New York: The Donnelly Press (1916), 8.
[19] *E.g.*, "[A]ll attempts at peace or compromise between Ireland and England were rendered impossible." George F.H. (Fitz-Hardinge) Berkeley, W.S. 971, 1.

claimed) in Ulster, and even more in England, signed a pledge called the "Sacramentum." This was a somewhat sanitized version of the old Scottish Covenant ("The Solemn League and Covenant") of 1643, when the Scots rebelled against the English because they feared the imposition of the Established Church of England. Even though the Sacramentum really didn't commit anyone to anything, many signed on their knees, some in their own blood.[20]

In a typical Irish paradox, Nationalist suffragettes in the south who supported Home Rule criticized northern Unionist suffragettes who opposed Home Rule. This was not because the northerners were against Home Rule, however. Rather, it was because they signed a special woman's pledge against Home Rule instead of demanding the equal right to sign that of the men.

It was no longer a question whether armed rebellion was a viable option. It was now the only option. The only questions were when and where.

Irish Volunteers and the War in Europe

Nevertheless, the authorities were far from worried in April 1916. The most powerful (and best-armed) potential troublemakers, the UVF, had been removed from the scene. With the outbreak of war with Germany, the UVF patriotically formed their own unit, the 36th Ulster Division, and went to France under their own officers and with their own regimental insignia and banners.

Exhibiting the sort of churlish tactlessness that has given certain types of English men and women a reputation for boorish stupidity, however, Field Marshal Horatio Herbert Kitchener (1850-1916), First Earl Kitchener, refused to grant the same honor to the Irish Volunteers, even though he badly wanted and needed the manpower. He also rejected Redmond's offer of the Volunteers as a Home Guard for Ireland to free British troops on garrison duty in the country for service on the continent.[21]

Even Redmond's impassioned speech on August 16, 1914, urging Irish men to enlist for King and country, failed to

---

[20] Dangerfield, *The Damnable Question, op. cit.*, 76.
[21] Cf. Vane, *Agin the Governments, op. cit.*, 252-253.

wring any concessions from the government — or many recruits for the British army. Redmond's actions, however, did divide the Volunteers. As Fionán Lynch (1889-1966), a good friend of Seán MacDermot (1883-1916), a member of the IRB's inner circle, recalled,

> The outbreak of the European War in August 1914, and the pro-recruiting attitude of Mr. Redmond and his Party made it inevitable that the nominees of that Party could not be retained in the Executive, and the split in the Volunteers duly followed.[22]

Approximately 13,000 of the 180,000 Volunteers seceded and kept the name "Irish Volunteers." The balance dropped "Irish" and added back "National," becoming the "National Volunteers."

Still, despite being openly snubbed by the British, the reorganized Irish Volunteers caused little anxiety. With MacNeill, a noted scholar, at their head, the authorities seemed to consider them almost respectable. MacNeill had already declared that he would resort to violence only if conscription were introduced into Ireland, or to oppose any other action he considered contrary to the interests of the Irish people.

Added to this was the fact that only one of the four key men in the British government of Ireland had any glimmering of what was going on: Ivor Churchill Guest, First Viscount Wimborne (1873-1939), Lord Lieutenant or Viceroy of Ireland, who had no effective power. The others were Augustine Birrell (1850-1933), Chief Secretary for Ireland in the Cabinet, Sir Matthew Nathan (1862-1939), Under-Secretary for Ireland, and Major-General Sir Lovick Bransby Friend (1856-1944),[23] General Officer Commanding the British Army in Ireland. Wimborne had argued with Nathan on Easter Sunday until midnight that something was about to happen, and ringleaders should be rounded up.

---

[22] Fionan Lynch, W.S. 192, 5.
[23] Charles Duff, on page 83 of *Six Days to Shake an Empire*, New York: A.S. Barnes and Co., Inc., 1966, referred to "Major-General Field, General Officer Commanding the British Army in Ireland," an individual who never existed; Duff evidently wrote "Field" instead of "Friend." Others, relying on Duff's account, have continued the error.

Nathan, a very efficient administrator with an ideal bureaucratic mind whose strengths complemented the easygoing and well-liked Birrell's policy of appeasement, put Wimborne off until he finally gave up.[24] Friend probably assumed that the British troops in the country, combined with the paramilitary RIC, could handle any eventuality with ease.

Consequently, the British all but ignored the marching and drilling by the Volunteers that took place throughout Ireland in 1915 and the first quarter of 1916. Any action taken was the result of Volunteers coming into conflict with the general population, who were far from friendly, given all the nonsense and disruption of daily life on top of everything else.

Volunteers were frequently being hauled before a magistrate not for any treasonable offense, but because they had gotten into fights with the locals, rarely getting the better of it. The Irish people themselves seemed to have matters well in hand, suppressing rebellion and disorder on their own. There was no need for the authorities to be wary of any potential danger from that quarter.

As late as March 20, 1916, for example, a bare month before the Rising, Volunteers in Tullamore, County Offaly, ran afoul of the Gaelic Athletic Association (GAA). Wives of servicemen were celebrating the return of their husbands from the Front, waving Union Jacks. Volunteers protested — and barely managed to make it to the Volunteer hall ahead of an angry mob shouting "Down with the Sinn Féiners!" Two police officers were wounded when they tried to force their way in. A number of Volunteers were arrested, and one, William (Liam) Joseph Mellows (1892-1922), was deported to Staffordshire.

Even a rehearsal for the storming of Dublin Castle, carried out in broad daylight by Connolly's Irish Citizen Army, failed to alarm the authorities. It did, however, get the attention of the Supreme Council of the IRB, which had already set the date for its own rebellion. Connolly was "kidnapped" — or not; it's not clear exactly what happened[25] — and persuaded

---

[24] Duff, *Six Days to Shake an Empire, op. cit.*, 82-83.
[25] Dangerfield, *The Damnable Question, op. cit.*, 155.

to coordinate the ICA rising with that of the Volunteers in a joint effort.[26]

Secret Revolutionary Organization

MacNeill, however, was not aware that he was not really in command of the Volunteers — nor was Redmond. In 1914, the majority of the Irish Volunteers had been solidly behind Redmond's constitutional strategy. By 1916, with king, parliament, and even Carson advocating partition, Redmond "was a lonely, disappointed, failing man."[27] Home Rule by constitutional means, even with a statute on the books, seemed a fading dream.

Effective control of the reorganized Irish Volunteers was in the hands of Pádraic (Patrick) Henry Pearse (1879-1916). Pearse, along with MacNeill a member of the Gaelic League, was a scholar and poet who also held a high position in the Irish Republican Brotherhood, the "secret revolutionary organization" that had engineered the formation of the Volunteers in the first place. As Younger described the situation,

> MacNeill had no idea that his word was not law in the Volunteer movement. Through its organization of circles within circles, the local circles contained within district circles, and the district within county, each with its own centre, the influence of the I.R.B. permeated the whole Volunteer structure. So the real power was in the hands of Pearse but, because it was a hidden power, the command of MacNeill also carried force.[28]

When the Irish Volunteers split off from the main body that then became the National Volunteers, Pearse was put in Redmond's former position. Unlike Redmond, however, Pearse took an active role in the Volunteers.

This split the leadership of the Volunteers, although most of the rank and file had no notion that there was any conflict of interest or divided command. On the one hand was MacNeill, a moderate whom Connolly called "anti-labor" due to his opposition to socialism — at least Connolly's Marxist va-

---

[26] Senator Séamus O'Farrell, W.S. 193, 2-3. O'Farrell put "kidnapping" in quotes in his statement.
[27] Seamus MacManus, *The Story of the Irish Race: A Popular History of Ireland*. Old Greenwich, Connecticut: Devin-Adair, 1921, 694.
[28] Younger, *Ireland's Civil War, op. cit.*, 28.

riety of it. MacNeill favored achieving Home Rule by peaceful, constitutional means, albeit backed up with a show of force, if necessary.

On the other was Pearse, a Fabian-style socialist, although it is not clear to what extent (if any) he accepted the more esoteric theories of Fabianism based on Madame Blavatsky's theosophy and New Age thought. He was acquainted with the poet and novelist James Stephens (1880-1950), a fellow socialist and republican who dabbled in theosophy.[29]

Pearse had initially favored the 1912 Home Rule bill enacted in 1914, but had become convinced that the government of Great Britain had no intention of ever allowing it to be put into effect. It would instead be postponed indefinitely on the grounds of one excuse or another, until allowed to die of natural causes.

Complicating matters further was Connolly, a Marxist who "worked at all times to bring about that violent revolt against the Capitalist system from which the new order was expected to rise."[30] His Irish Citizen Army could not be ignored. Despite its tiny size, the ICA had to be considered in making any plans, especially since it was known that Connolly was planning a rising of his own.

If any one man could be considered the "Father of the Easter Rising," however, that man would be Tom Clarke. In consideration of this, his name was first on the Easter Proclamation, and he was among the first to be executed by the British firing squads. As Younger described him,

> Clarke, prematurely old after fifteen[31] years' imprisonment in England and with his steel spectacles and soup strainer moustache, hadn't the mien of a revolutionary, but there was an unquenchable fire within him, and he saw in Pearse a smouldering power which marked him out for leadership.[32]

---

[29] "I read for some time in Madame Blavatsky's 'Secret Doctrine,' which book interests me profoundly." James Stephens, *The Insurrection in Dublin* (1916), Chapter I: Monday.
[30] MacManus, *The Story of the Irish Race, op. cit.*, 696.
[31] Fifteen and a half years; most sources round to fourteen, fifteen, or sixteen years.
[32] Younger, *Ireland's Civil War, op. cit.*, 27.

Clarke held meetings of the revived IRB in his small tobacconist's shop on Parnell Street in Dublin, where the Rising was first proposed and the initial planning carried out. Identifying Pearse as a kindred spirit, Clarke inducted him into the IRB in 1913.

We can probably safely assume that Clarke, arrested and sentenced to penal servitude for life for his part in the dynamite campaign of 1883, was instrumental in convincing Pearse that Redmond's and (later) MacNeill's reliance on constitutional methods was futile. Only by violence could the British government ever be brought to keep its word to Ireland — an opinion that Carson, the UVF, and their sympathizers in the British government and military had done their very best to foster.

In January 1916, becoming concerned about the union leader's plans, the Supreme Council of the IRB allegedly carried out its "kidnapping," bringing Connolly to meet with Pearse, Joseph Mary Plunkett (1887-1916), and Thomas MacDonagh (1878-1916). Connolly agreed to combine the ICA with the Volunteers and join in a coordinated attack on Easter Sunday, April 23, 1916. This seemed to bring things together and ensure a united front and effective action that had the optimal chance of success.

Plans Go Wrong

What the main conspirators failed to take into consideration, however, was that having so many different groups and individuals involved in planning and carrying out a coordinated operation is extraordinarily difficult in the best of circumstances — and these were not the best of circumstances. The goals of each were similar, but not the same.

What each one thought to gain by "Home Rule," for example, did not necessarily match what any of the others wanted, nor could even the socialists agree on what kind of socialism they intended to establish. Would it be Pearse's moderate and presumably more beneficent Fabian-style socialism (albeit purged of its anti-Christian elements), or would it be Connolly's oxymoronic Christian-Marxism?

And these were far from being the only problems.

As the day set for the Rising drew near, things started to fall apart. Of most immediate concern was procurement of an adequate supply of arms and ammunition. This had turned into a tragi-comedy of errors.

In October 1914, Sir Roger David Casement (1864-1916), a retired British diplomat who had adopted Ireland's cause as his own, had managed to make his way to Germany. His goals were to secure Germany's support in the form of trained officers and troops for an Irish uprising, recruit men for an Irish Brigade to fight in Ireland from among the British prisoners of war held by the Germans, and obtain sufficient arms and ammunition to ensure the success of the effort.

As Younger remarked, however, "Casement, it seems, was not taken very seriously."[33] This was fortunate for Germany, for British Intelligence intercepted and decoded nearly all the cables sent by Casement through the German Embassy in the United States.

The IRB didn't seem to take Casement seriously either, possibly considering him an unreliable dilettante. They sent two other agents to Germany to negotiate, Joseph Plunkett and Robert Monteith (1880-1956), bypassing Casement altogether, although Plunkett kept on very good terms with him.

When Monteith arranged for a cargo of 20,000 obsolete Russian-made rifles for the Volunteers, scheduled to arrive shortly before Easter to minimize the chance that the authorities would be alerted, Casement decided enough was enough. Discouraged and convinced that the arms were worthless, he decided the Rising was hopeless and had to be called off. On April 12, 1916, three days after the arms shipment left Germany on the *Libau*, disguised as an actual Norwegian timber carrier, the *Aud*,[34] Casement began making his way back to Ireland.

---

[33] *Ibid.*, 32.
[34] Hereinafter this vessel will be referred to simply as the *Aud*. It was built in 1907 for the English Wilson Line and christened the *Castro*. Trapped in the Kiel Canal in Schleswig-Holstein, the northernmost province of Germany, at the outbreak of the war, it was captured by the Imperial German Navy and rechristened the *Libau*. The German captain at one point asked, in semi-jest, what he should do if the false *Aud* met the real *Aud* on the high seas.

The Rising was already off track. The Supreme Council of the IRB had changed the date when they wanted the arms delivered. The original plan had been to land the cargo at Fenit Island in the Bay of Tralee in the County Kerry the night of April 20. This would allow sufficient time to distribute the rifles and ammunition to the Volunteer unit in Cork and others throughout the country so that a coordinated effort could be made on Easter.

This was changed to the evening of April 23, Easter Sunday, the date set for the rising in Dublin, with the distribution of the arms and munitions evidently to be carried out that night. As George Dangerfield explained in his book, *The Damnable Question*, "Having decided to begin the Rising on Easter Sunday, the [Supreme] Council [of the IRB] did not wish a premature landing of arms to put the authorities on guard."[35]

In any event, the *Aud* did not have a radio, and the convoluted system arranged for getting messages to and from Germany ensured that word of the change in plans reached Germany on April 18, six days after the *Aud* had sailed. When the *Aud* arrived in Tralee Bay on the evening of April 20, there was no one there to receive the cargo. Captain Karl Spindler (1887-1951), in command of the vessel, waited twelve hours, and then prepared to return to Germany.[36]

The British Navy captured the *Aud* almost immediately, and escorted the ship to Queenstown (now Cobh) in County Cork. Spindler scuttled the *Aud* on April 22 to prevent the British from seizing the cargo.

Ironically, apart from Dublin, Cork was supposed to be the focus of the Rising. Two future Lord Mayors of Cork, Tomás MacCurtain (1884-1920) and Terence MacSwiney (1879-1920), were in command of the local Volunteers. MacCurtain

---

[35] Dangerfield, *The Damnable Question, op. cit.*, 170.
[36] George Renwick, "German Describes Effort to Arm Irish," *The New York Times*, January 2, 1921, 3. Dangerfield noted that Spindler's account, published in German as *Das Geheimnisvolle Schiff* ("The Mysterious Ship"), (1920) and in English as *The Mystery of the Casement Ship* (1931) may be somewhat fictionalized, *e.g.*, Spindler claimed that he unsuccessfully tried to "befuddle" the British sailors who sailed the *Aud* to Cork as a prize crew with "expensive scotch." Dangerfield, *The Damnable Question, op. cit.*, 168.

was elected Lord Mayor in January 1920, and served until the Royal Irish Constabulary (RIC) assassinated him on March 20 of that year. MacSwiney was then elected and served until his arrest for possession of seditious documents in August. Sentenced to two years in Brixton Prison, London, he died following a hunger strike.

Meanwhile, Casement was having problems of his own. The U-Boat that was transporting him and his two companions, Monteith and Daniel Bailey, to Ireland broke down, and they had to transfer to another. Within a few hours after being put ashore in Tralee Bay early in the morning of April 21 — evidently just missing the *Aud* — Casement was captured by the RIC, the RIC having been alerted by finding the dinghy in which he and the others had come ashore.

Casement got a message to his contact, Austin Stack (1879-1929), who commanded the local Volunteer detachment. Possibly because Casement's landing was unexpected and he needed to verify it, Stack delayed taking action. He was himself arrested when he went to the RIC Barracks in Tralee to make "discreet inquiries."[37] Inexperienced and with their leader captured, the Kerry Volunteers were probably uncertain what they should do. They failed to make any attempt to rescue Casement, although he was lightly guarded. There may also have been orders circulated that nothing was to be done to alert the authorities before Easter Sunday.[38]

Monteith, who was supposed to command the Irish Brigade that Casement was supposed to raise among Irish POWs held by the Germans, escaped and made his way to the United States. Bailey was captured, but turned informer. Reporting on Casement's arrest, the headline in London's *Daily Express* of Tuesday, April 25, blared about the three-man landing, "Invasion of Ireland: Notorious Traitor Captured."

Command, Countermand, and Confusion

Not that things had gone smoothly elsewhere. Rumors had circulated through the country that something was in the air, and the authorities might round up Sinn Féin and Volunteer

---

[37] Younger, *Ireland's Civil War, op. cit.*, 33.
[38] Peter de Rosa, *Rebels: The Irish Rising of 1916*. New York: Fawcett Columbine, 1990, 194.

leaders. The question was raised whether the Rising should take place as planned.

MacNeill, ostensibly in command of the Volunteers, was not even aware what was in the offing, but his views had to be considered as if he were: as nominal commander he retained the loyalty of the rank and file. With Carson's UVF fighting in France and there being no direct threat from that quarter, MacNeill remained adamantly opposed to the use of violence, except in response to conscription or other danger to Ireland.

It's not entirely clear how many people voted, or who they all were, but reportedly Seán MacDermott, Thomas MacDonagh, and — of course — Tom Clarke were committed to the Rising, come what may. Connolly declared he and the ICA would attack before they could be disarmed. Reportedly, Joseph Plunkett, Éamonn Ceannt (1881-1916), and — surprisingly — Pádraic Pearse counseled moderation.

The leaders were allegedly evenly divided on whether to follow through on the Rising. Pearse then changed sides, evidently persuaded by Connolly and his own rhetoric about the need for sacrifice. The Rising would go forward as planned.

Carefully worded advertisements were placed in newspapers throughout the country with veiled references to parades and marches scheduled for Easter Sunday. Rory O'Connor[39] (1883-1922) — most sources say Plunkett[40] — forged a detailed plan, "the Castle Document," purporting to authorize the incarceration of key members of Sinn Féin and the Volunteers. When circulated, this not only aroused the indignation of the Volunteers, it persuaded MacNeill that violence was their only recourse, and he came out in favor of the Rising.

Patrick John "P.J." Little (1884-1963), the recently appointed editor of *New Ireland*, printed the document, evidently unaware it was a forgery. He seemed to be under the impression that making it public would somehow avoid the round up of Volunteer leaders without recourse to violence. As he related,

---

[39] Patrick J. Little, W.S., 1,769, 10.
[40] Younger, *Ireland's Civil War, op. cit.*, 32. O'Connor may have been acting under Plunkett's orders.

There was an episode I forgot to mention that took place early in Holy Week, 1916, either Monday or Tuesday. Eoin McNeill, I heard, had changed his mind about our publishing the document. Rory O'Connor, Skeffington, Seamus O'Kelly and myself took the text out to Woodtown where McNeill lived, and we persuaded him again that it was proper to publish it. He consented. When we came back, I dropped Skeffington at the top of Terenure Road, and I said to him, "Well, I hope that this thing will work out all right and that there isn't any attack on the Volunteers!" Skeffington said, "Please God, it will!" That was the last time I saw him. He was dead within a week, shot owing to his effort to stop looting.[41]

MacNeill, however, soon learned of the deception. Outraged, he countermanded the mobilization order. To avert any action in Cork city, he also sent a trusted lieutenant, Jeremiah Joseph "J.J." "Ginger" O'Connell (1887-1944), to take over command of the Cork Volunteers from MacCurtain and MacSwiney.

Pearse then took MacNeill into his confidence and informed him of the expected arms shipment on the *Aud*. In light of this, MacNeill acquiesced in the Rising, but resigned from the Volunteers. He turned command over to Pearse, who sent out new orders that the Rising was to take place as scheduled.

Early in the morning of Saturday, April 22, however, MacNeill learned the fate of the *Aud*. Despite the fact that he had resigned from the Volunteers, he sent out another batch of couriers with orders cancelling all Volunteer activity for Easter Sunday. His handwritten missive was brief and to the point: "Volunteers completely deceived. All orders for tomorrow Sunday are entirely cancelled." He also inserted an advertisement in the newspapers:

> Owing to the very critical position, all orders given to Irish Volunteers for to-morrow, Easter Sunday, are hereby rescinded, and no parades, marches, or other movements of Irish Volunteers will take place. Each individual Volunteer will obey this order in every particular.

Pearse immediately sent new orders that the Rising was to take place as originally planned, except that, due to the con-

---

[41] Little, W.S., 1,769, 13.

fusion caused by the flurry of contradictory orders and MacNeill's advertisement, it would take place on Easter Monday, April 24, instead of Easter Sunday.

The damage, however, had been done. The order for the Rising had been issued three times and countermanded twice. Most of the Volunteers had no idea what they were supposed to do, and so did nothing. As O'Casey's old man said, "Mac Neill put a stop to their gallop!"

The Cork Volunteers, however, had only received two sets of orders to proceed as planned, and one countermand. While wondering why there appeared to be no countermand in light of the loss of the *Aud* — the cargo had been intended primarily for them — they assembled according to plan. Just as they were about to mount their assault on key points in the city, however, MacNeill's second countermand arrived.

MacSwiney and MacCurtain decided to hold maneuvers instead of attacking, and then dismiss the men in the evening. A heavy downpour ended the march early, and MacSwiney and MacCurtain were still in the countryside when Pearse's final order for the Rising, now to take place on Monday, was delivered in Cork city on Sunday. Knowing nothing of this, the Cork Volunteers stayed home on Monday, for which some of those who had turned out in Dublin later (and very unfairly) accused them of not doing their part.

Instead of 10,000 Volunteers rising throughout the country, then, approximately eight hundred Volunteers and one hundred and fifty members of the ICA turned out Monday morning,[42] and around noon took up their assigned positions throughout Dublin. By the end of the week, with men coming in from the surrounding countryside, these numbers would swell to between 1,200 and 1,600.

The flags of the Irish Republic, one a bannerette of green, with the words IRISH REPUBLIC emblazoned in white letters, and the other the orange, white, and green Tricolor, were raised over the General Post Office. The battle for the future of Ireland and of the British Empire had begun.

---

[42] Dangerfield noted that documents rediscovered in 1927 after being hidden during the Rising listed one hundred and fifty-two ICA members definitely turned out, with seven "probable." *The Damnable Question, op. cit.*, 188.

Chapter 2: A Terrible Beauty

An "Irish bull" is a ludicrous or logically absurd statement that, nevertheless, vividly conveys an obvious truth. John Pentland Mahaffy (1839-1919), Provost of Trinity College in Dublin, explained it by saying, "An Irish bull is always pregnant." As one example, if the Easter Rising hadn't failed, it wouldn't have succeeded.

A well-planned and efficiently executed military campaign in which the combatants on each side have a fighting chance, even if it does not achieve its end, is one thing. A hopeless stand or charge against impossible odds on a matter of principle or in defense of others is quite another.

Thus, Gallipoli and Passchendaele in the First World War are remembered as instances of military incompetence, even though they seemed feasible and sufficient resources were committed to ensure victory. At the same time, the Three Hundred at Thermopylae, the Siege of Szegetvár, the Alamo, the Charge of the Light Brigade — the last-named the result of criminal stupidity — and countless other last stands or attempts that had no chance whatsoever of success are enshrined as examples of heroism and glorious self-sacrifice in pursuit of a greater good.

The Paradox of 1916

The objective good or evil of such things is not our concern here. We are only concerned with the facts — and the fact is that if the Easter Rising had been anything more than what it was, it would have been an utter failure instead of the spark that reignited the fire of a nation.

The leaders of the rebellion appear to have accepted the possibility or inevitability of failure, indeed, relied on it to reawaken the spirit of independence. Pádraic Pearse, Thomas Clarke, Joseph Plunkett, Seán MacDermott, Éamonn Ceannt, and Thomas MacDonagh claimed they knew they would fail, and spoke of a sacrificial offering. Connolly commented at one point that they were going out to be slaughtered.

This, however, stands in sharp contrast to what the Volunteers and ICA were told, raising a question as to whether everyone expected failure from the beginning, or if they changed plans as the situation began falling apart. Initially, there seems to have been the idea that they would attack, and then retreat from Dublin into the countryside to carry on guerilla warfare. As one Volunteer with Edward "Ned" Daly (1891-1916) later recalled:

> I believe there was a general plan for the whole Country and that such plan did not contemplate immobilisation in buildings as our instructions originally provided for a retiral [sic] to the Country, North County Dublin and Meath. These instructions were afterwards cancelled and we were ordered to fall back to the Four Courts.[1]

Connolly believed that the capitalists who in his opinion controlled the British Army through parliament would never permit artillery to be used against their own property.[2] The Volunteers and the ICA could, he was convinced, easily withstand assault by attackers armed no better than they were, which suggests he may also have changed his plans.

The inexperience of the Volunteers and the ICA was apparent from the start. The capture of Dublin Castle, for hundreds of years the heart and soul of the English overlordship of Ireland, was essential to the success of the operation, if only for symbolic purposes. The men sent to secure it, however, seemed unaware that the Castle was almost completely unoccupied, with the gates standing wide open — Easter Monday is a "Bank Holiday," that is, a public holiday, in Ireland.

The only resistance at the Castle was an unarmed Dublin Metropolitan Police officer named James O'Brien, who promptly held up his hands and surrendered. Seán Connolly, an actor with the Abbey Theater and not entirely at ease as a soldier, was in command of the detachment. He became nervous and shot and killed O'Brien, the first casualty of the Rising. Restoring a certain gruesome balance, Seán Connolly was the first to be killed on the Volunteer side in the Rising, being shot while attempting to raise a flag over the City Hall.

Seán Connolly's nervousness was somewhat understandable, although that does not excuse what he did. Some of the

---

[1] John F. Shouldice, W.S. 162, 1.
[2] Duff, *Six Days to Shake an Empire*, op. cit., 150.

Volunteers and ICA members had found out only a few hours before that the Rising was not just another drill. As John (Seán) Shouldice, who was out with his brother Frank with Daly at the Four Courts, recalled years later, "I would say that perhaps one-third of those who mobilised on Easter Sunday and the majority of those who mobilised on Easter Monday were aware that they were going into action.[3] Others contend that most of the Volunteers and ICA had no idea until after they marched out that it wasn't just another day of drilling and maneuvers.[4]

At around noon Pearse and Connolly led approximately one hundred and fifty Volunteers and ICA members to the General Post Office. Others would join them as the day wore on.

The GPO had been chosen over Liberty Hall as headquarters due to its central location. It was a poor choice. It was difficult to defend, and there was no clear field of fire. The surrounding buildings made advance warning of any attack virtually impossible. The only advantages were that it was a communications hub and a mere seven unarmed guards constituted the force that had to be overcome. These were quickly overpowered.

Nevertheless, it was from the portico of the GPO that Pearse read a proclamation of the Irish Republic. He had written most of it himself.

The Birth of the Irish Republic

Even after stripping away the accumulated reverence accorded it for a century, the Proclamation is a remarkable document. First and foremost, there is the establishment of an independent Irish Republic. No longer would long-delayed and half-promised measures such as the various permutations of Home Rule under the British Crown be acceptable. Ireland was by natural right ("in the name of God") and by heritage ("the dead generations from which she receives her old traditions of nationhood") a free and sovereign people in an undivided country ("the whole nation and all . . . its parts").

---

[3] Shouldice, W.S. 162, 2.
[4] De Rosa, *Rebels, op. cit.*, 247.

The fact that the signatories added their names "on behalf of the Provisional Government" has a significance that is often overlooked. This was a masterstroke, both politically and tactically. As Younger explained,

> The signatories knew very well that their Provisional Government would be short-lived but they signed, not as members of the Provisional Government which, in fact, they were, but simply on its behalf. It was a secret government within the Irish Republican Brotherhood, a government which would act as trustees until the people were in a position to elect a permanent National Government, and so long as there was an I.R.B. it could contain within it a provisional republican government. There was, therefore, an opportunity to maintain continuity, and it was not lost when the signatories themselves were to be counted among the dead generations.[5]

There is, of course, a guarantee of religious and civil liberty, although the civil liberties are not specified. This too is significant, for Pearse had to walk a tightrope between his and Connolly's socialism, and the Catholic sensibilities and beliefs of most of the people of Ireland and of his own men.

The Catholic Church had clearly and unequivocally condemned all forms of socialism many times. Many of the Volunteers had already gone as far as they dared by joining the IRB, a secret society, for the Catholic Church also condemned secret societies. Éamon de Valera (1882-1975), for example, had struggled with his conscience before joining the IRB.[6]

Thus, the key triad of natural rights (life, liberty, and private property) that constitutes the principal matter and substance of civil liberties could not be mentioned outright, an omission that would have serious consequences. Equivocation on slavery had kept private property out of the American Declaration of Independence, although it otherwise closely followed the Virginia Declaration of Rights in which private property has a prominent place.[7] Equivocation on social-

---

[5] Younger, *Ireland's Civil War, op. cit.*, 36.
[6] Dangerfield, *The Damnable Question, op. cit.*, 175-176.
[7] Although he was himself a slave owner, George Mason's original draft of the Virginia Declaration of June 12, 1776 was phrased in such a way as to nullify the basis for human chattel slavery, but was amended by reactionaries in the Virginia Convention. Having

ism allowed the mention of property in the Easter Proclamation to be taken either as abolishing private property or supporting it: "We declare the right of the people of Ireland to the ownership of Ireland . . . to be sovereign and indefeasible."

Need v. Opportunity

There was, nevertheless, an important addition that, understood properly from a natural law perspective, nullifies the usual socialist interpretation of the Proclamation: equality of opportunity. It clearly stated that, "The Republic guarantees religious and civil liberty, equal rights *and equal opportunities* to all its citizens." (Emphasis added.)

Equality of opportunity is the antithesis of socialism's equality of results. It is important to note in this context, however, that even the strictest Marxist does not interpret "equality of results" as meaning everybody gets exactly the same thing, no more, no less. Rather, it means that everyone has an equal right to what he or she needs, or (as Karl Marx put it), "From each according to his ability, to each according to his needs."[8]

Equality of opportunity necessarily implies that everyone has an equal opportunity to participate in the economic process on the same terms as everyone else, both as an owner of labor and as an owner of capital. This in turn implies equality of access to the means of participation in economic life as a capital owner (money and credit), as well as participation itself.

Equal opportunity to participate also implies that someone in a distribution of the results of production will gain or lose in strict proportion to the relative value of his or her inputs. If equality of opportunity means the same thing as distribution on the basis of need,[9] regardless of one's participation,

---

an inherent understanding of social justice, Mason knew that it would do little good to free his slaves if the slave system was not abolished at the same time.

[8] Karl Marx, *Critique of the Gotha Program*. Peking, China: Foreign Languages Press, 1972, 17.

[9] An exception is made in Catholic social teaching in "extreme cases" (see *Rerum Novarum*, § 22), but this is limited to emergencies that permit redistribution by duly constituted authority to avoid

then equality of opportunity means equality of opportunity to be a slave. As Abraham Lincoln pointed out in one of his debates with Stephen Douglas,

> That is the real issue. That is the issue that will continue in this country when these poor tongues of Judge Douglas and myself shall be silent. It is the eternal struggle between these two principles — right and wrong — throughout the world. They are the two principles that have stood face to face from the beginning of time; and will ever continue to struggle. The one is the common right of humanity and the other the divine right of kings. It is the same principle in whatever shape it develops itself. It is the same spirit that says, "You work and toil and earn bread, and I'll eat it." No matter in what shape it comes, whether from the mouth of a king who seeks to bestride the people of his own nation and live by the fruit of their labor, or from one race of men as an apology for enslaving another race, it is the same tyrannical principle.[10]

Finally, equality of opportunity means the right and the duty to correct the situation when people do not have equality of opportunity to participate, or they are not receiving distributions in strict proportion to the relative value of their inputs. This is social justice, the justice that addresses our institutional environment in order to repair or reform any laws, traditions, and customs that interfere with the exercise of civil and religious liberties. Social justice, it is important to note, does not replace justice or charity, but makes it possible for people to be just and charitable.

After reading the Proclamation, Pearse went back into the GPO. His and Connelly's men commandeered bedding from a nearby hotel, while the young ladies of the Cumann na mBan ("The Irishwomen's Council"), an independent organization that served as an auxiliary to the Volunteers, set up kitchens and aid stations.

The Flag Question

While hardly a critical issue, which flags were flown during the Rising has been a matter of controversy over the years. Fortunately in 1946, Diarmuid Lynch (1878-1950), a surviv-

---

harm to the common good. It is not meant to establishment and maintain the standard for a just society.

[10] Abraham Lincoln, October 15, 1858, Seventh Debate with Stephen Douglas.

ing member of the IRB Supreme Council and believed by some to be the last man to leave the GPO, went to a great deal of trouble to clarify matters.

In his Statement By Witness of December 30, 1947, after interviewing all the survivors he could locate and comparing their statements with his own recollections, Lynch reported that not one, but three different flags were used, and there were variations even among those. What caused the confusion was Pearse's "flag order" to the Volunteers of March 1915: "The authorised flag is a plain gold harp on a green ground."[11] He repeated this a year later, a month before the Rising: "This flag should be well in evidence on all occasions of formal parades."[12]

Why not the Tricolor that had been the banner of Irish Republicanism since the 1840s? Because it had become associated in the minds of the British with "extremism." Lynch believed that Pearse's order was a temporary expedient until the Republic could be proclaimed.

In Lynch's opinion, Pearse issued his flag order to allay the fears of the public — and to hide the fact from the authorities that there was a rebellion planned. In addition, as Pearse explained in March 1916,

> [I]t is believed that at this stage the recognized National Flag more fully symbolises what the Irish Volunteers stand for, and will gain a readier consideration and respect from Irishmen in general.[13]

On all "formal occasions," then, the green "National Flag" would be displayed, while on "informal occasions" the Volunteers were permitted to display either the National Flag or the Tricolor "Republican Flag." As a separate organization, the ICA had its own, third, flag, the "Plough and the Stars."

Volunteer units were therefore uncertain on Easter Monday exactly what flag should be flown. Complicating matters further was the fact that there were different versions of the National Flag, with and without the harp, and sometimes the addition of the words "IRISH REPUBLIC" in white or gold.

---

[11] Diarmuid Lynch, W.S. 120, 1.
[12] *Ibid.*, 2.
[13] *Ibid.*

Arriving at the GPO, Pearse discovered they had left their Tricolor behind at Liberty Hall. He sent a man back for it, and the man returned with the Republican Tricolor and a version of the National Flag without the harp. Both were hoisted, the Tricolor at the Henry Street corner of the GPO, and the National Flag at the Parnell Street corner.[14] Accounting for the subsequent confusion, some people saw one, the other, or both, depending on their vantage points.

The Occupation of Dublin

At the same time that the GPO was being occupied, other units were securing their objectives — most simply by walking in and taking over. Targets were not particularly well chosen, primarily due to the lack of manpower, but also as a result of inexperience. For example, the telegraph office in the GPO was seized, but the telephone exchange was not. The British were thereby able to enjoy swift and effective local communication throughout the Rising, while the Volunteers were limited to couriers, and a Post Office engineer was able to set up an alternate telegraph system so that the British could coordinate with London and other units.

Michael Mallin (1874-1916) and his second-in-command, Constance Georgine Gore-Booth Markievicz, Countess Markievicz (1868-1927), an Irish woman who had married a Polish nobleman, occupied St. Stephen's Green, a walled park in the center of Dublin. Mallin's men barricaded the entrances to the Green by turning over buses and trucks.

The "flamboyantly uniformed" Countess Markiewicz, whom William Butler Yeats described as spending her days "in ignorant good-will," was accompanied by twenty or so other ladies dressed in men's clothing, evidently ready to take active combat roles. As the newspapers reported, "A number of women accompanied the first body of Sinn Féiners. They wore green sashes and carried cartridge belts."

Although not a member of the inner circle — or, possibly, for that very reason — de Valera ("Dev") was given command of what turned out to be the most strategic post, Boland's Mill and Bakery, the largest such enterprise in Dublin. For commercial purposes Boland's was placed convenient to land, water, and railway routes.

---

[14] *Ibid.*, 3.

This made the mill and bakery key militarily, a fact of which Dev took full advantage. By positioning his men with great care, he was able to hold several buildings and a large perimeter for a week. He would have been able to hold out much longer if he had not been ordered to surrender after the fall of the GPO.

Éamonn Ceannt, with Cathal Brugha (1874-1922) — Charles William St. John Burgess — as his second-in-command, was assigned the Workhouse of the South Dublin Poor Law Union complex near Phoenix Park. Edward Daly occupied the Four Courts on the banks of the Liffy River, the heart of the Irish judicial system. Smaller units occupied a number of other buildings.

Thomas MacDonagh was given Jacob's Biscuit Factory, where the first resistance was encountered — but not from the British Army. A crowd assembled, waving Union Jacks and calling the Volunteers "[expletive deleted] slackers." They said if the Volunteers wanted to fight, they could go to France. One man grabbed at a Volunteer's rifle and was told by a lieutenant to keep his hands to himself, or he'd be sorry. He didn't take his hands off, and the officer shot him in the leg.

Monday, April 24

Although British estimates of the number of Volunteers varied wildly between 2,000-10,000, there was probably no more than 1,200-1,600 at most in Dublin. The confusion over what was going on even in the ranks of the Volunteers ensured that the 10,000 who were supposed to have turned out in the capital were not able to do so even after the situation became less chaotic. As Younger commented, "Had the Rising been widespread, the British would have been hard put to it to deal with it. But MacNeill's countermanding orders had saved them."[15]

There were only three military engagements on Monday. By a coincidence that has led to confusing two separate incidents, two of the three involved British cavalry.

The first involved a troop of Lancers escorting an ammunition convoy around noon that got caught in a crossfire be-

---

[15] Younger, *The Irish Civil War, op. cit.*, 37.

tween the Four Courts and a small detachment of Volunteers on the Church Street Bridge. Half a dozen troopers were killed. The rest scattered panic-stricken through the backstreets, one of them accidentally shooting and killing a child, until their commanding officer restored order and led them out of danger. One of the dead horses lay in the street the entire week.

Later that afternoon another troop of Lancers was ordered to clear the GPO. They charged the building, and if Volunteers hadn't started shooting before ordered, it is likely the troop would have been wiped out. As it was, four troopers died in the premature and wildly aimed volley, and the Volunteers suffered three casualties from their own fire, one man shooting himself in the stomach.

The third incident was the ambush of a company of the Dublin Veterans Corps, "the Gorgeous Wrecks" (from the "Georgius Rex" on their belts). These had been out on a march in the Dublin Mountains since early morning and were unaware of the turn of events.

Returning to their barracks on Northumberland Road, they were spotted by one of de Valera's outposts. Seeing uniformed soldiers carrying rifles, Dev's men opened fire, killing five and wounding eight, one of whom died later. The Volunteers had no way of knowing until too late that the middle-aged, part-time soldiers didn't have any ammunition.

A number of factors explain the initial lack of response by the British. For one, there were less than 2,500 troops stationed in Dublin.

Two, Easter Monday was a Bank Holiday, and most of the officers and men had taken full advantage of that fact. Many of them had gone to the races at Fairyhouse, as Yeats noted in his poem, "Easter, 1916."

Three, the authorities simply weren't expecting anything — their informers turned out to be as unreliable as their own assumptions.[16] They were caught completely by surprise. They had been maintaining a special force of four hundred just in case the Germans attempted to land more arms — a hundred at each of the four main barracks in Dublin. These

---

[16] Dangerfield, *The Damnable Question, op. cit.*, 161-164.

had been released when the *Aud* was scuttled and Casement's three-man invasion thwarted.

The civilian population was equally surprised, but the poor of Dublin were quick to realize their opportunity, and began looting. The high-end shops of Sackville Street, Dublin's main thoroughfare, were simply too much of a temptation to resist. There remained scarcely a shop that wasn't broken into, early on by the poor of Dublin, and later by the British soldiers, encouraged by their officers.

In an effort to restore order (or maybe out of boredom — a number of those who turned out didn't fire a shot at an actual adversary all week), Volunteers occasionally fired over the heads of the looters. The police were nowhere to be found. After three unarmed officers were killed, the Police Commissioner had pulled them off the streets.

One witness saw a man wearing a stolen full dress suit and carrying a set of golf clubs. Another recalled seeing a woman with her arms full of everything she could grab drop it all every time a shot seemed to come close. She would then fall to her knees and clasp her hands in prayer, gather up the loot again, and drop it when another bullet startled her.

Still, British reinforcements began arriving in Dublin Monday afternoon, 1,600 men of the Third Cavalry Brigade from the Curragh of Kildare. Soon after artillery arrived from Athlone, a large town in County Westmeath, near the center of Ireland.

In Galway, between six and seven hundred Volunteers under Liam Mellows attacked the RIC barracks at Oranmore, a village on the outskirts of Galway city, and Clarinbridge, a village south of the city. The attacks were unsuccessful, largely due to the loss of the munitions and arms on the *Aud* and the confusion caused by MacNeil's countermanding orders. The Galway Volunteers had only twenty-five rifles, sixty revolvers, three hundred shotguns, and sixty pikes — hardly effective assault weapons.

During the withdrawal, there was a skirmish at Carnmore, about eight miles east of Galway city, in the course of which a RIC constable was killed. The Volunteers occupied the town of Athenry, about fifteen miles east of Galway City, but felt the position was too exposed for defense with the firearms they had been able to muster. They retreated to Moyode Castle, a sixteenth century tower house, and Limepark, to the south of Athenry.

Tuesday, April 25

More reinforcements arrived in Dublin on Tuesday, but the British did not attack. Instead, they consolidated their positions and concentrated on cutting Volunteer lines of communications. A cordon was set up around the city, and the British dug in.

Looting continued throughout the day, and it was then that Francis Sheehy-Skeffington — "Skeffy" — the husband of the suffragette Hanna Sheehy-Skeffington, and a well-known and easily recognizable figure in Dublin, decided that something had to be done. As Hanna related,

> All Monday and Tuesday he actively interested himself in preventing looting . . . He saved various shops, posted civic guards and enlisted the help of many civilians and priests. He talked to the crowds and held them off. . . . He called a meeting [Tuesday] evening to organize a civic police.[17]

Unfortunately, Sheehy-Skeffington, easily identified by his unique style of dress and the large VOTES FOR WOMEN button he always wore on his lapel, was an advocate of Irish independence. The British troops were on the lookout for him. It didn't help that he was a known associate of the ringleaders — who viewed him with amused affection and did not take him too seriously.[18]

Ironically, on Monday Sheey-Skeffington had risked his life to run through a hail of bullets to try and save the life of a British officer who was bleeding to death after being caught in a crossfire.[19] Despite that, his description had been circulated and soldiers posted along the routes that he had to take to return home.[20]

---

[17] Hanna Sheehy-Skeffington, *British Imperialism as I Have Known It*. New York: The Donnelly Press, ND, 17; cf. Senator Séamus O'Farrell, W.S., 193, 3.
[18] William Ingoldsby, W.S. 582, Addendum, 2.
[19] Hanna Sheehy-Skeffington, *British Imperialism as I Have Known It, op. cit.*, 17.
[20] *Ibid.*, 18.

This was justified on the grounds that in 1914, Sheehy-Skeffington (a strict pacifist) had been arrested for making a speech "calculated to prejudice recruiting"[21] and sentenced to six months hard labor. He was released early after a six-day hunger strike on condition that he was to be subject to arrest at any time without trial to serve out the remainder of his six-month sentence.[22]

Séamus O'Farrell (?-1973) was near the Portobello Bridge on Tuesday evening when —

> . . . I overtook the late Francis Sheehy-Skeffington. We walked along together, discussing what had occurred. He suggested that I should go next day, about 4.30 p.m. to the rooms of the Irish Women's Franchise League, where he hoped to have a few others who might form a civil police force "to put down looting". He did not indicate how such a body could effectively act. We then parted, Skeffington going towards Portobello Bridge, I in the opposite direction.[23]

Sheehy-Skeffington was arrested on the Portobello Bridge between 7 and 8 pm by a section of the 11th East Surrey Regiment. As an eye-witness reported,

> I was in Dublin standing on Porto Bello Bridge when the soldiers came and arrested Mr. Sheehy Skeffington. He was giving out leaflets one of which was handed to me advising the people not to be looting and was not doing anything unlawful or political.[24]

Sheehy-Skeffington was taken to nearby Portobello Barracks, where he was held without charge. Sometime around midnight Captain John Colthurst Bowen-Colthurst (1880-1965), an officer of the Third Battalion, Royal Irish Rifles, acting without orders, decided to take forty or so men out on a raid. The officer on duty, eighteen-year old Second Lieutenant William Price Dobbin, commissioned only a few months, allowed Bowen-Colthurst, a ranking veteran of

---

[21] F. Sheehy-Skeffington, *A Forgotten Small Nationality*, op. cit., 15.
[22] *Ibid*.
[23] Séamus O'Farrell, W.S. 193, *loc. cit.* Hanna Sheehy-Skeffington stated that the meeting was to take place Tuesday evening — which have been Francis's original intention. Hanna Sheehy-Skeffington, *British Imperialism as I Have Known It*, op. cit., 17.
[24] Mrs. Julia Hughes, W.S. 880; cf. Michael Noyk, W.S. 707, 8.

many years' service, to do as he pleased without questioning his actions. Bowen-Colthurst took Sheehy-Skeffington along on the raid as hostage on his own authority, tying Sheehy-Skeffington's hands behind his back.

A fanatic Unionist, Bowen-Colthurst probably recognized Sheehy-Skeffington as the author of "A Forgotten Small Nationality: Ireland and the War," recently published (February 1916) in *Century Magazine*. The article was pro-Nationalist and extremely unfavorable to the Unionist position. Sheehy-Skeffington also had a letter published in *The New Statesman* on April 7, harshly critical of the British military and its "Prussian plans in Ireland."

Bowen-Colthurst and Lieutenant Leslie Wilson took Sheehy-Skeffington along on a raid to search for "Fenians." As the raiding party proceeded along Rathmines Road, the soldiers shot randomly at the buildings to prevent people from coming to the windows and seeing what was going on. Near the local Catholic Church on Lower Rathmines Road, dedicated to Mary Immaculate, Refuge of Sinners, they came across two boys returning home after attending a meeting of the Holy Family Sodality (a devotional association for Catholic laity) at the parish.

Bowen-Colthurst questioned the boys and told them that under martial law he could "shoot them 'like dogs'."[25] As one of the boys, seventeen-year old[26] James J. Coade, turned to leave, Bowen-Colthurst said, "Bash him." One of the soldiers broke Coade's jaw with his rifle butt, rendering him unconscious.

Bowen-Colthurst then shot Coade with his pistol and left him lying in the street. Coade died later that night. When Sheehy-Skeffington protested, Bowen-Colthurst told him "to say his prayers . . . as he would likely be the next."[27]

The Royal Commission of Inquiry established to investigate the case noted that Bowen-Colthurst may have killed one or more other persons besides Coade during his spree,

---

[25] Hanna Sheehy-Skeffington, *British Imperialism as I Have Known It, op. cit.*, 19.
[26] Some give his age as nineteen.
[27] Hanna Sheehy-Skeffington, *British Imperialism as I Have Known It, op. cit.*, 19.

but did not consider the matter worth investigating.[28] Bowen-Colthurst then had Wilson take Sheehy-Skeffington aside, possibly to prevent him from being able to bear witness later to what he, Bowen-Colthurst, intended to do next.

Bowen-Colthurst ordered Wilson to shoot Sheehy-Skeffington if they were attacked. Wilson later testified "he saw 'nothing strange' in the order and would have carried it out, and it was in fact a common practice with these parties . . . to take such 'hostages'."[29]

Bowen-Colthurst then proceeded to a tobacconist's at the corner of Camden Street and Harcourt Road, owned by James Kelly, a Unionist Dublin City Alderman. Bowen-Colthurst evidently confused James Kelly with another Alderman, Thomas Kelly, a Nationalist.

Inside were Kelly and two pro-British editors detested by the Nationalists,[30] Thomas Dickson (who was physically disabled) and Patrick MacIntyre. The soldiers threw hand grenades into the shop without warning, wounding one of the men inside. Bowen-Colthurst took everyone prisoner, while the soldiers looted the shop.

Ironically, had Bowen-Colthurst started his raid before nightfall, he would have captured Michael Noyk (1884-1966), solicitor to Sinn Féin founder Arthur Griffith (1872-1922), who later joined Sinn Féin himself, defended many Republicans in court, and was a high level advisor to the Irish government. Noyk was in the habit of frequenting Kelly's shop to hear the news. He was Jewish, however, and had to be home for Passover. He thereby escaped being killed or taken hostage.[31]

Rejoining Wilson and Sheehy-Skeffington, Bowen-Colthurst returned to Portobello Barracks with his hostages, where the prisoners were thrown into cells. Bowen-Colthurst spent the rest of the night in prayer.

---

[28] *Ibid.*; cf. Royal Commission of Inquiry, "Shooting of Three Men in Portobello Barracks," § 17, *Sinn Féin Rebellion Handbook*. Dublin, Éire: The Irish Times, 1917, 208.
[29] *Ibid.*
[30] Noyk, W.S. 707, *loc. cit.*
[31] *Ibid.*

Wednesday, April 26

About 3 am Bowen-Colthurst read Luke 19:27: "But those mine enemies, which would not that I should reign over them, bring hither, and slay them before me." He took this as a divine command to kill his hostages.[32] He is reported to have said, "'In any other country except Ireland it would be recognized as right to kill rebels."

The next morning, around 10:00 am, Bowen-Colthurst demanded that Sheehy-Skeffington and the two editors be turned over to him. He stated he was going to " 'shoot Skeffington and the others, that he thought 'it was the right thing to do.' "[33] Bowen-Colthurst then ordered Sergeant John William Aldridge, Tenth Battalion, Royal Dublin Fusiliers, to assemble a firing squad and had Sheehy-Skeffington, McIntyre, and Dickson shot.

The firing squad bungled the job, however, and either Sheehy-Skeffington alone, or all three were still alive.[34] Some sources say that another firing squad was assembled,[35] others that Bowen-Colthurst finished the job himself with his revolver.[36] The Royal Commission investigating the shootings concluded that Bowen Colthurst ordered the shooting, but did not participate. The bodies were wrapped in sheets and secretly buried in the barracks yard.

A number of individuals, however, alleged that the Commission suppressed evidence. Major Sir Francis Fletcher Vane of the Royal Munster Fusiliers, in charge of the defense of Portobello Barracks, was reprimanded by the president of the Commission for trying to "say things *which we do not want you to say*" [emphasis in original] and was prevented from testifying further.[37]

---

[32] Hanna Sheehy-Skeffington, *British Imperialism as I Have Known It, op. cit.*, 20.
[33] *Ibid.*
[34] Sergeant Aldridge testified at Bowen-Colthurst's court martial that he had examined the bodies and they were dead. Other witnesses claimed they saw movement.
[35] Hanna Sheehy-Skeffington, *British Imperialism as I Have Known It, op. cit.*, 21.
[36] Dr. Nancy Wyse-Power, W.S. 587, 5.
[37] Vane, *Agin the Governments, op. cit.*, 271-272.

Vane first learned of what happened as he was returning to Portobello Barracks after placing an observation post on the tower of the Rathmines town hall. As he related,

> While marching through a semi-hostile crowd on returning to Barracks, several men, with that directness which characterises the Irish, shouted: "Murderer, Murderer!" I have been called many names in my life, but had up to then never been accused of this offence. Perhaps this was the reason that it stuck in my memory, and consequently on arrival in Barracks, made careful inquiries among my young officers. Then the truth came out that this same morning Captain Bowen Colthurst had gone to the Guard house, ordered the three men out, and had them shot against the wall.[38]

Vane went immediately to the temporary deputy commander of the garrison, Major James Rossborough,[39] and demanded that Bowen-Colthurst be placed under arrest. Rossborough, however, had already requested instructions from his superiors at the Castle, and — unbeknownst to Vane — had been told to cover up the incident. All Rossborough told Vane was that he did not feel he could act against his superiors.

Vane then demanded that Bowen-Colthurst at least be confined to barracks. Receiving Rossborough's word of honor on that point, Vane then had all the officers assembled and lectured them on their duties under Martial Law — which included personal responsibility for any act deemed murder under common law. He then left to carry out other duties, clearly assuming he had dealt with the situation the best he could for the time being.

Although Vane believed he had "put the fear of God into them,"[40] later in the day Bowen-Colthurst was put in command of some troops in Camden Street when Richard O'Carroll, a Labour Party politician on the Dublin City Council, was brought in after surrendering to the soldiers. Bowen-Colthurst took O'Carroll into the barracks yard and shot him in the lung. O'Carroll died ten days later.

---

[38] *Ibid.*, 262-263.
[39] "Rosborough" in many accounts.
[40] Vane, *Agin the Governments, op. cit.*, 265.

Afterwards, Bowen-Colthurst questioned a young boy whom he believed had information about Sinn Féin. When the boy denied it, Bowen-Colthurst had him kneel in the street, and shot him in the back of the head as the boy started to make the sign of the cross. None of these later killings were investigated.

Wednesday also saw the beginning of the British offensive and the fiercest fighting of the Rising. An armed auxiliary patrol yacht, the *Helga*,[41] had been brought up the Liffy. The guns of the *Helga* and the artillery that been positioned the day before opened up on Wednesday morning, and the heart of Dublin was soon in flames.

The day had actually started out quite pleasantly for the British, though, almost a cakewalk — literally. The 176th and 178th Infantry Brigades of the 59th North Midland Division had embarked on Tuesday night in response to frantic messages from Dublin, and arrived in Kingstown Harbor at around 5:00 am. As they marched to the city —

> The first thing that took the troops by surprise was the arrival of dozens of Irish women bringing them tea and cakes and biscuits. "They were just like one of us," one of them still says in amazement. "They seemed as pleased as could be that we'd arrived." The troops were showered with bars of chocolate and fruit; they felt they "could have had ten breakfasts a day" if they wished.[42]

The British divided into two columns, the first of which, the 5th and 6th Battalions, marched around Dublin to the western side and encamped at Kilmainham. There they joined the cordon that was being drawn around the downtown area.

Unfortunately for the British, de Valera had the eastern approaches to the city covered. Even though he had few men to spare (and those he had were spread very thin), he had

---

[41] Originally *Helga II*, a fishery research and protection cruiser. In March 1915, the British Admiralty acquired the vessel, dropped the "II" from the name, and reclassified it as "His Majesty's Yacht *Helga*," an armed steam yacht. Renamed *Muirchú* ("Sea-hound"), in 1923 it became one of the first vessels in the Irish Navy.

[42] Robert Kee, *Ireland: A History*. Boston, Massachusetts: Little, Brown and Company, 1982, 165.

sent seventeen men under Lieutenant Michael Malone (1888-1916), to set a trap at Mount Street Bridge for the eight hundred Sherwood Foresters coming from Dun Laoghaire along the Northumberland Road.

Despite being grossly outnumbered, Malone and his men beat off one attack after another in a five-hour battle that lasted until dark. Malone and three other Volunteers died, with the balance being wounded or captured. Malone's men, however, accounted for four British officers killed, fourteen officers wounded, and two hundred sixteen enlisted men killed or wounded.

This was nearly half of all losses the British sustained during the Rising. The British were convinced until the very end that they faced two or three hundred men.

In the Mendicity Institution, an outpost of the Volunteers' Four Courts garrison nearer the city center, twenty men under Seán Heuston (1891-1916) were cut off on Wednesday by the tightening of the British cordon. They put up a stubborn fight for two days until forced to surrender, having only expected to hold their position for three or four hours.

Thursday, April 27

Edward Daly, however, in command of the Four Courts, soon made up the loss. His men captured two-dozen members of the Dublin Metropolitan police force whom they found hiding in the Bridewell Police Station, and also took the Linenhall RIC barracks. Unable to hold the barracks, Daly ordered them burned to prevent them from falling into the hands of the British.

Daly's men had barricaded a rabbit warren of small streets and tenements around North King Street, a primary route to the GPO. Starting Thursday the South Staffordshire Regiment under the command of Lieutenant-Colonel Henry Taylor attempted to clear them out.

Expecting to achieve a quick victory with overwhelming force, the British encountered stiff resistance. They began tunneling through tenement walls, thereby avoiding most of the direct fire from the Volunteers that seemed to come from every angle.

Progress was too slow, however, and a British Major ordered a frontal assault with bayonets. Baffled as to why anyone would give such an insane order, the Volunteers poured fire into the British platoon, inflicting fifteen casualties, including the Major who led the charge, who was killed. One of the Volunteers, Frank Shouldice, brother of John F. Shouldice, another Volunteer, said years later, "One by one we knocked them all over. It was a terrible slaughter and to this day I can't understand why they tried to rush things."[43]

Inspired by the news coming out of Dublin, the Volunteers of Enniscorthy, County Wexford, mobilized early Thursday morning. They raised the Republican flag (probably the Tricolor) over the town, and cut off the roads leading in. They captured the train station, tore up some track, and cut telephone and telegraph wires. Towards nightfall, there was a brief engagement with two RIC constables from the constables' position in the local branch of the Bank of Ireland, and the Volunteers attacked, but did not capture, the RIC barracks. They did, however, occupy Enniscorthy Castle, the private home of the Roche family, whom they evicted.

Back in Dublin, by Thursday evening the city center was in flames as a result of the British artillery bombardment with incendiary shells — the very thing that Connelly had been convinced that the capitalists would never allow. The major blaze appears to have begun in Abbey Street and spread to Sackville Street, completing the destruction begun by the looters. Volunteers began tunneling from one building to another on Sackville Street to keep ahead of the fire.

Friday, April 28

General Sir John Grenfell Maxwell (1859-1929) arrived a few hours after midnight on Friday morning from London as military governor with plenary powers under Martial law. From this point the tenor of the situation changed, especially with respect to the assault on the Four Courts.

Maxwell was a poor choice for the job. He had held a high position as commander of "The Force in Egypt," but was replaced by General Sir Archibald James Murray (1860-1945) in circumstances that Maxwell, probably rightly, regarded as the result of political favoritism. Thus, as Dangerfield noted,

---

[43] Max Caulfield, *The Easter Rebellion*. London: Four Square Books, 1963, 342.

"when [Maxwell] came to Dublin he was that quite dangerous person, a general with a grievance."[44]

Matters had not improved for the British in North King Street. They fought from house to house, the Volunteers retreating slowly before them. Even bringing up an improvised armored car did little to help. By midday Saturday, when the cease-fire was declared, they had advanced barely one hundred fifty yards at the cost of eleven dead and twenty-eight wounded.

From late Friday evening through Saturday morning, allegedly enraged at the slow progress they were making and purportedly driven temporarily insane, British troops broke into houses along North King Street. They began bayonetting, shooting, or taking prisoner any men or boys they found, none of whom were armed or had taken any part in the fighting.

Ellen Walsh later told how soldiers pounded on the door of home of Michael and Sarah Hughes in which she and a number of others had taken refuge, and demanded to know if there were any men in the house. A troop of soldiers burst in and ransacked the house, acting "like wild animals or things possessed."[45] As Sarah Hughes related,

> One of the soldiers that entered my place, a Corporal and a Sergeant, they searched my husband also the man Walsh, one of the soldiers said give those Irish pigs an ounce of lead. . . . The military put all women and children down to the cellars, including myself.
>
> I heard the man Walsh saying what are you doing that for. I understood they were taking the men prisoners and handcuffing them, let any human being think over it, one man taken into the drawing room and shot dead. My poor husband was brought to the top of the house and instantly shot dead for no crime at all, it was murder and cool blooded murder there is no other word for it.[46]

---

[44] Dangerfield, *The Damnable Question, op. cit.*, 197.
[45] Caulfield, *The Easter Rebellion, op. cit.*, 267-268.
[46] Peter Berresford Ellis (ed.), *Eyewitness to Irish History*. Hoboken, New Jersey: John Wiley & Sons, Inc., 2004, 214-215.

Anne Fennel, who had also given some people refuge in her home, told a similar story, with added details suggesting that the soldiers tortured some of their victims:

> I nearly fell on the ground and clasped the officer's hand in terror but he flung me off. As poor Mrs Ennis saw her husband being led upstairs she clung to him and refused to be parted from him, and said, "I must go up with my husband." One of the soldiers pulled her off and put a bayonet to her ear and uttered the foulest language. . . . After a long time, it must have been a couple of hours, we heard a noise at the parlour door, and to our horror, poor Mr Ennis crawled in. I will never forget. He was dying, bleeding to death, and when the military left the house he had crept down the stairs to see his wife for the last time. He was covered with blood and his eyes were rolling in his head.[47]

In all, fifteen men for certain, with a possible sixteenth in Little Britain Street a block away, were put to death for being in the wrong place at the wrong time. In most cases the bodies were stripped of anything of value.

At least one man, James Healy, was killed after the Rising was over in Dublin, last being seen by his wife as he went off to work late Saturday. Another, Patrick Bealen, who had been taken hostage, was probably killed at the same time as Healy. Christopher Hickey, killed with his father Thomas, was sixteen years old.

The soldiers buried a number of the bodies in shallow graves in cellars, to be found a week to two weeks later. Others were buried in backyards, some of which were later moved by the British to other locations. As Robert Kee commented, displaying a talent for understatement and factual inaccuracy,

> At the end of the week, making their way through North King Street towards the centre, the South Staffs Regiment gave the civilian population some rough treatment, killing twelve civilians in a number of houses there.[48]

"Rough treatment," indeed.

---

[47] *Ibid.*, 215.
[48] Kee, *Ireland, op. cit.*, 166.

The Beginning of the End

By Friday evening, April 28, with Dublin burning, it was obvious the end was near. Every Volunteer position except that of Daly in the Four Courts, where the resistance on North King Street held up the British advance, and Boland's Mill, where de Valera's position remained secure, was on its last legs. The GPO was in ruins and Connolly was wounded. Only the fact that the British were waiting for the smoke and heat to drive the Volunteers out — while the Volunteers waited for the British to storm their position — delayed the end.

Except for Connolly (who refused to go), and two nurses and Connolly's secretary, Pearse ordered the evacuation of the wounded and the women. They made their way through tunnels, holes in the walls of buildings, and over rooftops to the Coliseum Theater on Henry Street.

An hour or so later fire swept through the GPO. The Volunteers quickly moved their explosives and released fifteen prisoners . . . who were promptly machine-gunned by their fellow British soldiers when they came out of the GPO. One was killed and others wounded, one seriously.

The O'Rahilly — Michael Joseph O'Rahilly (1875-1916) — led a party of Volunteers to set up new headquarters. They got as far as Moore Street before being caught by fire from a barricade at the end of the street. The O'Rahilly (the Irish style of his title as head of the family) was badly wounded, but made his way to Sackville Street where he was able to scrawl a farewell note to his wife before he died.

The O'Rahilly (erroneously referred to as "the O'Reilly" in initial newspaper reports) had not been in favor of the rising, according to James Stephens. Nevertheless, "when insurrection was decided on, The O'Rahilly marched with his men, and surely a gallant man could not have done otherwise."[49]

Assuming that The O'Rahilly's group had run into trouble, another party led by sixteen-year old John McLoughlin[50] (1899-1960) and Michael Collins (1890-1922) — "the Big Fel-

---

[49] Stephens, *The Insurrection in Dublin, op. cit.*, Ch. IX: The Volunteers.
[50] Also spelled "MacLoughlin."

low" — went to the rescue. They arrived in Moore Street too late.

Additional Volunteers came out of the GPO, but were forced to take refuge in nearby buildings to escape from machine gun fire. Last of all, Pearse, the three remaining women, a small escort,[51] and Connolly on a stretcher managed to get through to the corner of Moore Street and Henry Place.

Later that night, Pearse and Connolly gave McLoughlin a battlefield promotion to commandant, and put him in charge, probably so they could get some rest. McLoughlin, to be remembered as "the Boy Commandant," was relieved of command the next morning. His promotion, however brief, made him senior to de Valera. McLoughlin was thus — technically — the highest-ranking survivor of the Rising after the other commandants except Dev were executed.

Somewhat ironically, on Friday while this was going on in Dublin, the Volunteers won their only clear victory outside of Dublin. Thomas Patrick Ashe (1885-1917), with his second-in-command Richard James Mulcahy (1886-1971), had originally raised a strong force and set out from Swords, County Dublin, on Wednesday to capture the radio station at Skerries, a small seaside town in Fingal, fifteen or so miles to the north of the capital. Seeing the British gunboats in the harbor, they gave up that idea. Two days later they crossed into County Meath, attacked the Ashbourne RIC Barracks, and ambushed a party of reinforcements. The RIC surrendered to Ashe after a five-hour battle.

Saturday, April 29

Saturday morning, back in Dublin, McLoughlin suggested to Pearse that they try again to tunnel out through the surrounding buildings, this time to link up with Daly who still held the Four Courts. At first Pearse was in favor of this, but then learned of the massacre of civilians by British troops on North King Street.

All heart seemed to go out of Pearse. He sent one of the two remaining nurses, Elizabeth O'Farrell (1884-1957) under a Red Cross flag to ask for terms. The only terms Major-General William Henry Muir Lowe (1861-1944), in charge of

---

[51] Among whom was Patrick Caldwell, see pages 198-199, below.

the British offensive in Dublin, would consider were unconditional surrender. After a few more attempts to treat with Lowe — who had given the order to take no prisoners that was allegedly responsible for the North King Street killings — Pearse signed the surrender at 3:45 pm, Saturday, April 29, 1916:

> In order to prevent the further slaughter of Dublin civilians, and in the hope of saving the lives of our followers now surrounded and hopelessly outnumbered, the members of the Provisional Government present at Headquarters have agreed to an unconditional surrender and the Commandants of the various districts in the City and Country will order their commands to lay down arms.[52]

Accompanied by a priest and three British soldiers, Nurse O'Farrell made the rounds of the remaining posts. The Four Courts had already fallen, but others — notably de Valera at Boland's Mill — still held out. When finally convinced of the authenticity of the surrender document, de Valera surrendered. As Dev and the others were being marched off to (almost) universal derision, he reportedly responded to the heckling,[53] "If only you had come out with [pitch] forks."[54]

---

[52] Younger, *Ireland's Civil War, op. cit.*, 43.
[53] According to the account in the *Sinn Féin Rebellion Handbook*, "An expression attributed to De Valera at the surrender was, 'If only the people had come out with knives and forks,' but afterwards this statement was said to have been made earlier in the proceedings to an employee of Messrs. Boland's, who had been detained by the Sinn Feiners to attend to that firm's horses." (25)
[54] Dangerfield, *The Damnable Question, op. cit.*, 200. This is usually quoted as "If only you'd come out with knives and forks," see Younger, *Ireland's Civil War, op. cit.*, 44. Dangerfield, citing the Earl of Longford (Francis Aungier Pakenham, Seventh Earl of Longford) and Thomas P. O'Neill's, *Eamon de Valera* (Boston, Massachusetts: Houghton Mifflin Co., 1971, 44-46), has "If only you had come out with [hay] (*i.e.*, pitch) forks," which makes more sense. Pitchforks as weapons were mentioned a number of times in the Witness Statements, *e.g.*, during the "Conscription Scare" of 1917: "When Cathal [Brugha] submitted that proposal [to go to London and "wipe out" the entire British Cabinet with bombs if conscription were imposed on Ireland] to a responsible committee, some of them would probably say it was madness. For his own sake, I would myself probably try to dissuade him, had I been there. But you must

In Galway, the Volunteers were running out of food and ammunition. With a British warship on the way carrying a large contingent of Royal Marines to reinforce the local RIC and military, they decided the situation was hopeless, and scattered. Many of them were arrested in the days following, while others, including Mellows, made good their escape. When the British reinforcements arrived, the Rising in the west was over.

That same day, the Enniscorthy Volunteers put together an expedition to Ferns, County Wexford, traveling by automobile. They captured the post office and the RIC barracks.

Sunday, April 30 and Later

On Sunday, evidently unaware of the surrender in Dublin the previous day, the Enniscorthy Volunteers all attended Mass. Later that day, however, what Séamus Mac Manus called "an interdenominational Peace Committee"[55] — RIC District Inspector McGovern and one Father Kehoe from Arklow[56] — informed them that the Rising was over. Like de Valera, they did not believe it. They were only persuaded to surrender after Captains Seán Etchingham (1870-1923) of Gorey and Séamus Doyle (?-1971) were taken to see Pearse and returned with the bad news.

A final "need-not-have-been" took place on Tuesday, May 2, at Bawnard House in East Cork. A squad of RIC went to arrest the four Kent brothers, Thomas, David, Richard, and William, all known Volunteers. They refused to be dragged from their own home, and resisted arrest. They fought the police, reinforced by the British Army, until they ran out of ammunition. Richard was killed trying to escape and David was wounded. William and Thomas were tried for treason. William was acquitted, but Thomas was convicted and exe-

---

remember the feeling of the country at the time — after Maxwell's butcheries — and the determination of everybody to resist the enforcement of conscription. Father O'Flanagan and others were going around asking suggestions from people on how to resist it. He received all sorts of suggestions even from grandmothers including the use of a four-pronged fork or any other weapon they might find at hand." John Joseph O'Kelly ("Sceilg"), W.S. 384, 40-41.

[55] Mac Manus, *The Story of the Irish Race, op. cit.*, 702.

[56] Others say nothing of Father Kehoe, but mention a RIC sergeant.

cuted by firing squad in Cork, being counted among "the Sixteen."

As the captured Volunteers were marched off to prison, it seemed to many the end of a disastrous, even ludicrous romantic gesture that some have described as a travesty. The question that arises, however, is how was this utter fiasco, this blood-drenched farce, transformed into a victory, a watershed in modern Irish history?

Chapter 3: From the Jaws of Victory

Despite the murderous rampage of Bowen-Colthurst and the massacre of civilians in North King Street, Dublin, the British had to all appearances (and certainly to popular acclaim, even in Ireland) successfully put down the Rising. Denunciations of the Volunteers came in from around the world. As James Stephens wrote in the first few days after the surrender,

> To-day, the 8th of May, the book is finished, and, so far as Ireland is immediately concerned, the insurrection is over. Action now lies with England, and on that action depends whether the Irish Insurrection is over or only suppressed.[1]

This would change very quickly.

Muddling Through to Defeat

If there is one thing at which the British government has proven itself adept, it is an unfailing refusal to make the best of a good situation. It has consistently managed to turn its greatest advantages into liabilities.

The habit of muddling through to defeat cost Great Britain its American colonies, most of Ireland, and, eventually, the Empire itself. As Stephens added in a postscript to his account of the Rising,

> Since the foregoing was written events have moved in this country. The situation is no longer the same. The executions have taken place. One cannot justly exclaim against the measures adopted by the military tribunal, and yet, in the interests of both countries one may deplore them. I have said there was no bitterness in Ireland, and it was true at the time of writing. It is no longer true; but it is still possible by generous Statesmanship to allay this, and to seal a true union between Ireland and England.[2]

The ruins of Dublin were still smoldering when the executions began. After secret drumhead courts martial, Pearse, Macdonagh, and Clarke were the first group to be shot on Wednesday, May 3.

---

[1] Stephens, "Foreword," *The Insurrection in Dublin, op. cit.*
[2] *Ibid.*

Almost immediately public opinion even in England started to turn against General Maxwell's harsh measures. On Thursday, May 4, the newspapers reported,

> The announcement in the house of commons by the prime minister that the leaders in the rebellion had been court martialled and summarily executed, created a profound feeling, although this action by the government was expected.[3]

Two days before, the newspapers had claimed that the Rising was "Hair-Brained [sic] and Only an Episode,"[4] "of no particular significance."[5] The administration of U.S. President Woodrow Wilson was particularly condemnatory, and a number of Catholics and Irish Americans, stalwarts of the Democratic Party, followed that lead:

> In the United States the attitude of the Church and the Catholic press towards the Easter rising was anything but cordial. There were some Catholic clerics who could detect the accents of God in the pronouncements of officials in the Wilson Administration and who quickly reflected the opinions of the President. Reverend John A. Ryan was typical of this group. He sharply denounced the Easter Rising and expressed the view that everyone who aided the Sinn Féiners should feel the heavy hand of the British Government. It is interesting to note that during World War II Dr. Ryan went to an extreme in his support of the Roosevelt Administration.[6]

Even the vociferous Unionist Edward Carson, now a Cabinet Minister, began expressing doubts about the wisdom of Maxwell's actions and called for clemency. Carson possibly recalled that, had it not been for the outbreak of the war in Europe that delayed implementation of the Home Rule bill, he might have been in Pearse's place as president of a provisional government in rebellion.[7] As Younger commented,

> The people of Dublin, and especially the Irish press, incensed by the destruction, had denounced the revolutionaries at first,

---

[3] "Irish Rebel Leaders Die/Executed by Firing Squad/Big Roundup Continues," *Meriden Morning Record*, May 4, 1916, 1.
[4] "Irish Revolt is But Hair-Brained, Tragic Absurdity — A Fracas," *The Montreal Daily Mail*, May 1, 1916, 1.
[5] *Ibid.*, 6.
[6] Charles Callan Tansill, *America and the Fight for Irish Freedom, 1866-1922*. New York: Devin-Adair Co., 1957, 204n.
[7] Younger, *Ireland's Civil War, op. cit.*, 50.

had clamoured for Maxwell to exercise a retributive hand, but the mood changed. Maxwell's calculated mercilessness caused revulsion, an emotional swing of sympathy towards the underdog.[8]

It is evident that the British government — or somebody — had badly misjudged the situation. Still, the executions continued.

Joseph Plunkett, dying of tuberculosis, was married in his cell just before being shot. Common belief has it that William "Willie" Pearse (1881-1916), Pádraic's brother, was condemned for not choosing his relations more wisely, John MacBride (1868-1916) for raising the Irish Transvaal Brigade, two units of commandoes who fought with the Boers against the British during the Second Boer War (1899-1902).

Connolly, whose wounds had turned gangrenous and who had only a short time to live in any event, was too weak to stand, so he was tied to a chair and shot on May 12. He and Seán MacDiarmada (1883-1916), disabled by polio and who took little part in the fighting, were the last to be executed in Dublin.

During his trial in England, Casement refused to defend himself on the legitimate grounds that he had hurried to Ireland in an effort to stop the Rising. Instead, he made a speech from the dock challenging the court's jurisdiction and asserting the right of the Irish nation to self-determination — allegedly the very thing in defense of which the British had gone to war against Germany.

Aftermath

De Valera, an American citizen only by a technicality, had renounced all citizenship except that of the Irish Republic, as had Tom Clarke, a naturalized U.S. citizen. Dev refused to plead for clemency.

Nevertheless, the outrage in the United States against the executions had reached a fever pitch. De Valera's sentence was commuted in part to assuage American feelings, and in part to prevent public opinion across the pond from going in favor of Germany. Public feeling was also clearly going

---

[8] *Ibid.*, 49.

against Maxwell. Countess Markievicz's death sentence was commuted due to her sex.

Eoin MacNeill had requested a meeting with Maxwell on Friday, April 28, 1916, to discuss ways to stop the fighting. For his trouble, he was arrested and sentenced to penal servitude for life on eight counts of attempting to cause disaffection among the civilian population and four counts of acting in a way prejudicial to recruiting.[9]

Both sides thus viewed MacNeill as a traitor. This lasted until he was transferred to the same prison where de Valera and a number of other Volunteers were incarcerated.

As MacNeill was being led into the yard where the others were taking their daily exercise (walking in a circle in silence), the commandant of Boland's Mill spotted his commander-in-chief, immediately stepped out of line, and ordered a salute: "Irish Volunteers, attention! Eyes left!" Outraged, the prison guards marched Dev off to a punishment cell.[10]

Today's historians and analysts are unanimous in declaring that the executions were a grave error on the part of the British. Many of them, however, claim that the authorities had no choice but to make that mistake. As Younger put it, "a policy of heaping ridicule on the rebels was just not possible. Too many lives had been lost and too much damage done."[11]

Still, had Maxwell waited even a short time before trying the leaders, and given them the full benefit of proper legal procedure, adequate counsel, and "the canvas and rigging of the law," much (if not all) of the outrage would have been quelled, if not avoided altogether, even had all the executions been carried out. It was the appearance not of justice that turned the Irish and even many English against the policy of the British government in Ireland, but the flavor of revenge, of vindictive malice that imbued the proceedings.

---

[9] Dangerfield, *The Damnable Question, op. cit.*, 210-211.
[10] Bill Severn, *Irish Statesman and Rebel: The Two Lives of Eamon de Valera*. New York: Ives Washburn, Inc., 1970, 41; cf. Dangerfield, *The Damnable Question, op. cit.*, 258-259.
[11] Younger, *Ireland's Civil War, op. cit.*, 47.

Even the Catholic hierarchy of Ireland, hardly sympathetic to revolutionary movements (especially those tainted with socialism and esoteric philosophies), was moved to indignation. It didn't help any when Maxwell wrote a letter on May 6, 1916 to Edward Thomas O'Dwyer (1842-1917), bishop of Limerick. In the letter Maxwell demanded that the bishop discipline some of his priests who had expressed their support of the Nationalist movement a little too forcefully for Maxwell's taste.

In response, His Lordship asked that Maxwell provide him with specific charges and evidence so that he could investigate. If the charges were true, O'Dwyer said he would take appropriate action.[12]

Clearly irritated, Maxwell sent another letter on May 12 in which he gave some unsubstantiated rumors about the two priests. He again demanded that the priests be punished, adding, "it should not be necessary for me to make definite charges, supported by evidence."[13] For Maxwell, suspicion and hearsay were sufficient to convict.

O'Dwyer then sent an open letter to the newspapers on May 17 with copies of all correspondence. Referring to Maxwell as "a military dictator of Ireland" he said, "You took care that no plea for mercy should interpose on behalf of the poor young fellows who surrendered to you in Dublin."[14]

Assuaging the scruples of many who had been worried that support for the Nationalist cause might be contrary to God's law, O'Dwyer added, "I regard your action with horror, and I believe that it has outraged the conscience of the country."[15]

Did Maxwell Blunder?

In hindsight, Maxwell's action in hurrying through the executions seems inexplicable. As Younger commented, Maxwell "may have realised, but probably did not, that his policy of wholesale executions was to present that brave, impassioned, improvised little army with the only victory it could have achieved."[16]

---

[12] *Ibid.*
[13] *Ibid.*
[14] *Ibid.*
[15] *Ibid.*
[16] *Ibid.*

But was Maxwell as obtuse as all that? Despite negative portrayals in literature and on stage, screen, and television, there is nothing inherently vicious about the military mind. Further, Maxwell was a more than competent officer, and a decorated war hero. Notwithstanding public opinion in Ireland and among historians, he was not a stupid man, although one with a grudge and something to prove.

There is one possibility that has never been fully explored, despite the fact that the Easter Rising is the pivotal event in modern Irish history. The following analysis is, of course, not by any means proof that this is what happened. It is presented as a possibility only, but it does fit all the facts of which we are aware.

Nevertheless, what happened on North King Street from late Friday through to Saturday, April 29, and Pearse's decision to surrender instead of fighting to the very end may be the key that unlocks the puzzle of Maxwell's otherwise incomprehensible actions. It was, along with the shooting of Pearse and the other leaders, and the murder of Sheehy-Skeffington by Bowen-Colthurst, the thing that most outraged the Irish and caused public opinion to go against the British.

A typical reaction was that of Michael O'Donoghue, later an engineer officer in the Irish Republican Army (IRA), Second Cork Brigade. (The Irish Volunteers officially became the IRA after Dáil Éireann, the Irish legislature, ratified the Easter Proclamation in 1919.) As O'Donoghue said, "A photo of some of the victims in a Dublin paper startled me. I recognised the faces of father and son butchered by English soldiers in their King St. home — William Hickey and his only son, Tommy."[17] Younger summed up the matter as follows:

> The Bowen-Colthurst episode[18] and the blood-letting by British troops in King Street remained to be dealt with and honest measures would have won back for England some of her lost ground. But when it was seen that, like a slovenly maid, Maxwell was busily sweeping the dirt under the mat, disillusionment grew among those whose loyalty was still swinging

---

[17] Michael V. O'Donoghue W.S. 1,741, 17.
[18] The murder of Francis Sheehy-Skeffington and others by Captain Bowen-Colthurst or at his orders.

on precarious hinges. Asquith himself had sense enough to force the Bowen-Colthurst issue into the open and this unhappy lunatic went to Broadmoor. The King Street incidents could not be so easily explained away and, although Maxwell was compelled to admit that "some unfortunate incidents, which we should regret now, may have occurred", he brushed them off as inevitable in the circumstances and, despite an elaborate inquiry, the culprits were never made to answer for their crimes.[19]

North King Street

The situation was almost custom-made for an atrocity. To begin with, Daly's Four Courts position with its heavily barricaded network of small streets centered around North King Street was, with the possible exception of de Valera's command at Boland's Mill and Bakery, arguably the best fortified and defended Republican post in Dublin. Outposts that the British expected to overcome in hours took days to reduce. As one Volunteer recalled, "There was little fighting in our area until the Wednesday, but from that [sic] on until the surrender on Saturday evening the fighting was intense."[20]

Gains — when they were made at all — were measured in inches and feet. As Maxwell later testified during the inquest investigating the civilian deaths in North King Street,

> With the one exception of the place at Ballsbridge, where the Sherwood Foresters were ambushed,[21] this was by far the worst fighting that occurred in the whole of Dublin. At first the troops, coming from one end of the street, were repulsed, and it was only when we made an attack at both ends that we succeeded, after twenty four hours' fighting, in capturing the street. The casualties were very heavy during this fighting.[22]

Maxwell later claimed that every effort had been made to persuade people to leave the area. As he stated, "We tried hard to get the women and children to leave North King Street. They would not go, their sympathies were with the rebels."

This statement, however, does not ring true. The British were completely unable to make any appreciable gains in the

---

[19] Younger, *Ireland's Civil War, op. cit.*, 53.
[20] Judge Fionan Lynch, W.S. 192, 12.
[21] The Mount Street Bridge outpost, under Lt. Michael Malone.
[22] Judge Fionan Lynch, W.S. 192, 13.

area until they brought up an improvised armored car late Friday. The soldiers were then able to shelter behind the vehicle, advance up North King Street, and begin breaking into houses.

Given these circumstances, there would have been no opportunity to "try hard to get the women and children to leave North King Street" until late Friday . . . and late Friday was when British troops began killing civilians. There is also the problem that neither during the court martial by the British government, nor in the hundreds of "Statements By Witnesses" collected by Buro Staire Mileata (Bureau of Military History) of the Republic of Ireland, did any of the surviving women and children ever mention being warned by the British to leave the area.

Instead, in a Proclamation issued by the Lord Lieutenant's office on Monday, April 24, the law-abiding portion of the civilian population was ordered to avoid "the danger of unnecessarily frequenting the streets or public places, or of assembling in crowds." People were lying low in their inner rooms and in cellars to avoid being hit by stray bullets.

As for simply leaving of their own accord, with some notable exceptions the civilian deaths during the Rising resulted from people disregarding the danger and going out to loot, hunt for food, or sightsee. Besides, by Thursday, British soldiers were shooting at anything that moved in the streets.[23]

Nevertheless, despite the absence of any corroboration or even plausibility of his claim, Maxwell continued to insist that the civilians who were killed by British troops on North King Street had only themselves to blame. As he rather disingenuously commented,

> No doubt in the districts where fighting was fiercest, parties of men under the great provocation of being shot at from rear and front, seeing their comrades fall from the fire of snipers, burst into suspected houses and killed such male members as were found. It is perfectly possible that some were innocent but they could have left their houses if they so wished and the number of such incidents that have been brought to notice is

---

[23] Duff, *Six Days to Shake an Empire, op. cit.*, 156-157.

happily few . . . Under the circumstance the troops as a whole behaved with the greatest restraint.[24]

Consistent with a cover-up, the story that came out of the official British government inquiry also had a great many holes in it — holes that were not filled in after the records were finally released in 1990, long after any redress was possible. Nor did it improve credibility when the individuals who participated in the incidents were spirited out of the country by being assigned to other units before the "South Staffs" were paraded before survivors to see if survivors could identify any of them.[25] As crafted for public consumption, the official story is as follows.

Early in the fighting, General Lowe had given orders that "no hesitation was to be shown in dealing with these rebels; that by their actions they had placed themselves outside the law and that they were not be made prisoners."[26]

After Maxwell arrived on Friday from London, the order to take no prisoners suddenly began to be interpreted very broadly. The soldiers in the North King Street fight allegedly and without any prior warning included in the category of "rebel" all the men they could find. As a report to the prime minister noted later, the soldiers allegedly "took [the order] to mean they could shoot anyone they suspected of being an active rebel."[27]

Consequently (so the story goes), on late Friday evening and early Saturday morning, British soldiers began forcing their way into houses along North King Street. They shot or bayonetted any men they found on the assumption that they were rebels. As Maxwell later declared in a statement,

> Always we found that the rebels tried to cloak themselves behind their women. When we began to search a house they threw away their rifles and joined the women herding at the back, pretending they had been there all the time. The rebels wore no uniform and the man who had been shooting at a sol-

---

[24] Charles Townshend, *Easter 1916 — The Irish Rebellion*. London: Penguin Books, Ltd., 2006, 293.
[25] Caulfield, *The Easter Revellion, op. cit.*, 293-294.
[26] Tim Pat Coogan, *1916, The Easter Rising*. London: Phoenix, 2005, 154.
[27] *Ibid.*, 156.

dier one moment might be walking quietly beside him at another.[28]

At the same time, the actions of the British soldiers were excused on the grounds that, having fought a fierce battle for two days with no end in sight, they were driven insane with rage. Out of control, they burst into the houses lining North King Street and, having temporarily lost their reason, began killing indiscriminately.

Thus, disciplined and highly trained British soldiers were, at one and the same time, being careful to follow orders *and* completely losing control of themselves.

Fact v. Fiction

The facts give a different story. Dealing first with the claim that the British soldiers were temporarily insane, it is not credible that soldiers who have lost the use of reason were able to distinguish between men, women, and children. When soldiers go berserk, they do not stop to think who or even what they are killing; they massacre anything that moves. The fact that only men were killed argues against the claim that the soldiers had gone out of control.

Then there is the belief that the soldiers did what they did under the impression that they were obeying an order to take no prisoners. This, too, does not hold up under examination.

The fact is that while a number of the men were shot or bayonetted in their homes or dragged into the street, some were taken hostage and held for many hours before being killed. This would be against the order to take no prisoners, and is inconsistent with the behavior of soldiers who have run amok. It agrees completely, however, with the testimony of Lieutenant Leslie Wilson in the Bowen-Colthurst investigation that it was "common practice" of the British troops in Ireland to take hostages and kill them if so ordered.[29]

The deaths of Patrick Bealen (or Bealin) and James Healy would appear to be instances of this "common practice."

---

[28] In his testimony Major Francis Vane refuted Maxwell's statement, declaring that the Irish Volunteers "fought clean," corroborated by Dr. C.M. O'Brien in a letter to the *Irish Independent*. Liam de Róiste, W.S., 1698, 339.

[29] Hanna Sheehy-Skeffington, *British Imperialism as I Have Known It, op. cit.*, 19.

Bealen had been dragged off by soldiers and not seen alive again, while Healy's wife had last seen him alive when he left for his job at Jameson's Distillery on Saturday evening, after the surrender.

Rosanna Knowles, a woman who lived on North King Street, told a reporter from the *Irish Times* that she had talked with a soldier about Bealen. She had asked him, "Was there much [sic] killed?" Again, inconsistent with the behavior of someone who has lost control of himself, the soldier answered, "There was a good deal of our men killed and a good deal of the others. I only felt sorry for the poor fellow at the corner. I pitied him from my heart though I had to shoot him. He had made tea for me." Knowles then stated,

> He said that [another] soldier had brought the prisoner downstairs in Mrs O'Rourke's [the pub where Bealen worked], the soldier said that the man had given him his pen knife and his ring. He produced the pen knife but he had lost the ring. He said that he brought him downstairs he had not the heart to shoot him straight and they told him to go up the stairs and they let bang at him from the foot of the stairs.[30]

Assuming Knowles's account is trustworthy, the soldiers shot Bealen and Healy on direct orders after the cease fire. A civilian inquest conducted on May 16, 1916 by Louis A. Byrne, Dublin City Coroner, returned the following verdicts:

> "[W]e find that the said Patrick Bealen died from shock and haemorrhage, resulting from Bullet wounds inflicted by a soldier or soldiers, in whose custody he was, an unarmed and unoffending prisoner." . . . .
>
> INQUEST ON JAMES HEALY. The adjourned inquest on the body of James Healy, which was also found buried in the cellar of 177 North King Street, was then resumed. The jury returned a verdict in terms similar to that recorded in the case of Bealen.[31]

Given that the official stories are contradictory, is there a more reasonable or even plausible explanation that fits the known facts? The following suggests itself.

---

[30] *Irish Times*, May 17, 1916.
[31] "Civilians Killed in the Rising," Irish Medals, http://irishmedals.org/images.html, accessed January 14, 2016.

It is evident from the fighting throughout Dublin that the Volunteers were prepared to carry on to the last man and woman. De Valera's post at Boland's Mill and Daly's around the Four Courts had demonstrated that, unless the British could gain some advantage or leverage, it could be days, possibly even another week or more, before the Rising could be suppressed.

Worse, although public opinion was, in the main, clearly against the Republican effort, it was only a matter of time before the estimated 10,000 Volunteers throughout Ireland were able to get organized and join the effort. Volunteer activity in Galway, Wexford, and Meath had shown what even disorganized, undermanned, and poorly armed groups could accomplish, especially with most of the attention and efforts by the British centered on Dublin.

Maxwell may well have decided that it was of the utmost importance to bring the rebellion to an end as swiftly as possible, regardless of the methods employed. His previous experience in putting down insurgencies in Africa and the difficulty of mounting an effective campaign against guerillas when the main British effort had to be in France, could have convinced him that any and all means were justified — the survival of the Empire demanded it.

The problem for Maxwell was that no means except death is effective against people who are prepared to die, or believe they have already forfeited their lives. They have nothing to lose. He needed leverage to be able to force the Volunteers to surrender unconditionally, and he didn't have any. He may therefore have decided to create some.

The timing of the massacre, eye-witness accounts, the "common practice" of taking hostages and killing them, and Maxwell's callous and evasive responses during the court martial all point to one thing. That is, Maxwell may have ordered the killing of civilians to gain the leverage he believed he needed to force the Volunteers to surrender.

Further, as his correspondence with Bishop O'Dwyer demonstrates, Maxwell firmly believed that suspicion, guilt by association, and supposition were sufficient to convict someone, especially a presumed rebel. By ordering the killing or taking as hostage people whom he believed were guilty anyway, Maxwell would be in a position to present Pearse with an ultimatum the provisional president could not ignore: surrender unconditionally, or more civilians will be killed, and their blood (according to Maxwell) would be on Pearse's hands.

Blackmail?

Pearse was preparing to move Volunteer headquarters to the Four Courts on McLoughlin's suggestion to continue the fight when he learned of the North King Street massacre. It was the deliberate killing of civilians by British troops that persuaded him to ask for terms from General Lowe.[32] At that time Pearse would not have been aware that Maxwell might have ordered the killings. Pearse would have believed that he, Pearse, not Maxwell, held the upper hand, or at least retained enough of an advantage to bargain for terms.

It would, however, have been made clear to Pearse after he surrendered to Lowe and was taken to Maxwell that he was being given no choice: either surrender all Volunteer forces unconditionally, or more civilians would be killed. This would explain the otherwise odd wording of the surrender document that put the primary reason for the surrender as being to prevent "further slaughter" of civilians, instead of "further needless deaths" or words to that effect. Pearse's use of the word *slaughter* seems to imply volition instead of accident.

It would also explain Pearse's acquiescing to an unconditional surrender when the Volunteers were prepared to fight to the end. He and the other Volunteers were willing to die for the cause, but he could not ask the same of innocent civilians.

The unconditional surrender astounded all the other commandants and their men, especially de Valera and Daly, as well as the Volunteers in Enniscorthy. None of these initially believed that the surrender was legitimate, and had to have it proved to them. As John Shouldice recalled,

> Earlier in the day, perhaps about 2 or 3 p.m., it was learned that negotiations were on foot for a conditional surrender and about 5 or 6 p.m. instructions came through from the Four Courts that we were to return there and surrender as directed by our Commanding Officer, Comdt. Daly. It was then ascertained that the surrender was unconditional which put us all

---

[32] Younger, *Ireland's Civil War, op. cit.*, 42-43.

in a very depressed state — knowing that we would meet with very little mercy from our old enemy.[33]

Once the surrender document was signed and accepted by all remaining Volunteer posts, there would have been no reason to retain any hostages, but a desperate need to hide the fact that hostages had been taken. A belief in the need for additional leverage would explain why Healy was taken after the cease fire but before all Volunteer posts throughout the country had surrendered, as well as the need to get rid of him once the surrender was complete.

It would also explain the haste with which the leaders were executed. If Pearse had been put on public trial instead of subjected to a quick, secret court martial, he would almost certainly have made some statement concerning any inducement he might have been offered to force him to surrender unconditionally against all his plans and his personal inclination.

Preferably, leaders of a rebellion are executed last. This presumably drives home the lesson that they are primarily responsible for what happened, and makes them suffer more by seeing their followers die before them. A show trial is also virtually a requirement to demonstrate to the world both the supposed criminality of the rebellion and to give an object lesson in the uselessness of opposing those in power.

If, however, Maxwell had blackmailed Pearse into surrendering by threatening to continue to kill civilians, he could not have risked a public trial in which Pearse might make a statement revealing the pressure that had been brought to bear. Maxwell would have had to stop Pearse's mouth, and thus Pearse would be among the first to be shot. Having started with Pearse, the others would have had to be executed quickly to cover up the fact that there was anything special about Pearse's execution.

The Bowen-Colthurst Cover-Up

Where the whitewashing of the North King Street massacre was coldblooded and despicable, the handling of the murders committed by Bowen-Colthurst was oafish and contemptible. Doubt can legitimately be expressed concerning

---

[33] Shouldice, W.S., 162, 9.

the rationalizations advanced for the former. No one, however, has ever denied that Bowen-Colthurst was outstandingly guilty — and serious questions can be raised as to the legitimacy of his insanity plea.

Nevertheless, it was clear from the very first that the response the British authorities decided on was to cover up the whole thing, from Major Rossborough's refusal to arrest Bowen-Colthurst, to the repairs made to the barracks. As Major Vane noted in his autobiography,

> On Sunday (30th April) a party of Royal Engineers, again without my knowledge, was sent from Dublin Castle at night to repair the wall against which the men were shot. They did their work very artistically, for I examined it afterwards, no doubt with the object that the facts might be denied. The next day I was summoned to the Orderly Room, and then was informed by a Colonel Maccamond, who had taken over command of the troops from Major Rossborough, that I would be relieved of my duties with the Defenses, and would hand them over to Captain Bowen Colthurst![34]

There were, however, three critical differences between the victims of the North King Street massacre and those murdered by Bowen-Colthurst.

One, chief among Bowen-Colthurst's victims was Francis Sheehy-Skeffington, a figure of some prominence in Dublin. He was a public figure, known to be a total pacifist; James Stephens related that he had often been subjected to physical abuse, and had never once borne his attackers even the slightest vestige of ill will.

Two, Sheehy-Skeffington's wife Hanna was a political activist, and in many ways the opposite of her husband. A militant suffragette — as her husband was a "fighting pacifist"[35] — she had no problem with recourse to violence, as long as she thought it was justified in the cause of right, and would pursue a matter to the bitter end.

In addition, Hanna's experiences in the votes for women movement proved that she could not be frightened off by threats or bribes. She, in common with a number of other

---

[34] Vane, *Agin the Governments, op. cit.*, 265.
[35] Hanna Sheehy-Skeffington, *British Imperialism as I Have Known It, op. cit.*, 17.

women connected with the Rising, was to become a terror to the British, and fully justified the equality of the sexes on which the Nationalists insisted.

Three, Vane had a strong sense of justice and a family tradition of championing human rights. He was also not someone who could be intimidated, even by authorities at the highest levels of the military or the government.

Hanna Sheehy-Skeffington's Investigation

At about 5:30 pm on Tuesday, April 25, 1916 Hanna had met Francis in a shop on Camden Street for tea. Francis had been full of plans to organize a "civic police" to stop the looting, and called a meeting for the next day.

Hanna returned home. Francis stayed behind doing paperwork, possibly preparing the text of the leaflets he distributed that evening.

When Francis did not return home Tuesday evening, Hanna began making enquiries. Coming to the attention of the authorities, she was put under surveillance, the police (who had returned to duty) evidently preferring that to stopping the systematic looting by British soldiers, some of whom were selling what they took, while officers pocketed "souvenirs."[36]

Hanna continued her efforts through Friday, when her two sisters went to Portobello Barracks on her behalf. Bowen-Colthurst immediately arrested them and put them on trial for having been seen talking to known Sinn Féiners, probably Hanna.[37] As Hanna related,

> They were refused all information by Capt. Colthurst, who said he knew nothing whatever of Sheehy Skeffington, and told them, "the sooner they left the Barracks the better for them." They were marched off under armed guard, and forbidden to speak till they left the premises.[38]

Her sisters' experience convinced Hanna that Bowen-Colthurst had guilty knowledge of her husband's fate. That afternoon, she found James Coade's father, and he told her

---

[36] *Ibid.*, 22-23.
[37] *Ibid.*, 23.
[38] *Ibid.*

that he had seen Francis's body in the barracks morgue when he went to claim the body of his son.

Hanna set out for Portobello Barracks, but met a priest on Rathmines Road, Rev. Francis E. O'Loughlin[39] (1868-1957), the barracks chaplain and curate of the Rathmines Catholic Church. Father O'Loughlin said he would make enquiries on her behalf, and a little later confirmed that Francis was dead. He gave no other details, evidently believing himself to be *sub siglo* ("under seal") and not free to divulge anything he learned while carrying out his priestly duties.

Returning home shortly after 6 pm, Hanna was putting her son, Owen, to bed when she saw her house surrounded by a squad of soldiers nominally under the command of Colonel H.T.N. Allat[40] and accompanied by Bowen-Colthurst, who appeared to be giving the orders. Evidently the enquiries had made the authorities nervous. They were anxious to gather incriminating evidence to justify Bowen-Colthurst's actions *post facto*. The Royal Commission later concluded "that the incident must be judged merely as an ineffectual attempt to obtain evidence which might justify or excuse the shooting which had already taken place at Portobello Barracks."[41]

As Hanna described the scene, "They broke in simultaneously all over the house — some went on the roof — and Capt. Colthurst rushed upon us — the maid, Owen and myself — with a squad with fixed bayonets, shouting 'Hands up!' to the boy and me."[42]

---

[39] Father O'Loughlin was born in Melbourne, Australia, and was ordained for the Dublin Diocese on December 11, 1892. After serving in various capacities, he became curate of the Rathmines parish in 1911, serving there until 1924, when he became Parish Priest of Donabate. In 1928 he became Parish Priest of Valleymount, where he served until his death.

[40] Given as both Allett (213) and Allat (259) in the Irish Times *Sinn Féin Rebellion Handbook*. He was later killed in the fighting at the South Union.

[41] Royal Commission of Inquiry, *Sinn Féin Rebellion Handbook*, op. cit., § 51.

[42] Hanna Sheehy-Skeffington, *British Imperialism as I Have Known It*, op. cit., 23.

Everything of value was taken, "books, pictures, souvenirs, toys, linen, and household goods,"[43] the officers making a joke of it. Hanna overheard one of the soldiers say, "I didn't enlist for this. They are taking the whole bloomin' house with them."[44]

Bowen-Colthurst raided the house again on Monday, May 1, and took Margaret Farrelly, the new temporary maid,[45] hostage, locking her up for a week for the crime of being found in the Sheehy-Skeffington home. Hanna was not molested beyond having any remaining valuables stolen. Lieutenant Leslie Wilson later said that he was sorry "that they had not shot Mrs. Skeffington while they were about it."[46]

Francis's body was reburied secretly on May 8. It had been handed over to his father on condition that Hanna not be told. He agreed when Maxwell assured him the murderer would be brought to justice.

Vane's Further "Adventures"

On Tuesday, May 2, Vane traveled to London after obtaining leave from the Adjutant General — who, in a conversation with Vane convinced the Major "that they were going to do even more stupid things" in addition to the Bowen-Colthurst cover up.[47] In London Vane used his connections to obtain a meeting with Lord Kitchener and Sir Maurice Bonham-Carter (1880-1960), private secretary to Asquith, the prime minister.

Vane was "relegated to unemployment" (relieved of duty), but persisted. Finally, on May 18, Rufus Isaacs (1860-1935), First Earl of Reading, Lord Chief justice of England, agreed that a court martial would be appropriate. It would have to be held in secret, however, to avoid embarrassing the government or the army.

After returning to Dublin, Vane met with Hanna to apologize on behalf of the Army, and assure her of his continued

---

[43] *Ibid.*, 24.
[44] *Ibid.*
[45] The former maid had resigned, "having been too terrified to stay." *Sinn Féin Rebellion Handbook, op. cit.*, 224.
[46] Hanna Sheehy-Skeffington, *British Imperialism as I Have Known It, op. cit.*, 24.
[47] Vane, *Agin the Governments, op. cit.*, 266.

assistance. Soon afterwards the authorities warned him not to be seen in her company.

Maxwell then suppressed a commendation Vane received for his assault on the South Union Workhouse. This had been under the command of William Thomas ("Liam"; "W.T.") Cosgrave (1880-1965), future Chairman of the Provisional Government (1922), and President of the Executive Committee (1922-1932).[48] Maxwell's action cost Vane a promotion to a command in France (ironically probably saving his life as the unit to which he would have been assigned was decimated), and again getting him relieved of duty. As Vane related,

> [Maxwell] apparently was a party to the concealment of the murder of Skeffington — for I had reported the events at once — the attempt of his chief Intelligence Officer to laugh at the murders, and it must have been with his connivance that Colthurst, six days after his crime, was appointed to relieve me in command of the Defenses. Above all, he presumably sanctioned the executions of the fourteen so called rebel leaders, one of whom a boy of nineteen[49] — which were carried out in the most brutally stupid manner.[50]

Nothing was done until June 2, when Maxwell sent a letter to Hanna requesting a meeting. During the meeting Maxwell offered Hanna £10,000 (nearly $50,000 at the time) in compensation if she would absolve the government of any need to fix guilt or apologize. Asquith repeated the offer when Hanna met with him on July 19.

Hanna refused what was to all intents and purposes a bribe, but did accept permission to leave the country without condition. This permission was required under the emergency powers granted to Maxwell in Ireland.

Hanna went to the United States, where she began raising funds for the care of the widows and orphans of the Volunteers and of the civilians killed in the North King Street

---

[48] Vane visited Cosgrave in 1917 after Cosgrave's release from prison and complimented him and his men on the fight they had put up. Cosgrave noted in his Witness Statement that Vane, who relied on memory for his autobiography after the government confiscated and destroyed his notes, got some details wrong. Liam T. Cosgrave, W.S. 268, 20-21.
[49] Edward Daly, the youngest executed, was twenty-five.
[50] Vane, *Agin the Governments, op. cit.*, 271.

massacre, and publicizing her husband's case. Vane offered to join her there at his own expense to (as he put it) "modify the natural rancour of her statements."[51] Hanna was willing to give the opposition a say, but the government refused Vane permission.

Hanna met with a number of eminent people, including former president Theodore Roosevelt. Although Roosevelt, who had something of a "love-hate" relationship with the Irish and Irish Americans,[52] condemned the Rising, he also had a strong sense of justice. Unwilling to condemn anyone without hard evidence, however, on January 18, 1917 Roosevelt wrote a long and detailed letter to Vane to verify Hanna's account, which Vane received in February through diplomatic channels.

The government and the military attempted to prevent Vane from responding, but he eventually got a letter through, confirming Hannah's account. Roosevelt corresponded with Vane "almost up to his death."[53]

Afterwards...

On June 6, Bowen-Colthurst was arrested and court martialed. To avoid being convicted on a charge of first degree murder, he successfully pleaded not guilty by reason of insanity.

This was allegedly the result of shell shock suffered during the Mons retreat in August and September 1914. "Shell shock" was a vague term that had been in use for less than a year. It was used to describe psychological trauma resulting from battle, whether the cause was physical or mental.

Bowen-Colthurst was sent to Broadmoor Hospital, a high security institution for the criminally insane, where he stayed for eighteen months. He was then sent to a hospital in Canada until his release as fully cured on April 26, 1921. He was granted a pension, remained in Canada, and died in 1965.

---

[51] *Ibid.*, 273.
[52] Roosevelt was a founding member of the American Irish Historical Society in 1897, and headed the Executive Committee.
[53] Vane, *Agin the Governments, op. cit.*, 278.

The verdict caused such outrage that a Royal Commission of Inquiry was convened on August 23, 1916 under Sir John Allsebrook Simon (1873-1954), later First Viscount Simon, to look into the Bowen-Colthurst affair and the North King Street massacre. Unfortunately, according to historian Sir Charles Petrie (1895-1977) and other authorities, Simon was "surely the worst [Foreign Secretary] of modern times," a very poor choice to handle a sensitive matter.

Ultimately, Maxwell sentenced ninety or so people to death, in courts martial lasting an average of five minutes each,[54] although most of the sentences were commuted. Approximately 3,000 were interned in various prisons and camps, many without trial and without specific charges being made, nearly half with no proven connection to the Rising.

The executions and internments are generally credited with turning the Irish against British rule, but the process appears to have started during the Rising itself. Younger, for example, related that two students who had started out to defend Trinity College against the Volunteers on Monday, ended up on Thursday in their own Republican outpost sniping at British troops, sharing a rifle between them.[55] As Lillian Stokes recorded in her diary on Sunday, April 30, 1916,

> [W]hen we thought it safe we . . . slipped back and were just in time to see 70 prisoners from Bolands [sic] march past, fine looking fellows, swinging along in good step. Of course they looked shabby and dirty, they had been fighting for seven days. Until I saw them I thought they ought to be shot, but I don't now — it would be [a] terrible waste of material [sic], if it was nothing else — it made one miserable to see them. The leader in Bolands was a fine looking man called the Mexican,[56] he is educated and speaks like a gentleman.[57]

Perhaps, then, it was not so much that the executions and internments were the cause of what looked like an abrupt about-face, but that they were the focus that united most of the Nationalist factions at a critical time. Had not the Rising

---

[54] Duff, *Six Days to Shake an Empire, op. cit.*, 188.
[55] Younger, *The Irish Civil War, op. cit.*, 40.
[56] De Valera; Stokes was confused — Dev was known as "the Spaniard" because of his surname.
[57] Stokes, *Personal Experience, op. cit.*, 8.

occurred, the Unionists would very likely have been able to take advantage of the differences of opinions among the Nationalists (with goals ranging from mild internal autonomy to complete independence) and divide — and weaken — them further. They would have been able to eviscerate the 1912 Home Rule bill, if not do away with it completely, especially after the official timidity in the face of the Curragh Mutiny.

As it was, the executions not only unified the Irish Nationalists and world opinion behind the Republican cause, they strengthened the Republican cause itself by eliminating potential divisions. It is probable that, had they lived, the leaders of the Rising would have had more of a falling out than what actually occurred, as happens with almost every revolution.

Clarke's radicalism, Pearse's Fabian socialism, Connolly's Marxism, and so on, would have all but ensured this. Men of such strong will and beliefs could unite on a specific objective, but once that objective was gained, there would have been nothing keeping them together. The fact that of the leaders only de Valera survived — and he not even of the inner circle — was a grim blessing in disguise.

By interning massive numbers of people the British also helped Sinn Féin, founded by Arthur Griffith as a political party, take full advantage of the situation. Sinn Féin clubs sprang up almost overnight, until there were some 1,300 with 250,000 members. De Valera, the obvious choice, became president of Sinn Féin.

The party ran men who were in prison as candidates for parliament. One campaign poster displayed Griffith full length in prison garb with the text reading "Put Him in to Get Him Out/Vote for Griffith/The Man in Jail for Ireland." Having had great success in by-elections, Sinn Féin won seventy-three of one hundred and five Irish seats in the 1918 general election.

Redmond died in March 1918, and with him died the hopes of a constitutional solution to "the damnable question" of Home Rule. It was no longer a question as to what form, if any, Home Rule would take, but what form of independence the Irish would accept.

Thus, the Irish situation that faced the British at the end of the First World War was, in a sense, the opposite of that which had faced them at the beginning. In 1914, the Unionists had vowed to fight to the death before submitting to any form of Home Rule, but had come to accept Home Rule for the south and partition for the north as a solution.

By 1918, the Nationalists had already proved that they were willing to fight to the death before submitting to continued British rule of any kind. Could they be persuaded to accept Home Rule for the south and partition for the North?

The British had their answer a few months after the end of the Great War in November 1918. No. The Irish War of Independence began on January 21, 1919 when Dáil Éireann ratified the 1916 Easter Proclamation, and (by coincidence) the IRA in Tipperary killed two RIC guards of a gelignite shipment who opened fire after being ordered twice to surrender.[58]

Making the job of the British government much more difficult than otherwise was the fact that Sinn Féin had established a parallel Republican government in Ireland, with its own parliament (Dáil Éireann), army, courts, and even tax collectors. In some instances the Republican tax men came through an area and collected rates ahead of the British, who, when they called, were presented with signed receipts for taxes paid, and had to go away empty-handed.[59]

The War of Independence quickly became a war of attrition. If the British could not afford to lose, neither could the Irish hope to win — at least in conventional terms.

The Republican strategy, therefore, focused on making it impossible for the British to govern Ireland. In this, they were helped not a little by the intransigence of the Unionists in Ulster.

Urged on by Carson, the Orange Lodges in the north that had formed the core of the Ulster Volunteer Force were persuaded that they stood between Sinn Féin and the dissolution of the British Empire. There would be (as they immortalized in their sloganeering) "No Surrender" to the forces of

---

[58] Duff, *Six Days to Shake an Empire, op. cit.*, 244-245.
[59] *Ibid.*, 241.

popery and Republicanism. The character of the northern statelet was established early:

> There followed an ugly and protracted campaign of terrorism in which many Catholic families were driven from their homes. 62 people were killed and 200 wounded. Long before the Government of Ireland Act came into force the following year there had thus been established the sad and bitter pattern which from the beginning was to dominate the life of the new state.[60]

Paradoxically, except for the somewhat limited evil of the riots against Catholics and Nationalists (often considered indistinguishable by Unionists), Ulster stayed relatively calm during the War of Independence. The British policy of coercion was carried out almost exclusively in the south — an act of hypocrisy that did not escape the extraordinarily effective Sinn Féin propaganda machine. Outlawing anti-government organizations, suppressing newspapers, and carrying out massive arrests and internments was a policy almost custom-made to outrage the media and the British public, which (like most people without the benefit of a modern, scientific education) have an inherent sense of fairness and justice.

Tans and Auxies

British policy in Ireland and the boycotting of its members by the public caused massive resignations from the RIC, many of whom quit in disgust. Faced with the need to reassert authority, early in 1920 the British began recruiting replacements from recently demobilized troops. As there were not enough complete uniforms to go around, the new recruits were dressed in bits and pieces of RIC uniforms, discarded military outfits, and civilian clothing. With grim humor someone called them "Black and Tans" after a noted hunting pack in County Limerick, and the label stuck.

In mid-1920 the "Tans" were supplemented with the Auxiliary Division of the RIC, the "Auxies." Bad as the reputation of the Black and Tans was to become, that of the Auxies was

---

[60] F.S.L. Lyons, *Ireland Since the Famine*. London: Fontana Press, 1973, 414.

worse, although they numbered no more than 1,418 at their height in January 1922.[61] As one historian described them,

> [I]n action they seem to have been every bit as tough and uninhibited as the Black and Tans, if not more so; indeed, their own commanding officer, Brigadier-General E.F. Crozier [sic],[62] eventually resigned his post rather than go on leading what he described as a drunken and insubordinate body of men.[63]

In countering such measures, the Republicans proved themselves every bit as ruthless as the British. Under Michael Collins, the Intelligence Squad ("The Squad") was formed to target key members of the British secret service for assassination.

This eventually led to "Bloody Sunday," November 21, 1920, following the discovery of how much information the British intelligence service (G-Division of the RIC) had collected on the IRA and Sinn Féin.[64] Collins decided it was better to try and take all the British agents out at once, rather than deal with them piecemeal. Early in the morning, eleven British "G-Men" were killed and three injured, most of them in their homes, in a successful effort to paralyze — for a time — the British intelligence operation in one "swoop."[65]

Later that day, truckloads of the Auxies drove to Croke Park, a GAA stadium, during a Gaelic football game between Tipperary and Dublin. Allegedly mistaking the uniformed ticket takers for armed insurgents, the Auxies opened fire on the crowd. They killed thirteen spectators and one player, and wounded approximately sixty others.

The Auxies then searched the men and took hostage two IRA members and another man with no involvement in the organization. These were taken to Dublin Castle where they

---

[61] *Ibid.*, 416n.
[62] Brigadier General Frank Percy Crozier (1879-1937), RIC Auxiliary Division Commander under Police Adviser/Chief of Police Lieutenant-General Sir Henry Hugh Tudor (1871-1965).
[63] Lyons, *Ireland Since the Famine, op. cit.*, 416.
[64] Charles Dalton, W.S. 434, 18-19.
[65] *Ibid.*, 19-21; cf. David Neligan, W.S. 380, 9.

were tortured, bayonetted, stood up against a wall, and (in the usual phrase) shot "while attempting to escape."[66],[67]

The British, however, soon regrouped. In particular, the "Igoe Gang" was a covert British squad that prowled the streets of Dublin. They targeted suspected Volunteers from out of town who would not recognize them:

> Igoe and his squad had adopted a technique of moving as a patrol through the streets of Dublin in a formation that was not noticeable to the pedestrians, and if they came across any country Volunteers in their strolls they either arrested them or beat them up and then arrested them. Needless to remark, as street activities became more general, this patrol became a menace to the Dublin Volunteers who were moving around the streets carrying out ambushes or other jobs.[68]

In 1920 — six years after the 1914 Government of Ireland Act granting Home Rule to a single Ireland passed parliament — Britain offered local autonomy within the Empire to both Dublin and Belfast. After the Rising, British Prime Minister David Lloyd George (1863-1945), First Earl Lloyd-George of Dwyfor, had led Redmond to believe that partition

---

[66] Duff, *Six Days to Shake an Empire, op. cit.*, 266.
[67] Some authorities maintain that Crozier resigned as a result of Bloody Sunday. In *Eyewitness to Irish History*, a compendium of historical documents, Crozier stated he resigned in February 1921, three months later, when Tudor reinstated a number of Auxiliaries whom Crozier had dismissed for looting. Ellis, *Eyewitness to Irish History, op. cit.*, 246. George F.H. (Fitz-Hardinge) Berkeley, a member of the "Peace with Ireland Council" 1920-1921, corroborated the grounds for Crozier's resignation as being Tudor's overriding his authority: "General Crozier resigned his commission because eighteen Auxiliaries whom he had dismissed for looting, were reinstated by the Government." Berkeley hinted Crozier may have been consumed by guilt for Bloody Sunday and other atrocities committed by the Auxies, for Crozier tried to explain himself a number of times: "He offered to tell me his whole story privately. But I never availed myself of the offer. But there were various people who heard everything that he had to say, and I cannot help supposing that fact must have caused some considerable uneasiness in Government circles." George F. H. Berkeley, W.S. 994, 119-120.
[68] Dalton W.S. 434, 23.

would be temporary, and at the same time promised Carson it would be permanent.⁶⁹

In any event, Belfast accepted the offer, and Dublin refused. The war continued.

The Civil War

By mid-1921, however, it was evident that the IRA could not carry on much longer. There was no real chance of victory, and it was becoming difficult to keep a campaign going with little in the way of resources. Given that the Republicans still believed partition was offered as a temporary accommodation until the differences between the north and the south could be worked out and the entire country established as an independent Republic, Dáil Éireann agreed to a truce.

During the negotiations in London, Lloyd George made it clear that partition was not only non-negotiable, he considered it permanent. Northern and Southern Ireland were to be "separate but equal." If the delegates did not agree, then the might of the British Empire would be brought to bear on them, and the war would continue with no end in sight.

Whether or not he believed Lloyd George was bluffing, de Valera (who had stayed behind in Dublin) gave explicit instructions to Collins, Griffith, and the other delegates that under no circumstances were they to agree to a treaty that included partition. Worn down by the protracted debates and faced with the prospect of an Ireland ruined politically and economically for a generation or more, however, the Irish delegates signed the treaty on December 6, 1921.

The British parliament ratified the treaty on December 16, 1921, but the Dáil debated until January 1922. Collins declared that the treaty gave the Irish more freedom than they had enjoyed in the past seven centuries, and they could eventually achieve full independence.

De Valera stood by his original position. As Volunteers and, later, as the IRA, they had fought for an independent and unified Irish Republic. Anything less was unacceptable.

---

⁶⁹ Dangerfield, *The Damnable Question, op. cit.*, 223-242; Younger, *Ireland's Civil War, op. cit.*, 50.

The Dáil voted on January 7, sixty-four in favor of ratifying the treaty, fifty-seven against. The Irish Free State, Saorstát Éireann, came into being.

The country divided and, on June 28, 1922, the Irish Civil War began.

Collins found himself in the position that the British had held during the War of Independence. He had plenty of resources that the British, doubtless relieved that the Irish could now fight it out amongst themselves, were happy to provide. De Valera occupied the place of Collins, using the same tactics that had served the Big Fellow so well — and with the same inability to bring matters to a successful resolution.

Collins's tactics caused divisions in the country and even in families that took generations to heal. He introduced military courts with broad discretionary powers. From September 1922 to April 1923, seventy-seven people were executed. By the end of the war he had imprisoned 12,000 people, while eight-hundred Free State troops, and an estimated 5,000 of the IRA, had been killed.

Adding to the cost was the loss of both Griffith and Collins within a few days of one another. Probably worn out by the stress of trying to lead a divided country and fighting against former comrades, Griffith, barely fifty years old, suffered a fatal heart attack on August 12, 1922. On August 22, Collins was killed in an ambush, probably in retribution for what many perceived as his betrayal of the Republic.

Finally, in April, De Valera gave his "Legion of the Rear Guard" speech and ordered his men to stand down and accept the treaty — for the time being. In May 1923, Frank Aiken (1898-1983), IRA Chief of Staff, issued a "dump arms" order.

Ireland was divided between the Irish Free State — which many did not consider free — and the rump statelet of Northern Ireland. Although the Free State did become independent in fact instead of legal fiction within a generation, the country remains divided to this day, a testament to the ability of anyone to make a bad system worse if the wrong guiding principles are used.

Nevertheless, Ireland, virtually an exemplar for what happens when bad principles, even with the best of intentions, guide a bad system, can also be a model for how even the worst situation (which Ireland most definitely is not) can be turned around by employing the right principles within a justly structured system. To do that, however, and to know what principles should be applied and how a just system should be structured, we need to know what went wrong and how.

This is somewhat difficult in Ireland, for the forces and influences that caused the present situation and that led up to the Easter Rising can, without exaggeration, be said to go back a thousand years or more. Still, by confining ourselves to more recent events, it should be possible to get an adequate grasp of the situation, and thus have a way to correct it in a manner consistent with the principles of economic and social justice.

So, although the story actually starts several centuries before then, we can begin, for convenience sake, in the closing years of the eighteenth century, in a little coastal village in Wales. . . .

Chapter 4: Back to the Beginning

As invasions go, it wasn't much, little enough to lead to the earth-shaking Easter Rising more than a century hence. Four French warships carrying between 1,200 and 1,400 French soldiers — *La Legion Noire* ("The Black Legion") — landed at Carregwastad Head near the village of Fishguard in Wales on Wednesday, February 22, 1797. The soldiers were predominantly the sweepings of the French prisons and other "volunteers," with a leavening of French and Irish regulars in the service of France. Many of the irregulars were not completely certain which end of a musket to point at an enemy. The Irish-American Colonel William Tate commanded the expeditionary force, while Commodore Jean-Joseph Castagnier (1753-1807) commanded the fleet. Such was —

The Last Invasion of Britain

What ended up being the "Battle of Fishguard" was supposed to be a diversion coordinated with and in support of another attempted rising in Ireland planned by Theobald Wolfe Tone (1763-1798). Tone was one of the founders of the United Irishmen. He is regarded as the "Father of Irish Republicanism."

The first landing spot selected was "near Bristol." The idea was that Tate (incorrectly described in most accounts as elderly) would take and burn Bristol, an important British seaport on the southwest coast of England. He would then cross into Wales and march against Chester and Liverpool. How this was supposed to be accomplished with a force of 1,400 ill-equipped and poorly trained recruits is not entirely clear.

Weather conditions were unfavorable for a landing near Bristol, so Tate decided to go straight to Wales, and had the tiny fleet set course for Cardigan Bay. When the French warships arrived at Fishguard Bay, a signal gun from the local fort fired to warn the townspeople was mistaken for possible resistance. Tate prudently had the vessels circle around to Carregwastad Head as the landing point, rather than let his troops (such as they were) be caught with their feet wet and slaughtered during the landing.

Troops and supplies were unloaded, and on Thursday morning, February 23, the French ships sailed away to report a successful landing. Their departure was possibly hastened by the distant sighting of a large number of women in traditional Welsh garb who came out to see the strange sight, whom the French mistook for red-coated British soldiers in the morning light.

The French soldiers almost immediately set about looting. They were unfortunate enough to be successful, the local folk having liberated a large quantity of food and wine from a Portuguese merchantman that had run aground recently. Still, Tate managed to get his troops two miles inland, and occupied a strong defensive position on the high ground of Garnwnda and Carngelli. This gave him a clear view of the surrounding countryside.

Discipline rapidly broke down. A number of men deserted Wednesday night, and the convicts began rebelling. Only the relatively few disciplined French and Irish regular troops remained, the rest being scattered throughout the countryside, falling-down drunk for the most part.

A few shots were fired and maneuvers carried out, but apparently most of the French were too dispirited to fight effectively — those that remained sober and stood by their colors. Tate unconditionally surrendered 2:00 pm Friday, February 24, to the local militia, the Pembrokeshire Yeomanry, led by John Campbell (1753-1821), First Baron Cawdor. Deserters continued to be rounded up for days afterward — a dozen or more by housewife, Jemima Nicholas, who entered local folklore as "Jemima Fawr," or "Jemima the Great" after herding her captives with the business end of a pitchfork.

On March 9, the British captured two of the French vessels, a frigate and a corvette (a vessel smaller than a frigate), and the other two French warships returned home. Tate and most of his men were later exchanged.

Financial Panic

As trivial as the episode might sound — if anything can be considered so when people are killed — the Battle of Fishguard had an enormous impact on the course of history that is little appreciated today, particularly on how new capital is financed. On hearing of the landing, people rushed to convert their Bank of England banknotes into gold and withdraw all of their savings (in gold, of course) just in case the diversionary raid in Wales turned out to be the opening move in a full-fledged invasion.

Gold reserves dropped so low that the government of Sir William Pitt "the Younger" (1759-1806) permitted (or ordered, depending on your source) the Bank of England temporarily to suspend convertibility of its banknotes into gold. This presumably temporary measure lasted for more than two decades. Convertibility of the paper pound into gold was not restored until 1821.

Prior to the suspension of convertibility, it was believed that backing any portion of the money supply with credit instruments, public or private, was sound only under certain conditions. First and foremost, issues of credit money ("banknotes") had to be strictly limited. Then, the banknotes backed by the credit instruments had to be convertible on demand into gold or silver. This meant that banks had to keep a store of gold and silver on hand — "in reserve" — to cover requests for convertibility when banknotes were presented for payment. With convertibility suspended, the politicians discovered that, as long as people had confidence in the faith and credit of the government, they could create money at will, backed only with their own future promises to pay: legal counterfeiting.

The amount of money that could be created by backing the money supply with private sector credit instruments representing actual existing and reasonably certain future wealth (mortgages and bills of exchange, respectively) had always been limited by the number of financially feasible projects available, and by the supply of gold and silver reserves, whichever was less. In contrast, the amount of money that can be created by backing the money supply with government credit instruments representing only the government's ability to redeem the credit instruments in the future (bills of credit) is limited only by the politicians' ability to spend (which is unlimited) and the willingness of the people to accept government debt as money — which lasts as long as people trust the politicians.

Not surprisingly, given the power that accompanies the ability to create money without having to own what backs the money, government credit instruments became the preferred backing for that portion of the money supply represented by the reserve currency. Control of money — which is supposed to represent and consist of all things transferred in commerce in the private sector — became the primary way in which the government (or the people who controlled the government) attempted to control the economy and impose desired results. By 1825, government "sovereign debt" (bills of credit) had become the single largest type of security traded on the world's key exchanges, London, Paris, and Vienna.

Unfortunately, most of the Spanish Empire had recently broken up, and the new republics in Central and South America floated massive quantities of sovereign debt just to keep their governments functioning. Much of this was of extremely dubious quality; even "the Republic of Poyais," a country that didn't exist, issued credit instruments.[1] The money supply was no longer connected to the marketable goods and services exchanged by means of money.

The bottom fell out of the market in the Panic of 1825 when a number of the new republics defaulted on their sovereign debt; the value of all debt and equity, public and private, plunged. Many experts consider this the start of the modern business cycle of "boom and bust." This was caused by the failure to link money and credit to the value of existing and future marketable goods and services through private property conveyed in contracts.[2]

Nevertheless, the idea persisted that government credit instruments representing a vague promise to pay at some unspecified future date, and not private sector credit instruments representing specific assets, payment for which is due on a certain date or occurrence of event, were an acceptable backing for a country's money supply. Ultimately, in the economic theories of John Maynard Keynes, this evolved into the fixed belief that government credit instruments are the

---

[1] David Sinclair, *The Land that Never Was: Sir Gregor MacGregor and the Most Audacious Fraud in History*. Cambridge, Massachusetts: Da Capo Press, 2003.
[2] Michael D. Greaney, (2015), The Business Cycle: A Kelsonian Analysis. *American Journal of Economics and Sociology*, 74: 379–418.

only possible backing for a country's money supply — thereby making all economic growth and development subject to government control.

Prelude to Rebellion

The British, however, were probably not thinking too much (or at all) about monetary theory or even pitchfork-wielding housewives in May of 1798. Rebellion was once again in the air in Ireland.

The situation had been unsettled for some time. During the American Revolution, with most of the regular troops out of the country, Great Britain had called for volunteers from the Anglo-Irish Ascendancy, as the Protestant ruling class was called, to form a local defense force. France had entered the war on the side of the United States, and the British were fearful that their old enemies would invade Ireland.

A militia was organized, the Irish Volunteers (with which the Irish National Volunteers of 1913 drew a conscious parallel), and thousands of men signed up. With their new political and military power, the Ascendency bargained for a measure of autonomy and more independence for their Anglo-Irish parliament. In 1783 pressure from the Volunteers forced the passage of a "Renunciation Bill" which guaranteed that Ireland should be bound only by laws passed by the Irish parliament and signed by the king, and that British courts had no jurisdiction.

The year 1791 saw the establishment of the Society of United Irishmen in Belfast, drawing its membership from all faiths and levels of society. Inspired by the ideals of the French Revolution, they sought Catholic Emancipation, an end to religious discrimination, and a more representative government — reforms that neither most of the Anglo-Irish nor the British parliament had any intention of granting.

Under Henry Grattan (1746-1820), the Irish Patriot Party pushed to extend the franchise to Catholics, urged parliamentary reform (a Protestant concern), and worked for economic reforms in a country in which most of the people owned nothing and lived in dire poverty. In 1793 under the Catholic Relief Act of the Irish parliament some Catholics gained the vote. Catholics with forty shillings (£2) in leased or owned wealth could now vote and run for parliament, but could not take their seats if elected, due to an oath that required they foreswear their religion.

The United Irishmen were forced underground when France and Great Britain were once again at war that same year. They then began agitating for an independent Ireland, and joined with the "Defenders," a Catholic movement working on land reform. By 1797 the Society claimed it had at least 200,000 members throughout Ireland.

Hopes were raised with the appointment of William Wentworth-Fitzwilliam (1748-1833), Fourth Earl Fitzwilliam, as Lord Lieutenant of Ireland on August 10, 1794. Fitzwilliam was a Whig and, although an Irish absentee landlord, wanted full political equality for Catholics. Arriving in Ireland in January 1795, he immediately began recommending Emancipation as a way to quell disturbances and institute good government.

Fitzwilliam was officially recalled in disgrace in a letter of February 23, 1795. When he left Ireland on March 25, the streets of Dublin were draped in mourning. Fitzwilliam blamed Pitt's desire to bring down the Whig government of Ireland as the immediate cause of his removal. George III (1738-1820), however, would never have signed an Emancipation bill in any event, as he believed it to be his sacred duty to uphold the Church of England, and may have exerted pressure on Pitt.

Fitzwilliam's removal convinced the United Irishmen that a peaceful, parliamentary solution was doomed to failure. Those in power would immediately quash any reforms. Violence seemed the only answer, and incidents between people of different faiths and philosophies increased dramatically.

In Ulster, the Presbyterians formed the Orange Order in 1795 to defend themselves against Catholics and Dissenters (primarily Methodists). The Order was named in honor of the Protestant Prince William of Orange (1650-1702), later King William III, who had defeated the forces of the Catholic King James II/VII Stuart at the Battle of the Boyne in 1690.

Still, even with their presumed numerical superiority, the United Irishmen thought it advisable to seek French aid. An attempted landing in December 1796 at Bantry Bay in the north of Ireland was called off due to stormy conditions and other factors. A second planned attempt a few months later, for which the Battle of Fishguard was planned as a diversion, never got anywhere.

1798: *Bliain na bhFrancach* **(The Year of the French)**

John Jeffreys Pratt, First Marquess Camden (1759-1840), replaced Fitzwilliam as Lord Lieutenant. Opposed to Emancipation, his policies fueled the growing unrest. In particular, his refusal to reprieve William Orr (1766-1797) of the United Irishmen, convicted of treason on highly questionable evidence, outraged the Irish.

To discourage republican agitation, Camden instituted a reign of terror, using torture, murder, and intimidation to quell revolutionary forces. He also adopted a "divide and conquer" policy with respect to the various faiths, and sowed suspicion between Presbyterian Orangemen and the United Irishmen, as the latter included Methodists and Catholics in addition to members of the Established Church. In March 1798 Camden had as many of the leaders of the Society as could be found arrested, and declared martial law.

One of the leaders arrested and later executed was Lord Edward Fitzgerald (1763-1798). As he was a member of the Ascendancy (the Anglo-Irish ruling class), every effort was made to avoid capturing him. John FitzGibbon, First Earl of Clare (*cir.* 1749-1802), Lord Chancellor of Ireland, told Fitzgerald's family to get him out of the country, assuring them that the port authorities would turn a blind eye to his movements. Fitzgerald refused to leave those whom he had led into danger, however, and was apprehended.

The only result of these measures was to convince the United Irishmen that they had to act before the British could suppress them entirely. An abortive uprising in Cahir in County Tipperary was easily put down, but a national effort was planned for May 23, 1798. The leadership felt they could not afford to wait for French aid.

Alerted by informers, the British broke the back of the rising in Dublin before it could begin, but there were other risings throughout the country, and panic spread. It was not until the end of June that the rebellion appeared to have been quelled — and then in late August, the French landed in the west of Ireland, starting the rebellion all over again.

After some initial successes, however, this too was suppressed, the main force of French troops and Irish irregulars surrendering on September 8, 1798. The French were treated as prisoners of war and exchanged, while the Irish, both guilty and suspected, were executed.

On October 12, 1798 a larger French force attempted to land in Donegal, but surrendered after being defeated by a larger British naval squadron. Wolfe Tone, the Irish leader, was tried for treason, but committed suicide before he could be hanged.

Camden resigned the Lieutenancy immediately after the rebellions were suppressed. Going from bad to worse, Charles Cornwallis (1738-1805), First Marquess Cornwallis, still rankling from his defeat at the hands of the Americans, replaced Camden in 1798. In the space of three years, Ireland had lost a man with a vision, and gained a man with a grudge.

The Act of Union

The story is told of the noted Irish advocate and jurist John Philpot Curran (1750-1817) shortly after the Acts of Union:

> Curran was standing one day outside the Parliament buildings. A nobleman — one who had been ennobled because he had voted for the Union — came up and said, "Curran, what do they mean to do with that useless building? For my part, I hate even the sight of it." "I do not wonder," rejoined Curran. "I never yet heard of a murderer who was not afraid of a ghost."[3]

Technically, there were *two* Acts of Union for Ireland, one for the Irish parliament to vote itself out of existence, and another for the British parliament to take over. As the rhetoric, history, and literature generally refer to the Act of Union in the singular, however, so shall we.

The risings of 1798 convinced Pitt that Ireland could no longer be permitted its own parliament. While many of the Catholic peasantry had joined the rebellion to be out from under the Established Church (and thus the legally enforced in-kind tithes that represented a significant portion of the

---

[3] Pádraic Colum (ed.), *A Treasury of Irish Folklore*. New York: Bonanza Books, 1967, 282.

annual produce of most farms), the upper classes were divided between a desire for parliamentary reform and full independence.

Pitt believed that maintaining a separate Irish parliament would eventually lead to a demand for independence, thereby provide a steppingstone for a French invasion of England. This was in spite of the example of Scotland and France, traditional allies for centuries. Even during the Jacobite Rebellion of Charles Edward Louis John Casimir Sylvester Severino Maria Stuart ("Bonnie Prince Charlie," 1720-1788) in 1745, when many Scots and English, antagonistic to a German ruling house, would have welcomed a French army, no aid had been forthcoming.

Thus, Pitt advocated integrating Ireland into the United Kingdom through an act of union, promising (and fully intending) to institute a sweeping program of reform. At the top of the list was Catholic Emancipation, that is, the recognition and protection of the civil rights of Catholics.

The principal argument against union with Great Britain was that Ireland had always been separate and intended by God to be a separate kingdom, albeit under the same king as Great Britain. Furthermore, where Scotland's 1707 Act of Union had been adopted during the reign of Queen Anne Stuart (1665-1714), of the Scottish royal house, an Irish king or queen had never sat on the English throne. Union would not be a joining of equals, but the establishment and maintenance of a permanently inferior status for Ireland, as had been the case with Wales.[4]

There were three ostensible arguments in favor of union. One, English capital would flow into Ireland, creating jobs and raising the standard of living. This would have been completely unnecessary had the country had a functioning commercial/mercantile banking system and a central bank that operated according to sound banking principles.

Two, enjoying the benefits of English culture and civilization, the Irish would transform themselves in "West Britons." This would presumably give stability to the social order. This

---

[4] Despite their name, the Tudors considered themselves English, and in any event based their claim to the throne on a "right of conquest" and a tenuous descent from the House of Lancaster.

was unlikely in light of the centuries-long failure to turn the native Irish into English, and the tendency of the older Norman and English settlers to become *Hibernicis ipsis Hibernior*: "more Irish than the Irish."

Three — assuming Emancipation was forthcoming — under an Irish parliament, there were three Protestants to eleven Catholics. As part of Great Britain, the proportion would change to eleven Protestants to three Catholics.

The real argument favoring union, however, was money. Peerages were created and pensions awarded as prizes for votes for union, with £1.25 million paid in "compensation for disturbance."

Adding insult to injury, the disbursements were charged to the Irish Exchequer, which was to remain separate.[5] Philip Yorke (1757-1834), Third Earl of Hardwicke, who succeeded Cornwallis as Lord Lieutenant, complained that he had been burdened with a "heavy mortgage on the patronage of the country." Money that should have gone into the pockets of the politicians and their supporters as graft had already been committed to pay the promised bribes.

The final betrayal, however, was the failure to grant Catholic Emancipation and other promised reforms. George III, a sincere if misguided and shortsighted ruler, again refused to countenance anything he felt would cause him to foreswear his coronation oath.

Those who had voted in favor of the Act of Union, trading nominal sovereignty for civil rights, were outraged. Pitt resigned in protest. Once again the peaceful, parliamentary approach had proved futile. Ireland had surrendered its last vestige of sovereignty, and gained nothing in return.

Emmet's Rebellion

Convinced that only armed force would be effective in gaining Catholic Emancipation and other reforms, a young Anglo-Irish Protestant, Robert Emmet (1778-1803), began planning an uprising in March 1803. Emmet had joined the Society of

---

[5] The Irish Exchequer was merged into that of Great Britain in 1817, although the currencies weren't amalgamated (made the same value) until 1821, and a separate coinage continued until 1826, when the specifically Irish coinage was officially withdrawn from circulation.

United Irishmen while a student at Trinity College, Dublin, for which he was expelled in April 1798. He went to France later that year to avoid arrest in the general roundup of members of the Society.

Returning to Ireland, Emmet assisted in reorganizing the United Irishmen, but again had to flee to the continent to avoid arrest when a warrant was issued in April 1799. He failed to interest Napoleon in supporting another rebellion, and returned to Ireland in October 1802. Five months later he began his own preparations for a rising.

Emmet established tiny munitions factories throughout Dublin to provide the insurgents with weapons and explosives. He invented a pike that was easy to make and could be folded for concealment under a cloak. Where the preparations for the 1798 rebellion were widely known, Emmet kept everything strictly secret, a lesson not lost on the Irish Republican Brotherhood in 1916.

Unfortunately, a premature explosion in one of his factories killed a man. This convinced Emmet that the rebellion had to be moved up in order to avoid arousing the suspicions of the government. It also created a serious problem, for he had not yet convinced enough people to join him, and those that did begin a march on Dublin turned back due to the lack of firearms they had been promised.

Despite this, Emmet decided the rebellion had to go forward. Again providing a model for the Easter Rising, he drew up a proclamation in the name of the Provisional Government and had approximately 10,000 copies printed. Most were seized and destroyed by the authorities before they could be distributed.

Emmet began his rebellion the evening of July 23, 1803 — due to its northerly latitude, the summer sun in Ireland does not go down until nearly midnight. Almost immediately he lost control of the situation, and the rebellion quickly degenerated into a localized civil disturbance characterized by mindless acts of violence.

Failing to bring a halt to what was now a riot, Emmet fled to Rathfarnam south of Dublin, and then to Harold's Cross, a nearby village. He could have escaped again to France had he not insisted on staying to convince his secret fiancée, Sarah Curran (1782-1808), the daughter of John Philpot Curran (who violently opposed the engagement when he discovered it), to elope with him to the United States.

Emmet was captured on August 25 and taken to Dublin Castle. He was later removed to Kilmainham Jail, where most of the leaders of the 1916 Easter Rising would be executed. Several failed attempts were made to effect his escape. He was brought to trial September 19, 1803 on a charge of high treason.

To ensure conviction, the authorities suborned Emmet's defense attorney, Leonard McNally (1752-1820), buying him off with £200 and a pension. Despite that, McNally's assistant, Peter Burrowes (1753-1841) refused a bribe and made the best case he could. In a trial that may have lasted longer than the rebellion itself, Emmet was found guilty, and sentenced to be hanged and beheaded.

In his "Speech from the Dock" on his conviction but before sentence was passed, Emmet declared he wanted no epitaph until Ireland had taken its place among the nations of the world. This inspired generations of Irish republicans, especially those who planned the Easter Rising. There are different versions of the speech, however, in the earlier of which Emmet declared he wanted no epitaph until he had been vindicated.

The Rise of Daniel O'Connell

Although Emmet was a Protestant, his rebellion was used to justify the failure to extend civil rights to Catholics on the grounds of their presumed inherent disloyalty. The failure of Emmet's rebellion was the last gasp of the United Irishmen, having been largely a spent force since 1798. Ireland seemed effectively cowed.

The promised economic benefits of the Union went largely to Belfast, a Protestant stronghold, while the south sunk deeper into squalor. Efforts by reformers to bring parliament to a sense of its responsibility were unavailing. Works such as Maria Edgeworth's *Castle Rackrent* (1800) painted a picture of utter despair. Conditions became so bad that people began looking back on the eighteenth century as a golden age.

In 1808, however, a Dublin attorney originally from County Kerry in the west of Ireland, Daniel O'Connell (1775-1847), came into the public eye. In 1806, during the "Ministry of All the Talents," Foreign Secretary Charles James Fox[6] (1749-1806) and Prime Minister William Wyndham Grenville (1759-1834), First Baron Grenville, introduced a bill that would implement a watered down version of Catholic Emancipation.[7] Grenville's government fell in March 1807 as a result of the wave of "no popery" hysteria that swept through England, and the anti-Catholic administration of William Henry Cavendish Cavendish-Bentinck (1738-1809), Third Duke of Portland, took its place.

The Catholic Committee of Ireland, composed of aristocrats, bishops, and wealthy merchants, had had great hopes for Grenville's bill. The members had even agreed that the British government could veto the appointment of Catholic bishops. Disappointed, the former Catholic leader, John Keogh (1740-1817) counseled "dignified silence" as the most appropriate response.

Outraged, O'Connell roused the country to protest what he regarded as betrayal. When it came to light that ten of the bishop trustees of Maynooth College, the Catholic seminary of Ireland, had secretly agreed to the veto in 1799, O'Connell forced the calling of a council in which the Irish hierarchy as a whole repudiated the agreement, and supported the independence of the Catholic Church from any form of State control.

It has been said that the history of Ireland in the first half of the nineteenth century is that of O'Connell, and *vice versa*. Utterly opposed to the use of violence (although he could be maneuvered into it and often threatened it), he combined a fierce love of Ireland, hatred of injustice, and an overriding respect for the law, with an adulatory, almost fawning love of the British Crown, the wearer of which generally feared or despised him. George IV once remarked that the Anglo-Irish Arthur Wellesley[8] (1769-1852), First Duke of Wellington, the enormously popular victor of the Battle of Waterloo, was the

---

[6] Fox had resigned with Pitt in 1801 over the issue of Emancipation.
[7] Grenville's government did succeed in abolishing the slave trade.
[8] Born Wesley.

king of England, O'Connell was the king of Ireland, and he was only "the dean of Windsor."

Catholic Emancipation

In 1811 O'Connell founded the populist Catholic Board as an alternative to the elitist Catholic Committee. The government suppressed the organization almost immediately, whereupon O'Connell reformed it as the General Committee of the Catholics of Ireland. He then began agitating for the promised grant of civil rights to Catholics.

The Roman Catholic Relief Act 1813[9] extended the provisions of the 1793 Act of the pre-Union Irish parliament to Irish Catholics living in England. Catholics now could to a limited extent bear arms, vote, and hold certain offices . . . provided they took the Oath of Allegiance and repudiated certain Catholic doctrines. Grattan considered the Act unacceptable, so with the support of George Canning (1770-1827) and Robert Stewart (1769-1822), Second Marquess of Londonderry, "Lord Castlereagh," introduced a Catholic Relief Bill that same year. Although Grattan conceded the veto, the Bill died in committee, and future motions were rejected.

Before then, however, O'Connell organized resistance to the Act. The government countered by negotiating directly with Giovanni Battista Cardinal Quarantotti (1733-1820), who was handling Church administration while Napoleon held Pius VII hostage.

In February 1814 Quarantotti issued a Rescript approving the Act in full. In England, Bishop John Milner (1752-1826), English Vicar Apostolic of the Midland District, traveled to Rome to appeal directly to the pope, who had been released following Napoleon's fall and exile to Elba. Bishop William Poynter (1762-1827), London Vicar Apostolic, joined Milner in Rome.

Pius VII recalled Quarantotti's Rescript and ordered a reexamination of the issue. Lorenzo Cardinal Litta (1756-1820), Prefect of Propaganda, sent a letter to Poynter during the Hundred Days condemning the Act, but allowing a veto under certain conditions, *e.g.*, as long as a veto did not constitute a positive nomination, a decision Milner accepted, alt-

---

[9] 53 Geo. III, c. 128.

hough opposed in principle. It did not come to actual conflict as the veto was never exercised.

In Ireland, O'Connell notified the Irish hierarchy that if they accepted the veto, the people would import friars from the continent and ignore their own bishops and priests. In any event, the Irish hierarchy, in common with the English Vicars Apostolic, opposed the veto, and never took advantage of the permission to accept it. From that point on, despite continuing efforts by the British government to impose some form of direct control, the rights of the Catholic Church in England or Ireland — and of Catholics — were non-negotiable.

Grattan died in 1820, and William Conyngham Plunket (1764-1854), First Baron Plunket, assumed Grattan's mantle on the Emancipation issue, more or less. Plunket persuaded the House of Commons to pass Grattan's Bill in 1820, but the House of Lords threw it out.

O'Connell on the Move

While Catholic Emancipation and Repeal of the Union were important issues, O'Connell's later efforts might not have had the success they did if he had not had the fortune to be one of the greatest lawyers and most skillful politicians of his day. In 1813, he won great public acclaim for defending John Magee, the Presbyterian owner of *The Evening Post*, who was highly critical of government policy in Ireland.

Sued by the government for libel, and tried by prejudiced judges with a packed jury, Magee's conviction was a foregone conclusion, and the sentence was harsh. O'Connell's speech, however, made the judges, jury, and, especially, the Attorney General, William Saurin (1757-1839), look like fools, for which Saurin never forgave him. Sir Robert Peel (1788-1850), future home secretary and prime minister, attended the trial, and acquired a violent dislike of O'Connell.

O'Connell's popularity soared. In an 1815 speech he made a disparaging reference to the "beggarly Corporation" of Dublin. A candidate for High Sheriff, the noted duelist John Neville D'Esterre (?-1815), seeking to score points with voters, threatened to horsewhip O'Connell when O'Connell refused to apologize for his comment. D'Esterre backed down when

O'Connell showed up for his chastisement with a blackthorn stick and a large crowd of spectators.

With the tacit consent of Dublin Castle, who wanted O'Connell out of the way, D'Esterre then forced O'Connell into a duel. It was D'Esterre, however, who was put out of the way.

Although everyone praised him for killing D'Esterre, the outcome haunted O'Connell for the rest of his life. It turned his opposition to violence into a near phobia, and undermined the effectiveness of his efforts.

Economic Insecurity

In 1821 the House of Commons passed another Catholic Relief Bill, the third in less than fifteen years. The Bill made Catholics eligible for parliament and for government preferment, but still included the veto. To this was added the requirement that priests take an oath only to elect bishops loyal to the British Crown — which violated the rights of both the pope and the Catholics of Ireland.

Virtually the whole of the Irish Catholic priesthood joined O'Connell in protesting the Bill. While a moral victory, the protest had no other effect. The House of Lords, refusing to grant any concessions to Catholics, exercised its permanent veto and threw the Bill out.

O'Connell then entered into negotiations with Richard Colley Wesley (1760-1842), First Marquess Wellesley, Lord Lieutenant of Ireland from 1821 to 1828, for a compromise form of the veto. If any candidate for bishop in Ireland was thought to be of questionable loyalty, he would be investigated and examined before two other bishops. The brother of the Iron Duke, now a supporter of Emancipation, agreed, but the government did not, and O'Connell was back to square one.

By this time the whole of the United Kingdom was in sad shape. The early 1820s saw yet another of the recurrent famines that plagued Ireland, and the flood of paper money backed by government debt instead of private sector assets used to finance the Napoleonic Wars had greatly inflated prices. Enclosure of the commons in England added to the distress, and advancing technology was depressing the price of labor. Radical politicians such as William Cobbett (1763-1835), a great admirer and supporter of O'Connell, advocated economic and monetary reforms, especially widespread capital ownership, in addition to Catholic Emancipation.

It was the heyday of the Luddites, Swing-Kettles, Pikies, Ribbonmen, White Boys, Defenders, and seemingly countless others, [10] secret societies that professed to champion the rights of the poor against landlords, the rich, the banks, the Jews, the government — anyone believed to be the source of the problem — and the country seemed about to dissolve in chaos. The fact that it was the system, especially how money was created and for what purpose, and the growing concentration of capital ownership in fewer and fewer hands, did not occur to desperate people anxious for a scapegoat, although reformers such as O'Connell and Cobbett did their best within their limited paradigm.

In 1823 O'Connell joined forces with Richard Lalor Shiel (1791-1851), a former opponent, to form the Catholic Association. The time seemed propitious, for George III was dead, and had been insane for years prior to his death. Memory of the rebellions of 1798 and 1803 had faded somewhat, and the threat of the Emperor Napoleon had ended with the Man of Destiny's exile and death on the distant island of Saint Helena in 1821.

In a move that particularly worried the government, the Association was organized by parishes, with the local pastor as the head. To finance the effort, in 1824 a subscription known variously as the Catholic Rent, the Penny Rent, or the Shilling Rent was levied. This consisted of one penny a month (one shilling a year), collected at the church door the first Sunday of every month.

The government suppressed the Association in 1825, but introduced yet another Emancipation Bill to soften the blow. The Bill omitted the veto, but included a provision that would have turned the Catholic clergy into government employees, and thus amenable to State control.

O'Connell, anxious for a victory, was willing to accept the Bill, but the clergy and the people were not. The Bill passed the House of Commons, but following an emotional performance by Prince Frederick (1763-1827), the Duke of York

---

[10] Caravats, Shanavests, Thrashers, Carders, Right Boys, Terry Alts, Blackfeet, White Feet — to name a few.

and Albany (George IV's brother), the House of Lords again threw it out. Another wave of anti-Catholicism swept through England, parliament dissolved, and in the ensuing general election of 1826 another anti-Catholic government was seated.

Emancipation Achieved

O'Connell now formed the New Catholic Association "for the purpose of public and private charity and such other purposes as are not forbidden by the statue of George IV, cap. 4." This wording circumvented the Suppression Act that had terminated the Catholic Association.

Ameliorating the anti-Catholicism of the new government was the realization that, while the "no popery" ticket had won in England, all the members from Ireland — every one a Protestant — while nowhere near a majority, favored Catholic Emancipation. Support was also growing in England. This gave pause to the powers-that-be, although Wellington, now prime minister, remained unconvinced of its political wisdom.

Although it was legal for Catholics to run for parliament, it was illegal for them to be seated without taking an oath that required them to foreswear Catholicism. To challenge this ludicrous provision, O'Connell ran for parliament in 1828 to fill a vacancy in the County Clare. He was elected by a landslide, and dared parliament not to permit him to take his seat without taking the oath. A significant number of the "forty shilling men" who voted for him were evicted.

Mass meetings were held throughout the country, and the Catholic bishops gave their approval to O'Connell's efforts. Tens of thousands of people pledged to oppose any candidate who supported Wellington's administration.

Wellington was now convinced, whatever his personal feelings, that Emancipation had become a political necessity, if only to avoid another rebellion — one in which the English Catholics and their sympathizers would join. Always a realist, he gave what many consider the finest speech of his career to the House of Lords in support of Emancipation in light of O'Connell's achievement.

In March 1829, George William Finch-Hatton (1791-1858), Tenth Earl of Winchilsea, Fifth Earl of Nottingham, accused

Wellington of "an insidious design for the infringement of our liberties and the introduction of Popery into every department of the State." They fought a duel on March 21, 1829, in which Wellington claimed to have deloped and Winchilsea refused to fire.

Putting pressure on Home Secretary Peel, whom O'Connell called "Orange Peel" for his vehement opposition to Emancipation, Wellington pushed through the Roman Catholic Relief Act 1829.[11]

The victory was not, however, complete. The Parliamentary Elections (Ireland) Act 1829[12] raised the property qualification for the franchise from forty shillings (£2) to £10. This reduced the number of potential Irish Catholic voters by more than ninety percent.

George IV (1762-1830) refused to sign the Emancipation act until Wellington threatened to resign and informed the king that he feared civil war if the Royal Assent was withheld. The king, weeping, signed the bill into law on April 13, 1829.

The Act was not made retroactive. O'Connell had to run for election again. He was reelected without opposition, but missed being the first Catholic member of parliament to be seated in over a century, beaten out by Henry Charles Howard (1791-1856) Thirteenth Duke of Norfolk and Earl of Surrey.

The Repeal Movement

The probably apocryphal story is told that one day O'Connell was out walking and met an old man breaking stones by the side of the road. Praised for his work on achieving Emancipation and for the effort to repeal the Act of Union, O'Connell said, "Whatever happens, you will still be breaking stones."

O'Connell viewed Emancipation not as an end, but as a beginning, as a means to an end: justice and good government for Ireland. As he declared in March 1829, "How mistaken men are who suppose that the history of the world will be

---

[11] 10 Geo. IV, c. 7.
[12] 10 Geo. IV, c. 8

over as soon as we are emancipated! Oh, *that* will be the time to *commence* the struggle for popular rights."[13]

From the 1830s until his death in 1847, O'Connell and the various permutations of his "Repeal Association" made nullification of the Act of Union and the reestablishment of a separate kingdom under the British Crown the focus of their efforts. His idea was to institute something similar to the "dual monarchy" of Austria-Hungary under the Hapsburgs.

O'Connell did not found the Repeal movement. As early as 1810 the Tory Anglo-Irish Grand Jurors of Dublin had begun agitating to repeal the Act of Union. Whig politicians prevented the Catholics as a whole from joining the Protestant effort by promising Emancipation.

Emancipation won, Catholics (with some notable exceptions) began supporting Repeal. Protestants (also with notable exceptions), resentful of the lack of Catholic support for earlier efforts, and realizing they faced loss of their privileged position in a country with a Catholic political majority, now opposed it.

No one was more effective in his opposition to O'Connell's efforts than Peel. His masterstroke was to declare in November 1830 to the House of Commons that O'Connell's Repeal agitation proved the Liberator's intention to gain his end by force. If unchecked, the movement would result in an upheaval even more violent than the French and Belgian revolutions of a few months previous.

In response, O'Connell declared, "France waded to liberty through blood, the Poles are wading to liberty through blood; but mark me, my friends, the shedding of one drop of blood in Ireland would effectively destroy all chance of repealing the Union. Ireland will be tranquil, Ireland will be quiet, and we shall obtain our freedom by uniting among ourselves."[14]

Thus reassured, and having learned its lesson from O'Connell's success in achieving Emancipation, the government did everything in its power to prevent O'Connell from

---

[13] Letter 1536, Volume IV, M.R. O'Connell, ed., *The Correspondence of Daniel O'Connell*, cited in Fergus O'Ferrall, *Gill's Irish Lives: Daniel O'Connell*. Dublin, Éire: Gill and Macmillan, 1981, 67.
[14] Denis Gwynn, *Daniel O'Connell*. Oxford, U.K.: Cork University Press, 1947, 200-201.

organizing effectively for Repeal — free association being key to carrying out peaceful acts of social justice. From then on, the power *élite* knew, for all his bombast and rhetoric, O'Connell would never condone violence.

O'Connell stuck with peaceful agitation. He first formed the Friends of Ireland Society. Confident it could do so with impunity, the government suppressed it. Then came Irish Volunteers for the Repeal of the Union. It was suppressed. No sooner did O'Connell establish one association than the government proscribed ("proclaimed") it, and he would found another:

> He started a weekly Repeal Breakfast, and promised that if it was suppressed, he would have Repeal Lunches, Repeal Dinners, Repeal Suppers in succession. Its next form was a General Association for Ireland. When that was proclaimed, he started A Body of Persons, in the Habit of Meeting Weekly for Breakfast, at a place called Holmes' Hotel. When this was proclaimed he had A Party Meeting for Dinner at Gray's Tavern.[15]

Next came A General Association for Ireland to Prevent Illegal Meetings and to Protect the Sacred Right of Petition. It was suppressed. The Irish Society for Legal and Legislative Relief was suppressed, as was the Association of Subscribers to the Parliamentary Intelligence Office.

At this point Henry William Paget, (1768-1854), First Marquess of Anglesey, Lord Lieutenant of Ireland, complained, "Things have now come to that pass that the question is whether O'Connell or I shall rule Ireland."[16]

On January 13, 1831, the government issued a proclamation forbidding all associations of any kind under any name. At that point, "[O'Connell] proposed to make himself the Repeal Association, with an assisting council of thirty-one people. He said they couldn't disperse an individual by proclamation."[17]

Edward George Geoffrey Smith-Stanley (1799-1869), Fourteenth Earl of Derby, Chief Secretary for Ireland, had

---

[15] Mac Manus, *The Story of the Irish Race, op. cit.*, 568.
[16] Seán Ó Faoláin, *King of the Beggars*. Dublin, Éire: Poolbeg Press, Ltd., 1980, 246.
[17] Mac Manus, *The Story of the Irish Race, op. cit.*, 568.

O'Connell arrested on January 19. The people of Ireland were outraged, and were ready to rise in revolt, as O'Connell less-than-diplomatically informed a friend in a letter was passed on (as intended) to Valentine Brown Lawless, (1773-1853), Second Baron Cloncurry, a member of Paget's private cabinet.

The letter, however, was also taken as O'Connell fully intended it should: an offer to push Repeal more slowly if he could wring other concessions from the government. Emancipation was, after all, only an empty shell, with most of the former eligible Catholic voters disenfranchised and no office of importance filled by a Catholic.

The Tithe War

After some negotiation, then, O'Connell shifted his efforts to support the English Whigs in their campaign for parliamentary reform. He believed that he would thereby gain their support for Repeal — later. Unfortunately, at the same time the issue of tithing came to the fore, and the protests quickly became violent.

The problem was that the Catholic Church of the majority was supported by voluntary contributions from Catholics. At the same time, the Protestant Established Church of the minority — the Church of Ireland — was supported by legally enforced "tithes" (a kind of religious tax) . . . collected from Catholics, who thus supported both churches.

Ironically, the richest Protestants often paid no tithe, because it was levied only on freeholders and tenants, not on landlords who did not farm their own land. The church of a rich minority was almost entirely supported by a poor majority.

James Warren Doyle (1786-1834), Catholic bishop of Kildare and Leighlin, told the people of his diocese that they should oppose the tithe by all legal means. As usual, most people heard what they wanted to hear, and quickly forgot the qualification. Violence escalated, secret societies (membership in which was forbidden by the Catholic Church) proliferated, and the government instituted coercive measures.

In 1832 parliament passed a Reform Act that reduced the number of Anglican bishoprics in Ireland. This, however, had little effect in Ireland. In England it provided the inspiration for the "Oxford Movement," which eventually led to a number of the intellectual lights of the Church of England to convert to Catholicism, among them Blessed John Henry Cardinal Newman.

In 1834 the Whigs passed their Reform Bill in part due to O'Connell's support, and put some minor church reforms in place with the Vestries Act and Church Temporalities Act. Presumably convinced by the ongoing Tithe War that the Irish could not be trusted to govern themselves, however, they reneged on their promised support for Repeal. Instead, they passed another Coercion Bill for Ireland, and reorganized the Royal Irish Constabulary in 1836 out of the provincial constabularies to put a stop to political and religious agitation.

Similar to the way the Pro-Life movement is today viewed in the United States, Repeal had by this time become identified in the public mind as a "Catholic" cause and, worse, purely an Irish issue in which English Catholics had no stake. Anti-Catholic feeling reached a fever pitch, whether directed at papal "Roman" or the neither-fish-nor-fowl "Anglo" Catholics.

O'Connell, however, remained convinced that the socially just parliamentary approach was the only one that could be effective and, at the same time, establish peace among the different parties and interests. He failed to take into account that social justice is to all intents and purposes impossible when others insist on maintaining their position through coercion and violence.

Suppressing his outrage over the Coercion Bill, O'Connell let himself be persuaded to throw his support again to the Whigs. They needed his help in light of the anger on the part of many English over the perceived betrayal of the Established Church. O'Connell then called on his followers to try an "experiment": hold off on Repeal for six years, and see what benefits the Whigs could deliver.

The results were disappointing. Most modern authorities (as well as O'Connell) believe the 1838 Poor Law Act increased poverty, and was inadequate for poor relief in the best of times in any event. Acts forbidding subletting and permitting evictions made land tenure even less secure than before.

Tithes were reduced in 1838 and made payable by the landlord instead of the tenant, but were changed from in-kind to cash. Most landlords simply raised rents to cover the expenditure. Tenants were worse off than before as agricultural prices fell, many going into arrears and facing eviction.

O'Connell's Bank

In the latter half of 1834 O'Connell undertook a project that most people to this day misunderstand — and of which O'Connell himself probably did not realize the full significance. He established "the National Bank of Ireland" to compete with the virtual monopoly of the Bank of Ireland and the Provincial Bank.

O'Connell's aim was twofold. His goal was "to reduce the domination of the Ascendancy in Ireland, and strengthen instead the nationalist-liberal-Repeal interest."[18]

This was not, however, merely a blow at the Ascendancy. It was a direct threat to those whom a generation later Walter Bagehot (1826-1877) would declare the *real* rulers of the British Empire. This was the oligarchy that controlled the Empire by controlling access to money and credit. They maintained their virtual monopoly by restricting financing of new capital to existing accumulations of wealth — which they owned or controlled — and through controlling parliament via the "pocket" or "rotten borough" system.[19]

A mercantile (commercial) bank such as O'Connell established threatened the *status quo* by making it possible to finance new capital formation without the use of existing wealth, by definition a monopoly of the *élite*. A mercantile bank that backed its note issues and demand deposits with the present value of future wealth also undermined the ability of government to maintain and extend its power by controlling money and credit by backing the currency with government debt.

The National Bank of Ireland was a financial success, and competed on equal terms with the existing Irish and English banks. There was, however, no attempt to use the bank's

---

[18] Oliver MacDonagh, *The Emancipist: Daniel O'Connell, 1830-1847*. London: Weidenfeld and Nicolson, 1989, 111.
[19] Walter Bagehot, *The English Constitution*. Brighton, England: Sussex Academic Press, 1997, 29.

money creation powers to extend capital credit to expand the number of owners in Ireland during the brief period when this would have been possible.

O'Connell's bank opened for business on January 28, 1835. Less than a decade later, Peel, Samuel Jones-Loyd, Lord Overstone (1796-1883),[20] and Colonel Robert Torrens (1780-1864) spearheaded the Bank Charter Act of 1844.[21]

The provisions of the Act were almost custom-designed to maintain the *status quo*, keep financial (and thus political) power in the hands of a tiny *élite*, and expand the economic role of government. The reserve currency of the Bank of England — what Peel, Overstone, Torrens, and others of the "Currency School" thought of as the money supply — was to be inelastic, and consist exclusively of gold and a fixed amount of paper currency (£14 million) backed with government debt.

Increases and decreases in the money supply were to be regulated by the import and export of gold. Existing banknotes backed by private sector assets issued by "country banks" (*i.e.*, private banks outside London) were to be gradually withdrawn from circulation and replaced with Bank of England notes backed with government debt.

No new note issues were authorized. Only the fact that the experts did not realize that demand deposits, bills of exchange, and mortgages are money prevented a depression. As it was, the lack of an elastic, asset-backed reserve currency into which all other forms of money could be converted on demand caused a series of "currency crises" in the latter half of the nineteenth century that were temporarily resolved by raising the debt ceiling so that more fiat money could be issued.

The Rebirth of Repeal

O'Connell's wife had died in 1837. The second Whig betrayal soon after and his loss of popularity threw him into a deep depression. Nearly sixty-five, and starting to feel his age in a day when fifty was considered old, at one point he considered retiring to a monastery. In 1839 he went on re-

---

[20] Lord Overstone, *The Evidence Given By Lord Overstone on the Bank Acts*. London: Longman, Brown, & Co., 1858.
[21] 7 & 8 Vict. c. 32.

treat to the Trappist monastery of Mount Melleray in County Waterford, and engaged in profound soul-searching.

Sincere as his faith and spiritual resolutions were, however, what appears to have revived O'Connell's flagging spirit and rescued him from depression was the eclipse of the Whigs. Because he had needed their political leverage against the Tories if he hoped to achieve anything through parliamentary means, O'Connell had allowed the Whigs to keep him dangling with promises they either failed to keep, or kept in a way that yielded no real benefit for Ireland.

Now, however, the Whigs needed O'Connell's support to remain in power. He had many times made the empty threat to abandon the alliance if the Whigs failed to accede to his demands. Now it was the Whigs who made the equally empty threat to cut O'Connell loose if he refused to come to heel.

Evidently deciding that there was little difference between allies who failed to keep their promises, and opponents who failed to make any, O'Connell struck out on his own. Having allowed the power *élite* to sidetrack and marginalize the Repeal movement for over a decade, he took his case to the people.

O'Connell thereby laid the foundation and provided the model for the popular mass movements of the twentieth century, such as Gandhi's policy of passive and non-violent resistance, the civil rights struggle in the United States, the Northern Ireland Civil Rights Association, and the anti-Apartheid movement in South Africa. The force of his mobilized "people power" was only stopped by his refusal to countenance violence, combined with England's refusal to consider anything other than coercion as the proper response to Irish agitation, peaceful or otherwise. As the Repeal movement gained momentum, O'Connell's old adversary Sir Robert Peel declared that if O'Connell gave England the choice of civil war or Repeal, England would unhesitatingly choose the former.

Nevertheless, O'Connell succeeded — or nearly. In the process, he roused the power *élite* to a terror that only a popular movement can instill. This was in spite of the fact that O'Connell went to great lengths to reassure queen and parliament that the revolution he led was peaceful, and that he demanded only justice. His "statements of principle" for the

National Association of Ireland he founded in 1840 pledged eternal and inviolable loyalty to Queen Victoria (1819-1901) and "her heirs and successors forever." To emphasize this, he renamed the Association in 1841, changing it to the "Loyal National Repeal Association." He also declared "[t]he total disclaiming of, and absence from, all physical force, violence, or breach of the law, or in short, any violation of the laws of man or the ordinances of the Eternal God whose holy name be ever blessed."

1843: The "Repeal Year"

O'Connell became more popular than ever. Under the new Municipal Reform Act, the people of Dublin elected a Nationalist corporation in 1841, throwing out the corrupt Orange administration. O'Connell became the first Nationalist Lord Mayor of Dublin, and the first Catholic to hold the office since 1690.

The Great Emancipator declared 1843 the "Repeal Year." Over the course of the summer forty and more of what the *London Times* labeled "monster meetings" took place. Seldom were there less than a hundred thousand people in attendance, with the average estimated at a quarter of a million. The largest took place in August at the Hill of Tara in County Meath, ancient stronghold of the High Kings of Ireland, where the *Times* claimed that over a million people came to hear O'Connell speak — more than ten percent of the estimated total population of the country.

The final meeting was to be held in October at Clontarf, today a suburb of Dublin. The meeting was set for a Sunday, but in midafternoon of the day before the government issued a proclamation cancelling the meeting. To ensure compliance with its demand, five regiments with artillery were posted, covering all roads leading to Clontarf. Seeing no alternative to having unarmed men, women, and children slaughtered in cold blood, O'Connell immediately sent messengers on fast horses along all the roads leading to Dublin to tell the people to turn back.

At first it seemed like just another temporary setback. Following up on its advantage, however, the authorities arrested O'Connell and a number of others on charges of conspiracy, sedition, and attempting to change the constitution through illegal means. As Seán Ó Faoláin commented in his biography of O'Connell,

> The indictment . . . contained eleven separate counts and referred to forty-three overt acts. It was so intricate and so inclusive that it was of a confusion impossible to elucidate, and no precision emerged from its phrases on which anybody could ever hope to agree, or ever did agree, or from which any victim could conceivably escape. "Criminal justice,' exulted the Quarterly, "once fished with a hook; she now fishes with a net." To ensure a verdict the jury, as everybody expected, was packed.[22]

O'Connell's defense was uncharacteristically weak. He was convicted, and sentenced to one year in prison and to pay a £2,000 fine.

Many historians blame O'Connell for losing heart, but they forget he was now seventy years old. Despite the vacation-like atmosphere of his short prison term, and the fact that Peel was forced to quash the sentence and release him, O'Connell was a broken man. He died shortly after, never regaining his lost momentum.

The Repeal movement could have recovered, however, except that in September of 1845, a year and a half before O'Connell died in Italy on his way to Rome, the potato crop failed.

---

[22] Ó Faoláin, *King of the Beggars, op. cit.*, 307.

Chapter 5: Down by the Glenside

All movements, if they are to effect institutional change in the social order that becomes an integral part of the lives of individuals and of society, must grow and develop their vision beyond that of their initial foundation. This is all the more true when the man is the movement, as Daniel O'Connell was for Catholic Emancipation and Repeal.

Movements do not live by one man alone. Unless a determinant number of people come together in solidarity and in conformity with the principles of social justice and the natural law and reform not merely their own lives but their institutions — their social as well as their individual habits — the cause, regardless how just and necessary, will die with that man.

The Rise of Young Ireland

Emancipation had been achieved ultimately because the English government of Ireland feared unless the promise to extend civil rights to Catholics was finally kept, the United Kingdom would dissolve in civil war. English Catholics, Irish Catholics, and their sympathizers — and they were many — were united on the issue. The fact that Emancipation, when it came, was an empty shell for many years was, in a sense, irrelevant. The government had been forced to keep its word, and (in time) would be forced to make that word mean something.

It was otherwise with Repeal of the Act of Union. For centuries, like the Jews for millennia, Catholics had been faced with the accusation that it is impossible to be both good citizens and faithful adherents of their religion. O'Connell's strength had been based in large measure on the fact that the Emancipation movement was inclusive. He made it clear he was fighting for civil rights not merely for Catholics, but for everyone. O'Connell's efforts on behalf of Catholics was key to the later extension of civil rights to Jews.

Repeal, however, was exclusive. Where Emancipation had brought people together and instilled in them the realization that institutional change for the better was possible, Repeal divided them. It confirmed the power *élite*, whether English or Ascendancy, in the opinion that if English Catholics could in some measure be trusted, to be Irish and Catholic was to be a natural rebel. Repeal, O'Connell's best efforts to the contrary, became linked inextricably with Catholicism.

If the failure of Repeal can be traced to one thing, however, it was O'Connell's insistence that violence was out of the question. Repeal was doomed the moment the power *élite* was convinced of the Liberator's sincerity on this point, and that they need not fear a rising.

Sensing these flaws, a number of younger men in the Repeal movement began working to make it more inclusive. They were also much less inclined than O'Connell to exclude violence, should they believe it was necessary.

Foremost among the group was Thomas Davis (1814-1845), a Protestant barrister from Cork. Joining him in an informal triumvirate were John Blake Dillon (1814-1866) and Charles Gavan Duffy (1816-1903). In his book, *Ireland and Its Rulers Since 1829* (1843), the writer Daniel Owen Madden (1815-1859) "mockingly" called the group "Young Ireland" from what he saw as their resemblance to the "Young England" movement, an elitist and nationalistic group that included Benjamin Disraeli (1804-1881), First Earl of Beaconsfield, and John James Robert Manners (1818-1906), Seventh Duke of Rutland.[1]

At first resisting the term as tending to divide the Repeal movement, members of the group took it as their own after O'Connell made a vitriolic speech applying the label to them. O'Connell believed the glorification of national heroes in the poetry and other literature of the younger generation would lead to violence, although they insisted they had no revolutionary intent — at first.

O'Connell and Davis had frequent differences of opinion. For example, where O'Connell, a fluent speaker, thought Gaelic unsuitable for "West Britons," Davis believed preservation of the language was essential to maintain a distinct Irish identity and character, even though few Young Ireland-

---

[1] James Quinn, *Young Ireland and the Writing of Irish History.* Dublin, Éire: University College Dublin Press, 2015, 1, 36-37.

ers could speak it.[2] Nevertheless, O'Connell, although suspicious of the movement as a whole, thought highly of Davis.

Dissatisfied with the Dublin *Morning Register* (the official organ of the Repeal Association) and the *Dublin Monthly Magazine* as outlets, Davis, Dillon, and Duffy founded *The Nation* in 1842. From the first the *Nation* was a newspaper devoted to restoring pride in being Irish. It soon had a circulation some authorities estimate at 250,000.

The *Nation* had a heavy infusion of Romanticism. Unchecked by common sense and orthodox religious faith (Catholic or Protestant), the romantic view of Ireland it fostered was eventually infiltrated by various schools of esoteric thought, *e.g.*, spiritualism, theosophy, and Fabian socialism that plagued the latter half of the nineteenth century.

The solid core of the publication, however, consisted of patriotic articles, essays, poems, and songs that linked the epic struggles of mythical, ancient, and medieval times to the Ireland of the 1840s. The Risings of 1798 were a special focus, particularly since they had led to the Acts of Union.

When the Repeal movement went into sudden eclipse with the cancelation of the Clontarf meeting and the arrest and conviction of O'Connell, the Young Irelanders stepped into the power vacuum. It became obvious, however, after his release that O'Connell was no longer the man he had been. A few years later he was diagnosed with "congestion of the brain." This was possibly an ischemic stroke or Alzheimer's, either of which can noticeably alter a person's behavior. The leadership of the Repeal Association began to dissolve in infighting.

With his good relationship with O'Connell, and the help of William Smith O'Brien (1803-1864), who joined the Repeal Association in 1843, Davis might have been able to bring the factions together, but he died in 1845 a month short of his thirty-first birthday. Within a year, the Young Irelanders under the leadership of Smith O'Brien and Duffy walked out of the Repeal Association, now headed by John O'Connell (1810-1858), Daniel O'Connell's son.

---

[2] *Ibid.*, 22,

This was after Thomas Francis Meagher (1823-1867), future acting territorial governor of Montana, gave his "Sword Speech," earning himself the sobriquet "Meagher of the Sword." The Young Irelanders formed the Irish Confederation in 1847 to replace O'Connell's Repeal Association.

While the politicians and agitators were arguing endlessly about proper tactics and methods to bring about repeal of the Act of Union, however, a more immediate problem surfaced with the failure of the potato crop in the Fall of 1845. What followed was to change the "Irish Question" from the abstraction of national survival, to the lives of actual children, women, and men.

An Gorta Mór

The Famine is the defining event in modern Irish history. It is impossible to understand Ireland today without knowing something about "The Great Hunger," *An Gorta Mór*, that ravaged the country from 1846 to 1852.

The Great Hunger can be described as the inevitable result of a system designed to fail. This is something the modern global economy shares with nineteenth century Ireland.

From the English invasion of Ireland in the twelfth century down to the 1840s, the effect of government policy had been to deprive the ordinary people of the country of ownership of productive capital, whether in the form of land, livestock, or technology. As a result of the prevalence of multiple levels of subletting and "rack renting," a system of extortionate rents, by the middle of the nineteenth century the vast majority of the people of Ireland subsisted on what would otherwise be sub-economic plots.

Only the potato made it possible for people to survive even marginally on such small plots of land as tenants-at-will with no rights, instead of owners with property rights or leaseholders of adequate farms with the "tenant-right." Consequently, poverty was widespread, and the country was subject to all the dangers of a one-crop subsistence economy.

In the 1820s Dominic Corrigan (1802-1880), a Dublin physician, warned the government of the problem. He predicted that "a pestilence and disease of unprecedented magnitude will befall us" unless some means was found to diversify crops and provide new sources of food.[3]

Disaster struck in September 1845. A blight — *phytophthora infestans* — that had affected the potato crop all across Europe reached Ireland. What caused hardship in Europe, however, triggered almost instant catastrophe in Ireland.

Hundreds of thousands of people died from starvation and starvation-related disease. The historian Cecil Woodham-Smith declared, "How many people died in the famine will never precisely be known. It is almost certain that, owing to geographical difficulties and the unwillingness of the people to be registered, the census of 1841 gave a total smaller than the population in fact was."[4]

Landlords, who should have had a generally good idea of the number of people from their rent rolls, and who were probably the primary source of data for the 1841 census, sometimes underestimated population by more than 400%. The later presumed exaggerations of Nationalists that more than four million died as a result of the Great Famine become, if not believable, at least understandable.

A Systems Failure

Ironically, there was more than enough food grown in Ireland to stave off the famine, just as in other parts of Europe where other crops were able to take up the slack when the potato crop failed.[5] Similarly, today's global, high-tech economy, capital produces marketable goods and services in almost unbelievable abundance, yet workers and their families typically live hand-to-mouth — when they have jobs.

Unfortunately, the Irish had something else in common with today's wage workers. The typical employee of modern times, like the Irish tenant of the mid-nineteenth century, owns little or none of the commercial and industrial capital

---

[3] Dominic Corrigan, "On the Epidemic Fever of Dublin, Part I," *Lancet*, 1829, 2:569-575; "On the Epidemic Fever of Dublin, Part II," *Lancet*, 1829, 2:600-605.
[4] Cecil Woodham-Smith, *The Great Hunger* New York: Harper & Row, Publishers, 1962, 411.
[5] Christine Kinealy, *This Great Calamity: The Irish Famine, 1845-1852*. Dublin: Gill and Macmillan, 1995, 354.

that produces the bulk of marketable goods and services in a modern developed economy. Neither, as a rule, did the Irish own the land on which other crops were grown.

Most of the food was shipped out of the country — under heavy guard — to generate cash income for the largely absentee landlords, and feed other people. Even had the food been retained in the country, Peel's government (possibly in revenge against O'Connell) had not included Ireland in the repeal of the Corn Laws, a system of tariffs and restrictions on imported grain intended to keep prices high. Instead, there was a new Coercion Act. Prices of other foodstuffs remained high, and the military was there to ensure that no involuntary redistribution took place.

The obvious step in any famine — prohibiting the export of food — was not taken. Ostensibly this was because politicians were afraid of interfering with the "free market" . . . so the government supported the "free market" with law and force of arms. The government even went to the extent of forbidding the import of American maize for free distribution because it might depress prices. This was mercantilism, the antithesis of a truly free market.

The Great Famine thereby dictated relations between Ireland and Great Britain down to the present day. As Young Irelander John Mitchel (1815-1875) commented, "The Almighty, indeed, sent the potato blight, but the English created the Famine."[6]

That is, in a sense, correct. It was not, however, due to active malice or even indifference on the part of the English people or government, except in a relatively few instances. In common with most people today who simply do not comprehend basic principles of sociology — the effect of institutions on people — the English of the mid-nineteenth century took their institutions (their social habits or tools) for granted. Completely misunderstanding Adam Smith's "invisible hand" argument, they assumed that any interference with the system would bring about a disaster worse than the Famine it-

---

[6] John Mitchel, *The Last Conquest of Ireland (Perhaps)* (1861), quoted in Peter Duffy, *The Killing of Major Denis Mahon*. New York: HarperCollins, 2007, 312.

self — even as they egregiously interfered with the system on a daily basis with laws and armed force.

The key to effective and just social change, however, is not simply to try and force desired results and then blame others for the inevitable failure. Rather, the solution is to join with others of like mind, discern the institutional flaws that have created barriers to the just operation of the social order, then organize to change social habits so that doing the right thing individually becomes possible.

This is the essence of social justice — not imposing desired results, but reforming or restructuring institutions to make desired results possible. Social justice does not, therefore, mean that the State or private organizations meet people's needs, even on the largest scale. Rather, the act of social justice involves people organized in free association and backed up by the State engaging in restructuring and maintaining the common good in a way that provides equal opportunity and means for all.

The Dismal Science

It would be a grave error, however, to think that there was no famine relief. Some landlords did as much as they could to relieve distress. Private associations, notably the Society of Friends (the Quakers) did a great deal. Even the government finally allowed the importation of American maize, although it has been estimated that the total amount allowed into Ireland would not have sufficed for the needs of a single county.

The problem was that the disaster was on such a gigantic scale that what was done amounted to tokenism. The only real famine relief for anything but short tem needs is to make ordinary people productive — and able to benefit from their own efforts.

The first part of a viable solution already existed in Ireland. The country was phenomenally productive. As noted above, however, the people producing the food did not own it. They derived little or no benefit from their efforts. In addition, there was wide and unquestioned acceptance of the work of the Reverend Thomas Malthus (1766-1834), especially his 1798 *Essay on Population*, which was interpreted to mean that what was happening in Ireland was inevitable.

Malthus's *Essay*, however, was nothing but a string of unproved assertions, *viz.*, poor people (such as the Irish) could not control themselves. They would always and everywhere breed up to the point where food supplies were just barely sufficient to keep them alive. Further, since food production increases arithmetically (1-2-3-4, *etc.*) and population increases geometrically (1-2-4-8, *etc.*), disaster is inevitable.

Food production and population do not, however, increase as Malthus claimed. Nor is explosive population growth the cause of poverty. Rather, all things being equal — such as equality of opportunity to employ one's labor and capital productively — population pressure spurs economic growth, which in turn slows population growth naturally.

In common with a number of other writers, John Weyland (1774-1854), had noted the correct relationship between economic growth and population in 1816 in *The Principles of Population and Production.*[7] Weyland observed that poor people tend to reproduce at great rates, the middle class tends to reproduce at replacement rates, while the rich tend to reproduce at rates less than replacement.

Weyland concluded, as did R. Buckminster Fuller[8] a century and a half later, along with Jane Jacobs,[9] that Malthus had confused cause and effect. Evidence indicated that the level of economic development and standard of living determines the rate of population growth, not the other way around.

The solution, then, was obvious. Raising living standards through economic growth in which everyone can participate as producers of wealth through direct ownership of capital and of labor resolves the "population problem"; reducing population growth does not raise living standards. The problem, of course, was how to finance expanded capital ownership when the rich who controlled money and credit weren't

---

[7] John Weyland, *The Principles of Population and Production.* London: Baldwin, Cradock & Joy, 1816.
[8] R. Buckminster Fuller, *Utopia or Oblivion: The Prospects for Humanity.* New York: Bantam Books, 1969, 200-201.
[9] Jane Jacobs, *The Economy of Cities.* New York: Vintage Books, 1970, 117-121.

about to deprive themselves of their monopoly financial power voluntarily.

Still, despite its obvious flaws, Malthus's *Essay* told the power *élite* in England and Ireland what it wanted to hear. As Joseph Schumpeter noted in his *History of Economic Analysis*:

> The teaching of Malthus' *Essay* became firmly entrenched in the system of the economic orthodoxy of the time in spite of the fact that it should have been, and in a sense was, recognized as fundamentally untenable or worthless by 1803 and that further reasons for so considering it were speedily forthcoming. It became the "right" view on population, just as free trade had become the "right" policy, which only ignorance or obliquity could possibly fail to accept — part and parcel of the set of eternal truth that had been observed once for all. Objectors might be lectured, if they were worthy of the effort, but they could not be taken seriously. No wonder that some people, utterly disgusted at this intolerable presumption which had so little to back it began to loathe this "science of economics" quite independently of class or party considerations — a feeling that has been an important factor in that science's fate ever after.[10]

The power *élite* took refuge in the belief that the Famine was a graphic, if regrettable, proof of Malthus's theories. Further, the Great Hunger persuaded subsequent generations that economics is "the dismal science," offering no hope, only despair. In this view of economics, common sense as well as common humanity had to give way to economic or political necessity.

A Viable Relief Proposal?

Countering Malthusian theory was the basis of a proposal by William Thomas Thornton (1830-1880), a clerk in the East India Company, who had become interested in the problem of poverty throughout the British Empire. This, naturally enough, led him to the theories of the Reverend Thomas Malthus that were taken as justifying the widespread poverty that accompanied the dispossession of the great mass of people.

---

[10] Joseph A. Schumpeter, *History of Economic Analysis*. New York: Oxford University Press, 1954, 581-582.

Thornton published his refutation of Malthus's theories, *Over-Population and Its Remedy*,[11] in 1846 just as the effects of the crop failure of 1845 were beginning to be felt. Briefly, Thornton's argument was that to slow population growth, it is necessary to raise living standards. And the way to raise living standards is to make ordinary people owners of productive capital, whether land or technology.

Immediately upon completing *Over-Population and Its Remedy*, Thornton set to work applying his theories to the situation developing in Ireland. He published the result as *A Plea for Peasant Proprietors; With the Outlines of a Plan for Their Establishment in Ireland*[12] in 1848.

Again briefly, Thornton's proposal was for the government to purchase large tracts of idle waste land in Ireland, divide them into economic plots, and either sell or lease them to families. An expert in agricultural development — he contributed the extensive article on agriculture to the 1875 Ninth Edition of the *Encyclopedia Britannica* — Thornton gave detailed instructions on how to make waste land productive, even what crops should be planted to facilitate the process.

Thornton also presented a detailed plan for financing the proposal. This would not only have reduced and, finally, eliminated the cost of famine relief, it would have yielded a profit to the government as well as broadened the tax base to increase future revenues.

So why was Thornton's proposal not implemented? In two words, Malthus and mercantilism.

As Thornton was fully aware, his facts, figures, and arguments flatly contradicted Malthusian assumptions. The power *élite*, however, did not want to hear what Thornton or any other "post scarcity" economist had to say. Malthus's theories were accepted economic orthodoxy, and any contrary position, regardless of its objective truth, was necessarily rejected without consideration.

---

[11] William Thomas Thornton, *Over-Population and Its Remedy*. London: Longman, Brown, Green, and Longmans, 1846.
[12] William Thomas Thornton, *A Plea for Peasant Proprietors; With the Outlines of a Plan for Their Establishment in Ireland*. London: John Murray, 1848.

More to the point, perhaps, Thornton's financing proposal would have required the government to issue bonds to purchase unused waste land at the fair market value, which would then be sold or leased to Irish families. This would have violated the limits on debt imposed by Sir Robert Peel's Bank Charter Act of 1844. It would also have increased geometrically the number of Catholics eligible to vote by raising hundreds of thousands of people almost immediately from dire poverty to the status of £10 freeholders and tenants.

It didn't matter that in this case the land would have secured the debt, and the land would have increased greatly in value as it was improved and put into production. Nor did it matter that several times over the course of the nineteenth century the government would increase the debt limit in order to bail out wealthy interests in England. Using the faith and credit of the British Imperial government to turn non-owners into owners — and generate potential votes for repeal of the Act of Union — was not merely not a priority, it was genuinely unthinkable.

Even if Thornton's proposal had been given serious consideration, however, it would have failed due to the refusal of the government to interfere in private interests for the general welfare. For the individual good of the propertied classes, yes, but not to make any inroads on private property for the good of the whole, even if the land was lying idle and the owner received its fair market value.

"Utterly Foreign to Christian Truth"

During "Black '47," the worst year of the Famine, a series of open letters appeared in the *Nation* written by James Fintan Lalor (1807-1849). Lalor's theme was the obvious truism that political power depends on economic power. Rather than work for the repeal of the Act of Union, Lalor believed the efforts of the Young Ireland movement should be directed to the establishment and maintenance of widespread ownership of productive capital, specifically land. As he explained,

> Society stands dissolved. In effect, as well as of right, it stands dissolved, and another requires to be constituted. To the past we can never return, even if we would. The potato was our sole and only capital, to live and work on, to make much or little of; and n it the entire social economy of this country was founded, formed and supported. That system and

> that state of things can never again be resumed or restored; not even should the potato return. . . .¹³
>
> Its theory contains itself in a single principle; its practical solution is comprised and completed in a single operation. Lay but the foundation and the work is done. . . . Lay deep and strong the only foundation that is firm under the foot of a nation — a secure and independent agricultural peasantry. A secure and independent agricultural peasantry is the only base on which a people ever rises or ever can be raised; or on which a nation can safely rest.¹⁴

All of this is, within limits, perfectly true. The problem was that, confusing the right to be an owner with what an owner may do with what he or she owns, Lalor's proposal was flawed by his belief that the right to be an owner is conditional, not absolute. This is because — in his opinion — all title ultimately derives from the collective, "the people."

Lalor's error is that on which all forms of socialism are established and maintained. The mistake is immediately obvious to anyone who understands private property and basic principles of natural law. It is an error that the Catholic Church has consistently condemned, describing it as "utterly foreign to Christian truth"[15] — or, for that matter, to the truth of any other system with a basis in common sense and human nature.

Specifically, the theory of socialism requires that a human creation — the abstraction of the collective, humanity, mankind, the State, community (whatever you want to call it) — has rights that actual flesh and blood human beings do not have. The contradiction here is that as a human creation, the collective can only have such rights as human beings grant to it. In other words, the socialist argument consists of a dog chasing its own tail and running around in circles.

The true understanding of private property is much more rational. As a natural right, the right to be an owner is built into human nature. It is therefore inalienable and absolute. The inherent rights of life, liberty, and private property can-

---

[13] Lilian Fogerty, ed., *James Fintan Lalor: Patriot and Political Essayist*. Dublin: The Talbot Press, 1918, 10.
[14] *Ibid.*, 21.
[15] *Quadragesimo Anno*, § 120.

not be taken away without making someone other than human.

The rights of property are a different matter. What an owner may legitimately do with what he or she owns can and must be limited; the exercise of property must never be absolute and unconditional. The rights *of* property — as opposed to the right *to* property — however, are conditioned upon the wants and needs of the owner balanced against the demands of the common good and the obligation not to harm others.

The Fall of Young Ireland

Lalor's theory was to influence the Nationalist debate down to the present day, and had enormous influence on the leaders of the Easter Rising. What was of more immediate importance, however, was the fact that, although Young Ireland had assumed O'Connell's mantle in the Repeal movement, the garment was hardly seamless. The leadership began dividing even before the official founding of the Irish Confederation in January 1847.

Smith O'Brien and Duffy, while in theory were prepared to use at least the threat of force to achieve Repeal, preferred Davis's tactic of reconciliation to bring together all the Irish, regardless of faith or economic status. Their special focus was to win over the predominantly Protestant landlord and mercantile class, and threaten violence only as a last resort.

Horrified at the Famine, influenced by Lalor, and inspired by the revolutionary movements in Europe, for his part Mitchel became convinced that only an armed insurrection would lead to the establishment of an Irish republic, bring about the end of landlordism, and secure the land for "the people." He resigned from the Council of the Irish Confederation. Having by this time become one of the most vocal and effective journalists writing for the *Nation*, he founded his own much more militant newspaper, *The United Irishman*, early in 1848.

What brought the Young Ireland movement back together for a time was the news from Paris of the "February Revolution" of 1848. The message was clear: successful revolution was possible. The *Nation* quickly became almost as radical as the *United Irishman*.

Still, the movement remained divided between those under Smith O'Brien and Duffy who put their hope in constitutional reform, and Mitchel, who advocated constitutional reform only as a first step toward the establishment of a socialist Irish republic. The situation was sufficiently fluid that there would probably have been a permanent split in the movement within a matter of weeks.

What saved the movement — briefly — was the arrest of Smith O'Brien, Mitchel, and Meagher in May 1848. Smith O'Brien and Meagher were found not guilty, but Mitchel was convicted of treason and sentenced to fourteen years' transportation. He was sent to Tasmania, then known as Van Dieman's Land, from whence he escaped in 1853 and made his way to the United States.

Having effectively brought the movement together in the face of a common enemy by removing Mitchel, the British arrested Duffy in July 1848 for seditious conspiracy. Defended by Isaac Butt, Duffy was freed after his fifth trial.

Although he continued to put his faith in constitutional reform, Duffy's arrest virtually guaranteed that the Nationalists as a whole would assume that armed revolution was the only viable option open to them. Duffy eventually gave up hope of reform in Ireland and emigrated to Australia, where he became Premier of Victoria.

The authorities also shut down the offices of the *Nation* and suspended habeas corpus. This last was to enable them to close the "Confederation Clubs" that had sprung up to support the Young Ireland movement without having to show cause.

Mrs. McCormack of the Cabbage Patch

Duffy's arrest left Smith O'Brien nominally in charge, but with others keeping things from him. Faced with the total dissolution of the movement, Smith O'Brien eventually allowed himself to be goaded into insurrection.

Effective revolution, however, was out of the question at this time. Confused, starving, and demoralized people are not the material out of which to fashion a successful rebellion.

Nevertheless, believing their backs to be against the wall, the Young Irelanders made the effort. Early on, Dillon proposed that the group fortify a large house and issue a proclamation. When the others rejected this plan, he left for Roscommon in the west of Ireland.

The principals seemed to lack the spirit of rebellion. In his book, *Ireland Since the Famine*, Francis Stewart Leland Lyons remarked that, "although individuals like Smith O'Brien and John Blake Dillon showed personal gallantry, their attitude to war was much too genteel to offer the slightest prospect of success."[16]

There were scattered outbreaks throughout the country, but the most serious one was in Ballingarry in County Tipperary. After a few days of ineffectual campaigning, the authorities issued a warrant for Smith O'Brien's arrest.

A band of approximately fifty Royal Irish Constabulary armed with rifles under Inspector Trant entered Ballingarry, but found barricades erected and a large number of people wandering aimlessly about. The constables retreated and occupied a house owned by a widow, Mrs. McCormack. The woman of the house was absent, but the men marched in, terrorizing and taking McCormack's five children hostage, and breaking up the furniture while singing *The British Grenadiers*.

Accompanied by a large crowd of curious spectators, Smith O'Brien and twenty or so peasants armed with an assortment of firearms and pikes tried to persuade the constables to surrender. While Smith O'Brien was negotiating for the release of the children, someone in the crowd shouted, "Slash away, boys, and slaughter them!" whereupon the onlookers began throwing rocks and sticks at the house.

Later claiming that someone in the crowd had fired first, the constables let loose a volley from the house. This scattered the crowd and forced O'Brien's men to take cover behind a low stone wall surrounding the widow's cabbage patch. The battle — such as it was — continued for an hour or so, until another body of constabulary arrived to lift the siege.

Badly outnumbered, having had two men killed and a number wounded, with the constables holding children as

---

[16] Lyons, *Ireland Since the Famine, op. cit.*, 110.

hostages, and unwilling to destroy the family's means of livelihood, Smith O'Brien and his men scattered. Smith O'Brien and the other leaders were captured within a few days.

Convicted of sedition, Smith O'Brien and the others were sentenced to death. Under pressure from the public, however, the sentences were commuted to transportation. They soon joined Mitchel in Van Diemen's Land, although sent to different settlements to prevent further collaboration.

Lalor had started a newspaper, *The Irish Felon*, in June 1848 after Mitchel's arrest and the suppression of *The United Irishman*. He was himself arrested after the suspension of habeas corpus, but released after a few months when it was clear that prison had ruined his already frail health.

Lalor immediately began planning a new insurrection, or a continuation of the existing one, depending on your point of view. This was in concert with John Savage (1828-1888), Joseph Brennan (1828-1857), John O'Leary (1830-1907), and Thomas Clarke Luby (1822-1901) in Tipperary and Waterford.

In September 1849 Savage and Brennan attacked the police barracks at Cappoquin, a town in west Waterford. Other leaders had neither the men nor the material to take action in their areas. Everyone scattered, and the second attempt at rebellion dissolved.

The Catholic Parliamentary Alliance

In the wake of the Famine and following the fiasco of the 1848 and 1849 Risings, organized efforts at reform or resistance virtually disappeared. The National Repeal Association dissolved in 1848, and the recognized leadership of the Young Ireland movement was scattered, in prison, or transported.

A political reaction set in. Irish Nationalism shifted its emphasis from independence or Repeal, to agrarian reform. This was a more popular and sustainable cause than rebellion in light of the horrors of the Great Hunger, and responded directly to the increasing agitation over long-standing grievances of the farmers.

The Tenant Right League ("Tenant League") formed in 1850. Anticipating Charles Stewart Parnell (1846-1891) and the National Land League, the Tenant League called for lower rents, fixity of tenure, and protection of the tenant right.

There was talk of a rent strike to force reforms, but nothing came of it. This was chiefly due to Duffy and Frederick Lucas (1812-1855), the two leaders of the tenants' rights movement, being convinced that the formation of an independent Irish parliamentary party without ties to any existing interest, would bring the necessary reform. O'Connell's unfortunate relationship with and reliance on the Whigs had not been forgotten.

The effort gained momentum when Pope Pius IX reestablished the hierarchy in England in 1850. This provoked a new wave of anti-Catholic hysteria, and the passage of the Ecclesiastical Titles Act 1851.[17] The Bill reiterated and clarified the prohibition contained in the Roman Catholic Relief Act 1829 against Catholic prelates (bishops) using "territorial titles."

Irish Catholic members of parliament voted against the Bill. The Bill passed anyway, but out of the effort developed an Irish "party in the making" that voted as a bloc in opposition to the Whigs at every opportunity.

What prevented "the Irish Brigade," as it came to be called, from becoming anything more than a loose alliance politically was its focus on religious issues. To emphasize their reliance on the Catholic Church, the members formed the Catholic Defense League in Dublin in 1851.

The Catholic Defense League joined in a united front with the Tenant League to promote lower rents and protection of the tenant right, dropping the more politically sensitive issue of fixity of tenure. Over the protests of the more ecumenically minded and politically astute "cradle Catholic" Duffy, the wishes of the fervent convert Lucas prevailed, and the parliamentary reform movement became specifically Catholic in character.

By 1852 the nascent Irish Catholic party had forty-eight members pledged to support its goals, making it the single largest voting bloc in Ireland. The fragility of the alliance was graphically demonstrated, however, when the Irish

---

[17] 14 & 15 Vict. c. 60.

Catholic bloc was instrumental in bringing about the fall of the Conservative government at the end of 1852. In a move widely taken as a betrayal, the two most prominent Catholic Defense leaders, John Sadleir (1813-1856) and William Keogh (1817-1878), were offered, and accepted, positions in the new coalition government.

A number of other "Irish Brigade" members followed suit, and the alliance dissolved. The Nationalist movement reoriented itself once again toward independence or Repeal. The only questions were the form of Ireland's political existence, and whether this would be achieved by peaceful, parliamentary means, or by violence.

The Irish Republican Brotherhood — Eventually

The dissolution of the Irish Catholic bloc set the stage for the advent of James Stephens (1825-1901). Stephens had been with Smith O'Brien at Ballingarry, where he had been seriously wounded. He managed to escape to France with Michael Doheny (1805-1863), and in Paris rejoined John O'Mahony (1816-1877).

O'Mahony, originally drawn into the Repeal movement by O'Connell, became by degrees a disciple of Lalor and Mitchel. O'Mahony was largely responsible for the romantic synthesis of socialism and "Celticism" that came to characterize Irish Nationalism. Fueled by sometimes naïve distortions of Ireland's myths and legends, this (as noted above) eventually became infected with elements of the spiritualist movements and half-formed scientific theories of the late nineteenth century "New Age" movement.

Admittedly, the combination, which reached its apogee with the Celtic Revival of the late nineteenth and early twentieth centuries, seemed to promise a higher ethnic consciousness than had been permitted among people who for centuries had been denied a recognized national identity. This, however, often degenerated into pseudo mysticism and a false racial (as opposed to cultural) pride as damaging to the image of the Irish people as the ubiquitous "stage Irishman" that afflicted the American theater for so many decades.

O'Mahony and Doheny made their separate ways to New York, where they met in 1854. Four years later Stephens, O'Mahony, and Doheny were back in Ireland, faced with the task of rebuilding the movement from the ground up. O'Mahony persuaded Stephens to lead the renewal. On March 17, 1858 Stephens formed a new secret society dedicated to forming Ireland into an independent democratic republic. O'Mahony later established this "Fenian" movement in New York.

At first the society had no official name, being known variously as "the Society," "the Organization," or "the Brotherhood." It was organized in "Circles," each commanded by a "Center," with each level being a section of nine, supposedly (but frequently not) entirely secret from all other sections.

Eventually the society became known as the Irish Brotherhood under the acronym IRB. Whether the R stood for Revolutionary or Republican, however, was unclear until 1873, when IRB was defined as the Irish Republican Brotherhood. The term Fenian came from O'Mahony's romantic fascination with the heroic age, and the Warriors of the Fianna under Fionn mac Cumhaill (Finn McCool) who defended Ireland from foreign enemies.

The Growth of Fenianism

Few other members of Young Ireland became involved in the Fenian movement, and everything had to begin all over again in both Ireland and America. For the time being, however, the effort was focused in Ireland, and Luby, back from France and Australia after the failure of the 1849 rising, greatly assisted Stephens in getting the new society under way, both of them touring the country to enlist new members.

While engaged in recruiting in the summer of 1858, Stephens and Luby visited Cork and came across the Phoenix Society. This was a political and literary group Jeremiah O'Donovan Rossa founded in 1857. With O'Donovan Rossa's group absorbed into Stephens's organization, the movement began spreading quickly.

This caused alarm among the local clergy, and there were warnings from the pulpit in many areas against getting involved. At the same time, Alexander Martin Sullivan (1830-1884), had taken over as editor of the *Nation* after Duffy's arrest and transportation. Sullivan was forceful in separating the constitutional nationalism he advocated from what he considered the extremism of the Phoenix Society.

Secrecy was not maintained as well as participants thought, and a number of Phoenix Society men were arrested. Determined on armed insurrection and seeing the opportunity to undermine Sullivan's attempt to rebuild a constitutional party, Stephens spread the rumor that Sullivan was a "felon setter" — an informer — and had been in touch with the authorities.

An avid self-promoter, Stephens seems to have had difficulty in separating Ireland's cause from his own career. This resulted in dissension in the movement, particularly when he took credit for every gain, and blamed others for every setback.

Stephens's ego also caused him to make claims that could not be supported, such as grossly inflated figures for numbers enrolled in Ireland, Great Britain, the United States, and the British Army. As Lyons summed up the situation,

> Insurrection . . . remained the goal. But the approach to this grand climactic event was marred by bitter disagreements within the movement, by personal rivalries, by hesitancies and last-minute changes of plan, and, it must be added, by moments not far removed from farce. . . . A secret revolutionary organization [publicly] proclaiming its doctrines within a stone's throw of Dublin Castle is not without its comic side.[18]

Much of the acrimony among the leadership core was due to Stephens's desire to publicize the effort. O'Mahony in America agreed that there were short term benefits in such a program, but insisted that in the long run it was counterproductive to the maintenance of a presumably secret movement.

Stephens as usual had his way, and in 1863 established a newspaper, the *Irish People*. Although Stephens had grandly announced that he would be the principal contributor, his contribution was limited to a few leading articles. Luby did most of the work, assisted by two recruits who became important to the movement, John O'Leary (1830-1907) and Charles Kickham (1828-1882).

---

[18] Lyons, *Ireland Since the Famine, op. cit.*, 127.

The work of O'Leary and Kickham was more difficult than it need otherwise have been due to the opposition of the Catholic hierarchy. The duo put forth a great deal of effort to convince people that they had not only the right, but the duty to rebel against a tyrannical government, and that the clergy had no role in politics, even to commenting or advising on the morality of public acts.

For its part, the Church was deeply suspicious of secret societies, and rightfully so, particularly in light of the spread of socialism and freemasonry in Europe, both of which tended to target organized religion in general, and the Catholic Church in particular. There was also the question as to whether the right of rebellion against even the most tyrannical government is justified if there is the possibility of a peaceful alternative.

That there were misunderstandings on both sides of the question is beyond dispute. A similar situation exists today in many countries.

From the middle of the nineteenth century on, politics everywhere, not just in Ireland, would become increasingly radical and State-oriented, the economic order would increasingly become controlled by a smaller and smaller private or State *élite*, and organized religion would be infiltrated by the doctrines of modernism and the New Age.

It was not, however, the Catholic Church, but the informer that nearly brought the movement to a halt. On September 15, 1865, the authorities raided the offices of the *Irish People* and arrested Luby, O'Donovan Rossa, O'Leary, and a number of other leaders.

Stephens, who was living outside Dublin, escaped capture for another two months, but the back of the movement seemed to have been broken. And so it would have been, had it not been for John Devoy.

Devoy, a deserter from the French Foreign Legion (in which he had enlisted to learn infantry warfare), had joined the staff of the *Irish People* in 1863. Seizing the initiative, Devoy engaged in the risky business of persuading Irish soldiers to mutiny. It was not the ideal time for a rebellion, but, in Devoy's judgment, unless something were done immediately, all momentum would be lost, and the chance to establish an Irish republic gone for at least a generation.

Stephens, his ego bruised by Devoy's activities, refused to heed any of the younger man's advice. Following Stephens's capture on November 11, 1865, Devoy engineered his escape with the help of secret Fenians among the prison guards, and again tried to persuade "the chief organizer of the Irish republic" to authorize a rising on the grounds that it was now or never.

Stephens felt the time was not ripe, and escaped to America. Devoy was himself captured in February 1866, and imprisoned until 1871. He was convinced to the end of his days that Stephens was a coward. Historians have not agreed with Devoy's assessment of Stephens, but most believe that the period between the raid on the *Irish People* offices and Devoy's arrest was the most favorable time for a rising that Ireland had seen in decades.

"I Remember '67 Well"

Shortly after Devoy's arrest the government suspended habeas corpus in Ireland and arrested hundreds of known Fenians. Organizing and drilling continued, however. Canon Sheehan of Doneraile recalled that as a boy he would see the men secretly marching and drilling in the woods near his home. As he wrote shortly before his death in 1913 in *The Graves at Kilmorna*, the Fenians were

> . . . strong silent men into whose character some stern and terrible energy seemed to have been infused. There were no braggarts among them. Their passion was too deep for words and that passion was all consuming, fierce unswerving love for Ireland.

Fenians in America were able to purchase large quantities of surplus weapons, ammunition, and other military supplies left over from the American Civil War. A large body of Fenians under General John O'Neill crossed into Canada near Buffalo, New York. They captured Fort Erie on May 31, 1866, but little else was accomplished.

American munitions were also shipped to Ireland, where Stephens's successor as "Chief Organizer," Thomas Joseph (1833-1908), tried to organize a rising in County Kerry in

February 1867. The idea was to initiate a guerilla campaign throughout Ireland and make the country ungovernable.

At the same time, elements in Dublin would join with Irish soldiers in the British Army that were expected to mutiny in support of the rising. Unfortunately, the movement had been infiltrated by large numbers of informers, and virtually every move made by the insurgents was known well in advance.

On March 5, 1867 there was another attempt that was thwarted in part by informers and also by the unexpected occurrence of a twelve-day blizzard. The effort dissolved in a series of minor skirmishes. When it became obvious that the coordinated rebellion had failed, most of the Fenians simply went home.

In a symbolically important move, the Fenians declared a Provisional Government and issued a proclamation, but this had little practical effect. Significantly, they declared they had resorted to violence only because they saw no other option.

In September 1867, Kelly and Timothy Deasy (1839-1880) went to England to attend a meeting of Centers, but were arrested. Edward O'Meaher Condon (1841-1915) organized a rescue, during which a guard was accidentally killed when the lock on the van in which the prisoners were being transported was blown off.

Kelly and Deasy escaped, but five men, Condon, Thomas Maguire, William Philip Allen (1848-1867), Michael Larkin (1837-1867), and Michael O'Brien (1837-1867) were arrested and put on trial amidst a wave of anti-Irish hysteria. All five were convicted on extremely dubious evidence, and Allen, Larkin, and O'Brien were executed on November 22, 1867. Condon's sentence was commuted the night before his scheduled execution. Maguire, a Royal Marine home on leave who had been arrested in a general roundup by police and who had taken no part in the rescue, was pardoned when it became obvious that the witnesses had perjured themselves.

Allen, Larkin, and O'Brien are the "Manchester Martyrs." They became an important symbol of nationalism to the Irish, and of the sinister nature of Fenianism to the English. It convinced many politicians of the United Kingdom that coercion was the only language the Irish understood, and a large number of Irish Nationalists that the English were equally deaf to anything except violence.

Others, more thoughtful, paused and considered what could have driven the Irish to such acts of desperation, and whether a more constructive program of reform might be more effective in reconciling the two peoples. One of these was William Ewart Gladstone (1809-1898), soon to become a key figure in the struggle for what would become known as "Home Rule," the trigger issue leading directly to the Easter Rising.

Chapter 6: The Irish Question

"Ireland, Ireland! that cloud in the west, that coming storm, the minister of God's retribution upon cruel and inveterate and but half-atoned injustice! Ireland forces upon us these great social and great religious questions — God grant that we may have courage — to look them in the face and to work through them."[1]

The Wake-Up Call

So the Liberal Gladstone wrote to his wife in 1845, summing up his attitude to the "Irish Question." His Conservative counterpart Disraeli had characterized Ireland as saddled with "a starving population, an absentee aristocracy, and an alien church, and in addition the weakest executive in the world."[2] By the time the Fenian uprising of 1867 brought the Irish Question into the glare of public opinion — and thus to the attention of parliament — however, Disraeli's main efforts were directed to other ends, although he did make an effort to correct some abuses and address Irish concerns after a fashion.

It was left to Gladstone to deal more effectively with Irish issues. Combining a genuine sympathy for the Irish and a better understanding of the situation, with the political base from which to work, Gladstone made significant progress in resolving the Irish Question justly.

Unfortunately, Gladstone's efforts were not sufficient. Too much had happened over the centuries for even full measures to be completely adequate, although they might have been good enough under the circumstances to satisfy everyone except the extreme Nationalists. Gladstone, however, for all his work and goodwill, was unable to achieve even half measures.

Although a failure in conventional terms, the Fenian Rising brought home to most of the factions and interest groups

---

[1] J.L. Hammond and M.R.D. Foot, *Gladstone and Liberalism.* New York: Collier Books, 1966, 84.
[2] Robert Blake, *Disraeli*. New York: St. Martin's Press, 1966, 178-179, quoted in Lyons, *Ireland Since the Famine, op. cit.*, 141.

in Great Britain and Ireland the desperate need for reform. The Fenians had — as intended — apparently validated the claims of Young Ireland that only by force of arms would Ireland's grievances gain a hearing.

Whether that hearing would be directed to the right questions, whether Ireland's advocates would be effective, and whether it would be adequate, are other issues. The message, however, was clear: continue on the path laid out by centuries of injustice, and the violence would not only continue, it would escalate.

The Rise of Home Rule

The "Home Rule" movement that replaced Repeal as the constitutional issue of Irish politics was, to all intents and purposes, the creation of one man, Isaac Butt (1813-1879). A lawyer-economist, he believed that Union with Great Britain was essential for the peace and prosperity of Ireland. The only questions for Butt were what form Union should take, and how to ensure that the people who tilled the land had rights in the land.

Prior to the Famine Butt had advocated land reform and disparaged the presumed *laissez faire* (actually mercantilist) policies of the government in Ireland. The disaster, however, persuaded him that simply pointing out problems was not the answer. As the popes Leo XIII and Pius XI would later make clear, the proper response to social injustice is to identify the real problem (not merely the symptoms), organize effectively, and carry out acts to reform the institutions — social habits — that inhibit or prevent people from doing the right thing.

This does not mean that short term needs are to be neglected. When people are starving, you feed them by any legitimate means. That, however, is not *social*, but *individual* justice and charity.

The goal of social justice is long term. It is not enough to address the symptoms of the problem, whether famine, lack of ownership, or crimes political or civil. Unjust institutions — the social environment — must be changed to make virtuous action possible, even optimal. Social justice means equality of opportunity and means, not the imposition of desired results, regardless on how vast a scale direct needs are met.

Butt seemed to grasp this essence of social justice. In 1847, the worst year of the Great Hunger, he warned that ignoring Ireland and failing to give effective relief in the short term would lead to serious political consequences in the long term.

The Young Ireland rebellion the next year confirmed Butt in his theory, and he defended Smith O'Brien and others at their trials. Significantly, he made his defense on both legal and economic grounds. He then went beyond that to advocate a form of federalism for Ireland, which would create a separate parliament for Ireland subordinate to the British parliament in London. This would, Butt believed, address the Irish demand for self-determination and at the same time preserve the Union.

Butt gained sufficient renown from his defense of the Young Irelanders to be elected to parliament. Instead of pushing for reform, however, he spent the next twenty years or so reveling in the fleshpots of London. Still a relatively young man at the time of his election, he proved able to resist anything except temptation, and acquired habits that would later undermine his effectiveness as a leader. Both penny and pound foolish, in the mid-1860s Butt was forced to return to Ireland to restore his finances by resuming the practice of law.

The fact that Butt increased his popularity and furthered his own career by advocating amnesty for Fenian political prisoners and defending them in court (for which he refused a fee) takes nothing away from the sincerity of his beliefs and actions. The laws and characteristics of social justice do not require that acts of social justice be disadvantageous to one's self or to others — just the opposite, in fact.

Circumstances also favored Butt. In the election of 1868 two issues were paramount: the disestablishment of the Church of Ireland, and more just relations between landlords and tenants. Butt had published his analysis of the Land Question, *The Irish People and the Irish Land*, the year before, linking the rise of Fenianism to centuries of misrule and mismanagement.

Gladstone, however, fell out of favor in Ireland as the result of Conservative outrage over the Church Act. To this was added Liberal dissatisfaction with his inadequate response to the demand for amnesty for the Fenians. Capping it all was the failure of his Land Act of 1870 ("Landlord and Tenant (Ireland) Act 1870") to address the crucial issue of tenant rights.

The situation was ripe for effective action. On May 19, 1870 Butt called a meeting at the Bilton Hotel in Dublin to organize the Home Government Association. He brought together the disparate elements of the current power structure and, to all appearances, fused them into a solid bloc in support of federalism. Butt's concluding motion was adopted unanimously:

> That it is the opinion of this meeting that the true remedy for the evils of Ireland is the establishment of an Irish Parliament with full control over our domestic affairs.[3]

The Idea of Home Rule

Unfortunately, for all the apparent solidarity of the new movement, the actual formation of the Home Government Association in July 1870 carried within itself the seeds of its own dissolution. Nowhere was this more evident than in the adoption of the term "Home Rule" to describe the goal of the Association.

First applied to Butt's federalist concept by Joseph Allen Galbraith (1818-1890), the term had previously been used in *The Celt* in 1858 and in *The Nation* in 1860. Unlike the specificity that Pius XI was to give to the previously indeterminate term "social justice," however, the "transfiguring vagueness"[4] of "Home Rule" to replace "federalism" and "Repeal" was seen as an advantage in bringing together disparate elements — at first.

Butt seems to have envisioned an arrangement similar to the system in the United States in which each state has a legislature, executive, and court, but also representation in the national legislature. This would mean a separate legislature for each of the four constituent parts of the United Kingdom, England, Wales, Scotland, and Ireland, as well as seats in the Imperial Parliament.

---

[3] Michael MacDonagh, *The Home Rule Movement*. Dublin, Éire: The Talbot Press, 1920, 10.
[4] *Ibid.*, 13.

To others, Home Rule meant repeal of the Act of Union and a completely separate government with the queen (Victoria was reigning-but-not-ruling at the time) as head of state. To still others, it meant independence in all but name.

And so on. One of the difficulties about the Irish Question was the fact that coming up with an answer was hampered by the fact that no one seemed able to agree on what was being asked. Consequently the harmony Butt achieved among the different groups was superficial, a development for which Butt himself was largely to blame. He knew he needed to be inclusive, and attract not only his fellow Protestants, but also the alienated Conservatives, Liberals, Constitutional Nationalists, and moderate and extreme Fenians to the cause.

Butt achieved inclusiveness by sacrificing substance, ending up trying to please three broad interest groups by telling each what they wanted to hear. The Protestant Ascendancy and the Conservatives formed a group that we might very loosely consider "the right." They were suspicious both of too much Catholic involvement, whether Constitutional Nationalist or Liberal (the middle), and the Fenians, whether Catholic or Protestant, moderate or extremist (the left).

The Catholic-Liberals and the Fenian moderates and extremists were suspicious of the Protestant-Conservatives, as well as of each other. The Catholics and Liberals viewed the Home Government Association as a Protestant lobbying organization, while the Fenians viewed it as a compromise on independence.

Fortune favored Butt, however. The Irish Catholic hierarchy had supported Gladstone and the Liberals in the hope that they would gain a national Catholic university. Gladstone failed to deliver to their satisfaction, and then started attacking the decrees of the First Vatican Council.

The bishops cautiously turned to Butt. This gave him the political clout to reorganize the Home Government Association as the Home Rule League for a more effective lobbying organization. The League had the same goals as the Association, but aimed at a much broader, national membership. Full members paid £1 per year, and associate members one shilling (12 pence), the same as for O'Connell's Repeal Association.

Butt was gaining ground. He had been reelected to parliament in 1871, while in the general election of 1874 — the first since the adoption of the secret ballot in 1872 — Home Rule candidates won fifty-nine seats. Many of these, however, were rather tenuous adherents, as the election had come soon after the formation of the Home Rule League and solid candidates had been difficult to surface in a hurry. At the same time, Gladstone's Liberal government fell, to be replaced by Disraeli's conservatives.

Still, while the candidates were overwhelmingly from the privileged classes, two tenant farmers were elected, and the small farmers and business owners were beginning to be a power in politics for the first time. The Home Rule bloc Butt attempted to form turned rapidly into an uneasy alliance between the landlords and the small owners, with all members having varying degrees of commitment — hardly what was needed to achieve the stated goal.

Only a strong political organization would be able to effect the sweeping and revolutionary economic and social reforms Ireland required if further violence was to be avoided down the road, and Butt had already failed as an organizer and as a leader. Further, while Gladstone's liberalism had been difficult to work with, the conservatism of Disraeli's new government was almost impossible, despite Butt's own leanings toward Disraeli's imperial policies.

The Rise of Parnell

This was the environment within which obstructionism evolved. Having little patience with Butt's gentlemanly approach to politics and its genteel but ineffective debating, and unwilling to continue exacting promises that never seemed to be kept except when the powers-that-be had no choice in the matter, the Home Rule bloc began falling into line behind the much more aggressive — and ungentlemanly — Joseph Gillis Biggar (1828-1890).

A convert to Catholicism, Biggar was at odds with Butt almost from the day of his election in 1874. A major conflict was that Biggar had demanded that any candidate running on the Home Rule ticket be required to sign a pledge to act in concert, a proposal Butt rejected.

Biggar had two great advantages over Butt. He regularly attended sessions of parliament, and was unafraid of upsetting the establishment or outraging English public opinion. Butt was frequently absent, either trying to make money or avoid his creditors, and to engage in acrimonious confrontation was alien to his nature.

Still, Biggar was not the man to replace Butt. He was of the wrong religion and social class. Nor did he look or sound the part. In 1875, however, a by-election in County Meath returned Charles Stewart Parnell, who had recently joined the Home Rule League.

A Protestant, landlord, educated in England — Parnell seemed the least likely of Irish Nationalists, especially with his pronounced English accent. He also had trouble speaking in public, hated crowds, and had a temper he had never been forced to curb.

What seemed to be almost Parnell's sole assets were that he looked the part, and he despised England, possibly because of his American mother and his English education. He also had a family tradition of going against the grain in political matters.

It became apparent after his initial stumbling, however, that Parnell had the one quality no leader can be without: an overriding passion for the cause. This drove him to overcome all obstacles, whether personal or political, and rank him with O'Connell and de Valera as the three most important Irish leaders since the Act of Union.

Parnell allied himself with Biggar and John O'Connor Power (1846-1919), a Home Ruler representing Mayo. He adopted the obstructionist tactic of filibustering to prevent bills from being passed in order to force concessions for Ireland. As might be expected, Butt objected to obstructionism, considering it counterproductive.

Among Parnell's first interventions in the parliamentary debates was to assert that the Manchester Martyrs were not guilty of murder. This, together with his association with Biggar (along with O'Connor Power a senior member of the IRB), brought Parnell to the attention of the Fenians.

In 1877 Butt threatened to resign from the League if the obstructionists continued their tactics. This created a rift between him and Parnell, and Parnell was elected president of the Home Rule Confederation of Great Britain in Butt's place. Butt had founded the Confederation to build support for Home Rule among the Irish in Britain, and the Fenians had quickly infiltrated the organization.

The Balkan Crisis (1875-1878) presented Home Rulers with another dilemma. Should they support the government in the hopes of addressing Irish concerns later? Or walk out of parliament to demonstrate "no community of interest" with Great Britain's foreign interventions while ignoring critical domestic (*i.e.*, Irish) issues?

During a January 1878 Home Rule conference in Dublin, John Dillon (1851-1927), soon to become one of Parnell's chief lieutenants, advocated a walkout. Butt violently opposed Dillon's proposal, and for the rest of the year ignored calls for united action by Home Rulers.

In December 1878, during the debates on the Second Anglo-Afghan War (1878-1880), Dillon harshly criticized Butt for refusing to embarrass the government by blocking legislation. In a Home Rule League meeting in February 1879, Dillon charged that Butt was a traitor and called for what was in effect a vote of no confidence.

Butt managed to retain nominal leadership of the League, but it was a Pyrrhic victory, as he well knew. Seriously ill, he suffered a stroke and died in May 1879. William Shaw (1823-1895), who had often acted as Butt's deputy, was selected as the new League chairman.

The New Departure

The field was now wide open for Parnell, but he faced the same problems as had Butt. His own class viewed him as a renegade, the Catholics were suspicious of a Protestant, and the Fenians rejected the constitutional approach on principle. It was then that the Irish-Americans shifted from a mere source of men, money, and material for an armed uprising, to being a potent force in Irish politics.

Where the failure of the 1867 Rising led many Nationalists in Ireland to abandon Fenianism and support a constitutional strategy, in the United States it led to a reorganization of the movement. Jerome James Collins (1841-1881) formed Clan na Gael (also known as the United Brotherhood), as a more effective secret organization. It eventually affiliated with the IRB in Ireland.

The two key members of Clan na Gael were William Carroll (1835-1926), a Philadelphia physician, and John Devoy. It was Devoy who would make Irish-American nationalism such a potent force in nineteenth century American politics — Tammany Hall in New York could not make a move without consulting Irish interests or the gangs — and leverage it to help bring about a revolution in Ireland.

In August 1877 as Parnell was beginning to show his leadership qualities and his devotion to the cause of Irish independence that made him "the Chief," he met with a Fenian, James Joseph O'Kelly (1845-1916) while in Paris. O'Kelly reported to Devoy that Parnell was cool and resolute. In January 1878 Carroll spoke with Parnell in London and got the impression that Parnell was in favor of complete independence.

It was Carroll who arranged a meeting with two members of the IRB a few months later for Parnell and two other obstructionists. These were John O'Leary, who had been involved in Lalor's abortive 1849 Rising, and John O'Connor (1850-1928). The meeting was significant on at least four counts.

First, it confirmed the absolute refusal of the IRB to compromise with constitutionalism. Only armed revolution was acceptable. Just the year before, Biggar and O'Connor Power had been expelled from the Supreme Council of the IRB, and John Barry (1845-1921) and Patrick Egan (1841-1919) had resigned over the issue of force versus constitutionalism.

Second, the meeting demonstrated that, while committed to revolution, Clan na Gael was willing not to abandon the pure principles of the IRB, but to add to them. Reasonable alternatives would be considered as long as nothing was done to rule out armed force — O'Connell's refusal to countenance violence was well within living memory, and widely viewed as emasculating the Repeal movement.

Third, it marked the clear ascendance of the American Clan na Gael — and Devoy — over the Irish IRB. Having marginalized itself by refusing to compromise on tactics, the IRB began its long decline until revived by Tom Clarke under the direction of Devoy and Clan na Gael. The center of constitutional nationalism would remain in Ireland, but the revolutionary initiative now shifted to the United States.

Finally, it identified Parnell as the man with whom the American Fenians and moderate Irish Fenians believed they could work. Parnell had not said much during the meeting, but by his silence had managed to convey a willingness to listen.

Devoy optimistically took Parnell's silence as agreement. Having refined the movement's goals after discussion with another rising figure, Michael Davitt (1846-1906), Devoy sent Parnell a telegram offering him the movement's support if he would adopt the major Irish-American objectives.

These were to, one, abandon federalism in favor of a general commitment to Irish self-government (carefully unspecified as to both form and substance). Two — the real power issue — settle the Land Question by pushing for immediate protection of tenant rights, but ultimately working toward widespread ownership of land to form a peasant proprietorship.

Astonishingly for a landlord, Parnell had already committed himself to widespread land ownership. Where in 1875 he had been content to speak of fair treatment of tenants, by 1877 he viewed fixity of tenure and fair rents only as a stopgap. The ultimate solution was for tenants to purchase the land they farmed at a fair price from the owner.

Davitt and Devoy had previously met in June 1879 with Parnell in Dublin to persuade Parnell to adopt land reform as a main plank in his platform. Influenced by Lalor's somewhat vague agrarian socialism, Davitt was himself the son of a man evicted during the Great Hunger from a farm in County Mayo. By April 1879, when he participated in a mass meeting in Irishtown, Mayo, Davitt had already made obtaining justice for tenant farmers the focus of his efforts.

The next day, October 27, 1879, Devoy declared that this "New Departure" was not an abandonment of revolutionary principles. Instead, by coming out into the open, the movement would educate the people to demand that their representatives withdraw from the Imperial Parliament when the time was right and set up a parallel legislature in Ireland. If this precipitated a war for independence, then so be it.

The Irish National Land League

What helped bring the ownership issue to the forefront of the Irish Question and usher in the "Land Wars" (agrarian agitation and violence directed to land reform) was the failure of the potato crop in three successive years, 1877 through 1879, combined with falling agricultural prices. While nowhere near the scope of the Great Hunger, people were starving.

Credit, even from the notorious gombeen men (moneylenders), dried up, and evictions escalated. Violence increased dramatically, targeting landlords, agents, and "grabbers" who leased farms from which others had been evicted.

A number of local land leagues were organized to protest the exorbitant rents being charged, especially in Connaught, the province hardest hit. The Mayo Tenants Defense Association organized in Castlebar in October 1878, and in April 1879 held the demonstration in which Davitt participated, the first of a series.

On October 21, 1879, a week before Devoy announced the New Departure, Davitt brought the various organizations and initiatives together under one roof with the founding of the Irish National Land League, *Conradh na Talún*, with Parnell as president. The short term goals were to stop rack renting and evictions. The long term goal was land ownership — although, like the term "Home Rule," what each person meant by "ownership" was subject to an almost infinite variety of meanings.

The early program was straightforward: help the starving and destitute. This rapidly expanded to assisting families evicted for non-payment of rent. In addition to direct assistance, the League from the very first organized demonstrations against evictions and put pressure on grabbers. Within two years the League became the center of a mass movement based on moral suasion with the goal of "the land of Ireland for the people of Ireland."

Consistent with the New Departure, the League stressed non-payment of unjust rents and refusal to take a lease on a farm from which another had been evicted. Those who violated these principles were to be shunned, sent to a "moral Coventry." This latter became known as "boycotting" from its effectiveness against Captain Charles Cunningham Boycott (1832-1897), land agent for John Crichton (1802-1885), Third Earl Erne, a large landowner in Mayo. It cost the government an estimated £10,000 to harvest crops worth £500 when Boycott could not force anyone to associate or even speak to him, much less work.

Despite the rhetoric of the League leadership that physical force should be avoided, however, instances of ribbonism (rural violence) increased in response to evictions. This was actually helpful up to a point. The more moderate Fenians became very active in the League, while Irish-Americans tended to view incidents as justified in self-defense — and very useful to the League leadership when raising money and garnering support in America.

Arriving in the United States the first week of January 1880, Parnell and Dillon were able to raise an estimated £30,000 [5] ($150,000) for relief of the distressed and the League's political war chest; donors were asked to specify how they wanted their contributions used — financing violence was explicitly repudiated.[6] Back in Ireland, Home Rulers in parliament, their constituents, the newspapers, even many of the Catholic clergy and members of the hierarchy gave their support.

The Parliamentary Land War

While the general election of 1880 that returned the Liberal Gladstone to power was carried on against the Conservative Disraeli ("Beaconsfieldism") in England, the land issue was paramount in Ireland. Thanks to the introduction of the secret ballot and, especially, the growing popularity of the

---

[5] Lyons, *Ireland Since the Famine, op. cit.*, 168. Others give figures as high as £72,000, Alvin Jackson, *Home Rule: An Irish History, 1800-2000*. New York: Oxford University Press, 2003, 41. Lyons (178) stated that the total receipts from October 1879 through April 1882, mostly from the United States, "so far as they can be accurately known" were £233,420, although Davitt claimed that the American contribution alone was £250,000.
[6] "Parnell in New York: His Appeal to the American Nation," *The Irish Canadian*, January 7, 1880, 5.

League, the Parnellites (as they were becoming known) constituted a more democratic and aggressive minority than parliament had previously experienced — some had fought duels or served as mercenaries.[7]

It also presented Gladstone with a problem. He was genuinely dedicated to improving the lot of Ireland and the Irish — but also responsible for maintaining law and order. He could not afford to be perceived as giving in to violence or the threat of it.

If Gladstone was trapped by circumstances, however, so was Parnell. The latter had not yet attained the personal popularity that would have allowed him to weld the dozen or more major interest groups supporting the League, each with its own agenda, into a unified whole. Parnell was still a figurehead, and he knew it. He had to be very careful about being too specific about anything, or of showing favoritism to anyone, and yet still advance the goal. This, naturally enough, led to charges of "aloofness" and "inscrutability."[8]

Gladstone and the Chief Secretary for Ireland, William Edward Forster (1818-1886), were developing a new land bill that they hoped would be an improvement over the failed effort of 1870. They felt, however, that they could not make progress until order was restored.

Forster went so far as to hint that he needed "special powers" to deal with the situation. An initial attempt late in 1880 to prosecute League leaders for allegations of conspiracy in encouraging violence failed, however, when Dublin juries refused to bring in a verdict.

Then in January 1881 parliament opened with the queen's speech focused on Ireland. It referred to an "extended system of terror," and promised an "Additional Powers" Bill and a Land Bill. Parnell moved to amend the address so that a Land Bill would precede any Coercion Bill. He argued that justice should be tried first, especially since the League provided a peaceful outlet for action that would otherwise take violent form. After debates lasting nearly two weeks, Par-

---

[7] Lyons, *Ireland Since the Famine, op. cit.*, 169-170.
[8] Conor Cruise O'Brien, *Parnell and His Party, 1880-90*. London: Oxford University Press, 1957, 36-37.

nell's motion was defeated four hundred thirty-five to fifty-seven.

Forster wasted no time. He immediately introduced the Protection of Person and Property (Ireland) Bill. Davitt wrote to Devoy that, in his opinion, another suspension of habeas corpus would destroy the movement in a month. The Parnellites dramatically increased the intensity of their obstructionism.[9]

Unfortunately, with a few exceptions, the parliamentary inexperience of the Parnellites resulted in a crude, even inept handling of the effort. Consequently, on February 2 Henry Bouverie William Brand (1814-1892), First Viscount Hampden, Speaker of the House, after secretly consulting with Gladstone, suspended the rules. As Chair, he refused to recognize any more members, and put the question from the chair. The Bill passed the first reading.

The next day Gladstone moved to adopt a new Standing Order to legitimize Brand's action. At the same time, Sir William George Granville Venables Vernon Harcourt (1827-1904), Home Secretary, anticipating suspension of habeas corpus, announced Davitt's arrest.

Outraged, Dillon took the floor without being recognized, was suspended for flouting the chair's authority, and ejected from the House by the Sergeant at Arms. No doubt attempting to demonstrate the hypocrisy of an *ex post facto* rule change that validated silencing debate, Parnell then interrupted Gladstone.

Parnell moved that Gladstone "not be heard." This was a parliamentary procedure that had not been used for centuries until Gladstone resurrected it during the previous session to silence Francis "Frank" Hugh O'Donnell (1846-1916). As might be expected, Brand refused to recognize Parnell's motion.

Parnell continued to insist that the question be put, and was "named" (a vote to suspend a member for an infraction of the rules) by the Speaker. "Indescribable confusion" reigned.

---

[9] *Ibid.*, 58.

Parnell and thirty-four others were suspended with Dillon and ejected from the House.[10]

The first Coercion Bill[11] passed February 28. The second, the Peace Preservation (Ireland) Bill ("the Arms Bill"), passed March 11.

Revolution or Social Justice?

Matters had now reached a crisis, and Parnell faced a decision. Withdrawing from the Imperial Parliament and setting up an independent government in Dublin had been discussed as a possible strategy. With the country now united as never before behind Parnell, the Parnellites could have turned their temporary suspension and ejection into secession. Brand's rule change and Gladstone's validating motion took away the Parnellites only effective parliamentary weapon, and Davitt's understanding of the New Departure was that the constitutional strategy would eventually lead to separation.

Nor was such a move entirely without precedent. During the Wars of the Roses in the fifteenth century Richard Plantagenet (1411-1460), the Duke of York (father of Edward IV and Richard III), issued what amounted to a declaration of independence for Ireland. He struck his own coinage, and consolidated his power for an eventual return to England.

Parnell, however, faced a much more justifiable — and more difficult — task than coming out Number One in a power struggle between dynastic factions to see who would grab the spoils.[12] His immediate goal was to obtain economic justice for the Irish, thereby making the ultimate political goal of Home Rule (however defined) possible.

On February 14, League leaders met in Paris, during which Dillon told Parnell that they wanted him to go to the United States on a promotional and fund raising tour. Fully aware that if he went he would have to make speeches advocating secession to please the Irish Americans, while at the same time providing the League with the financial resources

---

[10] *Ibid.*, 59.
[11] 44 & 45 Vict., c. 4.
[12] That's a little unfair to the House of York, which on the whole had a better record of good government in Ireland than the House of Lancaster, but still hardly democratic.

to carry on without him and reduce or remove his influence, Parnell declined.

Instead, he declared that his first duty to the cause was to return to parliament, while Egan should stay in Paris beyond the reach of English law and act as liaison with the Americans. This put Davitt (who was in prison) and Egan, both of whom opposed constitutionalism, out of the way instead of Parnell.

Parnell then wrote an open letter to the League setting out three points:

- It was his clear duty to stay in Ireland, not go to America,
- Parliamentary action was still to be preferred over acts that would precipitate violence, and
- The "area of agitation" should be universalized to include those English suffering from similar injustices.[13]

This last was a masterstroke. A year earlier Davitt had declared that Ireland's cause was that of humanity, while throughout 1880 there had been demonstrations in England in support of Irish grievances in ways that expanded them to the English, Scottish, and Welsh poor. Davitt could hardly complain when Parnell was simply following Davitt's own recommendation.

Nor was Parnell wrong. Within a short time a number of individuals and groups in England announced their support for Ireland's cause, and would continue to do so — although they were less than influential and Parnell took their declarations with a grain of salt. It did, however, give Gladstone pause.

Parnell's decision to remain with the constitutional approach was therefore not such a mystery or an about-face as many authorities have supposed. Rather, what he did was in strict accordance with the laws and characteristics of social justice.

Acts of social justice must, above all, be *effective*.[14] They are not symbolic acts, but practical reforms of institutions in-

---

[13] O'Brien, *Parnell and His Party, op. cit.*, 61-62.

tended to make an ultimate goal possible. Attempting to force desired results, regardless of the consequences, is not socially just, however gratifying it might be to one's ego or satisfying to a desire for revenge.

The 1881 Land Bill

Having gotten two Coercion Bills through parliament, Gladstone could hardly delay introducing his Land Bill, and did so in early April. As anticipated, it went further than any previous attempt at reform. Had its provisions been adopted in 1870, the Bill would probably have been satisfactory.

The Bill did not, however, go to the lengths now considered acceptable by the extreme Nationalists, however much it went beyond what the landlords and social conservatives thought safe. Further, with the landlords protected by the Coercion Acts, the number of evictions had risen sharply, and outbreaks of violence became more frequent. This is what Parnell had predicted, and was directly contrary to Gladstone's expectations.

The League membership, its supporters, and even the Parnellites in parliament divided on the Bill. Moderates thought that it should be supported, while extremists wanted it rejected. Even the Catholic clergy and hierarchy split.

Davitt had warned as early as December 1880 of the divisive nature of any measure short of the full program.[15] Parnell temporized, stating it would be unfair to comment until there was specific legislation.[16]

Dillon, however, forced Parnell's hand. During the Easter Recess he went to Ireland and made a series of speeches condemning the Bill, continuing his activities even after parliament reassembled in late April. He was arrested under the Coercion Act on May 2 after a particularly violent speech.

This put Parnell into an even more difficult position, especially since he had promised to call for a general rent strike if anyone was arrested for political activities. The alternative was to instruct his party to abstain from voting on the second

---

[14] Rev. William J. Ferree, S.M., Ph.D., *Introduction to Social Justice*. New York: Paulist Press, 1948, 51-52.
[15] O'Brien, *Parnell and His Party, op. cit.*, 66.
[16] *Ibid.*

reading of the Bill, a symbolic protest that could have no effect on the final outcome. Either move would alienate the conservatives and moderates, while only the former would placate the extremists. He chose the latter.

The Parnellites approved his motion, eighteen to eleven, after he threatened to resign as party leader. Not unexpectedly, Parnell was forced to explain the meaninglessness of his motion in an open letter to Thomas William Croke (1824-1902), Archbishop of Cashel, a strong, if conservative, League supporter. Croke had been instrumental in garnering the support of the Catholic clergy.

It was to no avail. When the division (a separation by groups to estimate the number of members voting each way) came on May 19, fourteen Parnellites went against the party and voted in favor of the Bill.

Nor did this end the matter. Having failed to mollify the extremists, Parnell had to deal with the increasingly vocal protests from the conservatives and moderates. In response to the pressure, he took no more actions to conciliate the extremists.

Instead, Parnell got down to the work of amending the Bill in committee to conform more closely to League demands. At the same time he had to prevent English and Irish reactionaries from emasculating the Bill with their own amendments.

Carefully refraining from anything that smacked of obstructionism, Parnell left it to individual party members how they would vote. Nearly all of them voted in favor of the Bill on its third reading on July 29. The Bill then went to the House of Lords, where it was again amended, and was signed into law ("received the Royal Assent") on August 22.

The Paradox of the Bill

Viewed objectively as possible, the Land Law (Ireland) Act 1881[17] was both an astounding victory for the League and the cause of Irish Nationalism, and an abysmal failure.

On the one hand, had anyone said at the beginning of the nineteenth century that the Irish, a people without civil rights and not even recognized as persons in a court of law,

---

[17] 44 & 45 Vict. c. 49.

would not only demand reform but obtain it, it is likely that no one in either Ireland or Great Britain would have believed it. Further, the fact that this had been done without resorting to armed revolt (the threat of it is another matter) was a very hopeful sign for future progress.

Moreover, the Great Hunger that had boded well to destroy not merely the distinct identity of the Irish as a people, but the nation itself, was starkly and harshly within living memory, and a grievance that bides to this day. After the horror of Black '47 it seemed as if Ireland would soon become "West Britain," and the country erased from the map, as Poland had been half a century before.

Gladstone's Land Bill was a great victory . . . but it was the wrong battle or, rather, the wrong objective. Like the civil rights movement in the United States in the early 1960s, essential gains were made, but then movement stopped.

The civil rights movement was satisfied with the vote, jobs, and welfare. The Land Bill — at least on paper (practice would turn out to be another matter) — secured "the Three Fs" of Fair Rent, Fixity of Tenure, and Free Sale.

Both the civil rights and the Home Rule movement, however, failed to take into account three "new things" that a decade later in the encyclical *Rerum Novarum* (1891) would be the focus of Catholic social teaching. These were the lack of capital ownership on the part of most people, money and credit,[18] and the effects of advancing technology.

As a rule, access to money and credit determines who owns productive wealth other than human labor. When land is the more productive asset that can legitimately be owned, those with control over money and credit own land. When technology is the more productive, they own technology.

With the Industrial Revolution, and accelerating through the nineteenth century, the balance of power began shifting away from an aristocracy based on concentrated ownership of land, to a new aristocracy based on concentrated ownership of industry and commerce. At the same time, those who con-

---

[18] "Money and Credit are essentially of the same nature; Money being only the highest and most general form of Credit." Henry Dunning Macleod, *The Theory of Credit*. Longmans, Green and Co., 1894, 82.

trolled access to money and credit became even more powerful than the industrial and commercial magnates who relied on those with "money power" to finance new capital formation.

The problem was exacerbated after Peel's Bank Charter Act of 1844[19] locked the British Empire into the demonstrably false past savings assumption. This is the fixed belief that only by producing more than is consumed is it possible to finance new capital . . . thereby restricting new capital ownership to those who can afford to save the enormous amounts of money needed to purchase capital.[20]

As a result, as Bagehot explained in *The English Constitution* (1867) and *Lombard Street* (1873), the "real" rulers of the British Empire were the financial interests, with the commercial and industrial interests a close second. This established and maintained a new dictatorship of control over money and credit that replaced the old dictatorship of concentrated land ownership.

Consequently, the landlord class no longer had the political power to prevent land reform as technology took over the bulk of production from land and labor. At the same time, the industrial, commercial, and, especially, financial magnates acquired immense political and economic power, making (lack of) worker ownership and labor relations the key issue.[21] This was a situation of which Gladstone took full advantage even while he probably did not grasp the implications.

Further, available land in the United States was disappearing. America had always provided a refuge to the Irish. As Frederick Jackson Turner pointed out in his "Frontier Thesis," the uniqueness of the land frontier in America cre-

---

[19] Ironically, Daniel O'Connell approved of the Act. "Ireland: Repeal Agitation," *The Head Quarters*, Fredericton, New Brunswick, May 28, 1845, 2.
[20] Cf. Hilaire Belloc, *The Servile State*, London: T.N. Foulis, 1912, 72-74.
[21] As early as 1854 the investment banker Charles Morrison had pointed out that unless workers could become owners, their economic condition would continue to worsen. Charles Morrison, *An Essay on the Relations Between Labour and Capital*. London: Longman, Green, Brown, and Longmans, 1854.

ated an environment within which democratic institutions not only could flourish, but were almost inevitable — as long as democracy was supported by ownership of productive assets: "So long as free land exists, the opportunity for a competency exists, and economic power secures political power."[22]

The land frontier had made America both a refuge and a power base for the Irish as well as for other oppressed peoples. With that safety valve gone, land being displaced by the productive power of technology, and new capital formation monopolized throughout the world by those who controlled past savings, there could only be one result. Wealth would become increasingly concentrated, and the gap between rich and poor would become a virtually impassible Grand Canyon.

The 1881 Land Bill addressed only a part of the problem, and that one of diminishing importance. This made Gladstone's task easier, although still not easy. It still left unresolved, however, the problem of concentrated control over the ever-expanding frontier of industry and commerce through control of the money power. Agrarian violence and unrest would decrease through the rest of the century, to be replaced by labor agitation, culminating in the 1913 Dublin strike and lockout.

Kilmainham and Treaty

Following the third reading of the Land Bill and the defection of so many of his party, Parnell engineered a tactical retreat from parliament by protesting a trivial matter and being suspended on August 1, 1881. Needing to counter the growing apathy of the moderates among the Nationalists and the dissatisfaction of the extremists with his own performance, within two weeks Parnell started a weekly newspaper, *United Ireland*, edited by William O'Brien (1852-1928). It achieved a wide circulation almost immediately.

A crisis had now been reached. Gladstone's tactics had split the Nationalist movement. Moderates and most of the

---

[22] Frederick Jackson Turner, "The Significance of the Frontier in American History," *Annual Report of the American Historical Association for the Year 1893*. Washington, DC: Government Printing Office, 1894, 223.

Catholic clergy were in favor of the Act, Irish extremists and the Americans were against it, and Parnell was caught in the middle. Coercion had done nothing to stop ribbonism and the activities of "Captain Midnight" — an Irish euphemism for agrarian violence, especially under cover of darkness.

Unexpectedly, Parnell came up with a solution that satisfied everyone except the Americans. At a League conference in Dublin on September 11, he announced that they would "test the Act" — submit selected cases of abuse to the newly established Land Commission.

Parnell justified this move to the extremists and the Americans on the grounds that the test cases were specially selected to expose the "hollowness" of the Act — which they did. It quickly became apparent that the Act as promulgated was almost worthless to those most in need of redress of their grievances.

The "American allies" were, however, still not convinced. Parnell then began mixing his actual qualified acceptance of the Act with a policy of verbal intransigence for show. Not appreciating Parnell's situation, Gladstone retaliated by attacking Parnell and the League in a speech at Leeds on October 7 — and restored Parnell to popularity.

Following up on the opening the prime minister had handed him, Parnell made his own speech in Wexford. He referred to "the perfidious English enemy" and Gladstone in particular as a "masquerading knight-errant." He raised the specter of the 1798 Wexford Rebellion and the Fenian Rising of 1867. At the same time, and in spite of his rhetoric, he was prudently considering a trip to the United States, as the League had been urging him since February.

Gladstone then made another misstep and had Parnell and a number of other League leaders arrested under the Coercion Act on October 13, and sent to Kilmainham Jail in Dublin. This caused outrage on both sides of the Atlantic, and brought the movement back together for the time being.

Parnell had not planned on being arrested, but it came at the right time. The problem was that British hamhandedness provided only a temporary respite — and it left the extremists in the movement in a good tactical position. To demonstrate the uselessness of the peaceful constitutional approach, it was only necessary to point to the victims of British perfidy sitting in Kilmainham.

According to Conor Cruise O'Brien in *Parnell and His Party*, however, Parnell managed once again to turn matters to his advantage.

To the extremists, the time seemed ripe to revive the idea of a rent strike. According to Parnell's mistress, Katharine "Kitty" O'Shea (1846-1921), he was against the "No Rent Manifesto," but allowed himself to be persuaded. According to William O'Brien, who drafted the Manifesto, Parnell was "most resolute" in favor of it.

Conor Cruise O'Brien suggested a middle ground, one that sounds quintessentially Parnell. In Conor Cruise O'Brien's opinion, Parnell believed the tactic would fail miserably. This would cause the extremist-leaning League to collapse, leaving the field to Parnell and his policy of moderation, eventual land ownership, and constitutional nationalism.[23]

At first it seemed to be working as Parnell expected. Archbishop Croke and the *Freeman's Journal* condemned the Manifesto, and the government suppressed the League on October 20 under the Coercion Act. Tenants either paid their rents, or went to the Land Commission to have a fair rent set. Violence increased, the New Departure was discredited, and the way seemed clear for a policy of moderation — if the British would agree to release Parnell and the others.

Finally, after months of secret negotiations that frustrated Parnell ("this wretched government have such a fashion of doing things by halves that it has managed to keep things going"[24]) an agreement was reached. This was the "Kilmainham Treaty."

The British agreed to deal with the problem of tenants in arrears in their rent, extend the Act to leaseholders, and implied that coercion would be ameliorated; dropping it completely was out of the question until law and order could be restored. Parnell agreed that he would regard an amended Act as "a practical settlement of the land question."

---

[23] O'Brien, *Parnell and His Party, op. cit.*, 73-75.
[24] *Ibid.*, 75.

Having gotten the camel's nose under the tent on the Land Question with the Land Bill and the promise of future amendment of the Act to extend the gains, Parnell shifted to a focus on Home Rule. To advance this, he further agreed to cooperate with the Liberal Party in their program of general reform.[25]

Politically speaking, the Treaty was probably the most that could be accomplished — for the time being. Increased ribbonism and political agitation on either the Land Question or Home Rule would almost certainly have led to another armed rebellion in the relatively near future. It is a virtual certainty that such an effort would have failed, far more repressive coercive measures implemented, and all that had been won would be lost.

Parnell probably knew better than anyone, however, that the Treaty was not a solution. It was a temporary measure to buy time in which to regroup, consolidate, and gather strength. That matters did not turn out as expected in the short term is not something that can be laid at Parnell's door, however much he was ultimately responsible for his own fall a decade later.

---

[25] *Ibid.*, 77.

Chapter 7: Home Rule All Round

On his release from Kilmainham Jail on May 2, 1882 along with Dillon and O'Kelly, Parnell wasted no time. The next day he and the others traveled to London where they put in "a brief but spectacular appearance in the House of Commons."[1] On May 6, the trio traveled to Portland Prison, located on a tiny island off the coast of Dorset in the English Channel, to escort Davitt back to London.

A Brief Ray of Hope

Davitt was far from pleased with the "Kilmainham Treaty." This may have been due in part to the influence of the American agrarian socialist, Henry George (1839-1897). Davitt had read George's recently published *Progress and Poverty* (1879) with great enthusiasm, and had become acquainted with the author, who was visiting the United Kingdom at this time.

George promoted nationalization of land as the solution to all economic and social ills. This was a view to which Davitt was increasingly committed, especially after George spent a great deal of time with him during his visit.

The problem for Davitt was that the Treaty and the Land Act had the potential to give Parnell both the power and the means to bring about the "peasant proprietorship" he sought as the foundation for Home Rule. With George, however, Davitt was increasingly convinced private ownership of land was the cause of, rather than the solution to Ireland's problems. In light of the increasing productiveness of technology over that of land and labor, and the consequent decline in the value of the latter two in competition with advancing technology, Davitt and George were just right enough to be wrong.

Both land and labor were increasingly insufficient to generate an adequate and secure income. Few people, however, seemed ready to advocate widespread ownership of technology, and none could see a way to finance new capital formation other than with past savings.

---

[1] Lyons, *Ireland Since the Famine, op. cit.*, 176.

Nevertheless, both Parnell and Gladstone were ready to move forward. The prime minister had even mentioned in a note to John Poyntz Spencer (1835-1910), Fifth Earl Spencer, the new Lord Lieutenant of Ireland, that he was preparing a list of suspects to be released from prison. This was so Parnell — who in Gladstone's opinion was "remaining true" — could put them to work restoring law and order in conformity with the Treaty instead of working against a peaceful resolution to the Irish Question.[2]

The Phoenix Park Murders

Davitt was not alone in his dissatisfaction with the Treaty. Forster, a firm believer in coercion, had resigned the office of Chief Secretary for Ireland in protest over what for different reasons he thought to be a misguided action.

By coincidence, Forster's replacement, Lord Frederick Charles Cavendish (1836-1882), arrived in Dublin to take up his new post the same day Davitt was released from prison. That evening, Cavendish and Thomas Henry Burke (1829-1882), Permanent Under-Secretary, were walking in Phoenix Park within sight of the Viceregal Lodge when members of a secret society known as "the Invincibles" attacked them with knives and killed them. Spencer, a probable target who had ridden to the Lodge by a different route, learned of the murders within moments.

Arriving in London that same evening, Parnell, Dillon, and Davitt separated. Parnell went to his mistress's house in Eltham.[3] Dillon and Davitt went to the Westminster Palace Hotel where they were staying. After they arrived, a newspaperman burst into the room waving a telegram and announcing the murders.

Although shocked by the news, Dillon and Davitt dismissed it as a hoax, and went to bed. It was not until five o'clock the next morning, when Henry George woke them with the news, that they were convinced of its truth.

Parnell knew nothing until Kitty O'Shea drove him to Blackheath Station in the morning and he stopped to buy a

---

[2] Lyons, *Charles Stewart Parnell, op. cit.*, 206.
[3] Parnell's and O'Shea's newborn child had recently died, and he probably felt it was his duty, as it was his inclination, to be with her.

newspaper to see what it said about Davitt's release. Stunned, he made his way to the flat of Captain William Henry O'Shea (1840-1905), his mistress's husband — the intricacies of these relationships are fortunately outside the scope of this work. There he penned a note to Gladstone, hand-delivered by O'Shea, offering to resign his seat if the prime minister thought it best.

Gladstone fully appreciated Parnell's motives and position, but considered him essential to the success of any reform program for Ireland. The prime minister told Parnell that he felt his, Gladstone's, duty did not permit him to accept the offer to resign.

Parnell then went to the Westminster to meet with Dillon and Davitt, who had been joined by Justin McCarthy (1830-1912). They immediately drew up a "Manifesto to the Irish People," signed by Parnell, Dillon, and Davitt, condemning the murders in the strongest possible terms.

Predictably, the government's response to the murders was to enact a much harsher Coercion Bill than originally anticipated in light of the Kilmainham Treaty, and to move up the timing in advance of the Fall expiration of the Protection of Person and Property Act. The unpalatable provisions of the Bill were not made any easier to swallow by the crudeness and "verbal brutality" of Sir William George Granville Venables Vernon Harcourt (1827-1904), Home Secretary, in his motion introducing it on May 11.

Georgism and the Irish

Parnell's situation was made worse by the fact that the murders followed hard on the heels of his release from Kilmainham. Extremists assumed the Land League had somehow inspired the senseless violence, while moderates, the general public, and the media concluded Parnell had lied or cut a deal to get out of prison.

Politically, Parnell was effectively neutralized for the next two years, and was in danger of fading from the scene completely, despite Gladstone's need of his help. He might well have lapsed into obscurity had it not been for O'Brien's staunch and uncritical support of him in *United Ireland*, Harcourt's callous oafishness in pushing through the new

Coercion Bill, and Davitt's growing fascination with socialism.

Possibly thinking that Parnell was in permanent eclipse, Davitt decided to throw his lot in with George's proposals and abandon his commitment to widespread ownership of land. On May 21, 1882 Davitt chaired a meeting in Manchester during which George made a speech.

Davitt announced that he had converted to George's theories and now advocated communal property in land instead of the League's goal of peasant proprietorship. In a speech in Liverpool on June 6, Davitt followed up his declaration with a more explicit call for the abolition of private property in land.

Although the specific methods Davitt advocated differed from George's "single tax" (all profits from land ownership taken by the State),[4] George was at this time more interested in the goal than the precise means of achieving it. As George commented in response to Davitt's abandonment of the League's position, "I think we may fairly say that we have done something, and that our theory(!) [sic] is at last forced into discussion. . . . I have gained the point I have been quietly working for."[5]

People were baffled. They demanded to know whether Davitt had separated from Parnell and distanced himself from the original goal of expanded ownership, on the strength of which Davitt had originally convinced Parnell to become League president. Evidently in all sincerity Davitt declared that he had done neither. Virtually no one believed him.

Some of the confusion (as well as Davitt's own lack of clarity) may have resulted from George's attempt to manipulate the Most Reverend Dr. Thomas Nulty (1818-1898), Catholic Bishop of Meath, a strong supporter of Parnell. Nulty had read *Progress and Poverty* a number of times and (according to George) claimed to agree with every word.

In 1881 Nulty issued a pastoral letter, "Back to the Land," in which he advocated George's program to abolish private

---

[4] Henry George, *Progress and Poverty*. New York: Robert Schalkenbach Foundation, 1935, 405-406.
[5] Henry George, Jr., "Starting the Revolution in Great Britain," *Life of Henry George, Third Period*, Chapter IV (1904).

property in land. Nulty appeared to be contradicting the basic Catholic doctrine that natural rights such as life, liberty, and private property are inherent in each human person.

George's position was that the right to be an owner is not inherent in individual human nature, but only in the abstraction of the collective, which then vests that right in individual human beings as expedient or necessary.[6] That some or all rights are vested in the collective and granted to human beings, instead of vested in human beings and granted to the collective, is the fundamental principle and error of all forms of socialism.

The logical fallacy involved[7] confuses the concrete with the abstract — the particular with the general, or the principle with the application of the principle — and is therefore contrary to reason. This is why the Catholic Church considers the theory of socialism a "concept of society . . . utterly foreign to Christian truth."[8]

Nulty's letter seems to have raised eyebrows among other members of the Irish hierarchy. Leo XIII's encyclical on socialism, *Quod Apostolici Muneris*, had been promulgated only

---

[6] Cf. "[N]atural justice can recognize no right in one man to the possession and enjoyment of land that is not equally the right of all his fellows." George, *Progress and Poverty, op. cit.*, 338-339.

[7] Socialism relies on "logical fallacies of equivocation," that is, when a key term or phrase in an argument is used in an ambiguous way, with one meaning in one portion of the argument, and another meaning in another portion of the argument. Thus, "property" in socialist theory means at one and the same time the natural and inalienable right to be an owner *and* the bundle of rights that define how an owner may exercise that right, while "man" means both individual human being *and* the collective, without making it clear which sense applies in the context.

[8] *Quadragesimo Anno*, § 117. Specifically, socialism relies on the theory that God built natural rights into the abstraction of the collective instead of into individual human nature. In Catholic doctrine, God does not deal in abstraction in His speculative knowledge. As a Perfect Being, God's speculative knowledge is limited to Himself and is perfect and therefore indistinguishable from His omniscient practical knowledge. This precludes dealing in any way with abstractions, or God would not be Perfect, that is, He would be at one and the same time both God and not-God, which is impossible. *Summa Theologica*, I, q. 14, a. 11.

a short time before, in December 1878. Certain aspects of George's theories appeared questionable in light of the encyclical, and would (at least according to George) be condemned within a decade in *Rerum Novarum*.[9]

Still, Nulty gave George an interview that George published in the *Irish World*, a Fenian newspaper in New York City, edited by Patrick Ford (1837-1913). This was picked up and (according to George) garbled by a London paper.

Although warned Nulty would be angry, to correct what he considered an error George had placards printed for distribution without the bishop's permission. He later explained, "I did not ask his permission, . . . I merely told him it was being done, and he made no objection."[10] Nulty, however, seems to have been unaware that George informed him of anything.

George's action publicly embarrassed Nulty, and the bishop issued a statement on December 31, 1881. Possibly in an effort to repudiate any connection or acquaintance with George, Nulty stated he did not know who was responsible, although he knew full well. He declared his words had been taken out of context and that he was —

> . . . enter[ing] an emphatic protest against an unfair as well as an unauthorised use made of an extract from one of my letters in a placard which I have just learned has been circulated and posted extensively in England and Ireland by some agency to me quite unknown.[11]

After this, Nulty seems to have lost his enthusiasm for georgism. In 1885, during a private audience with Leo XIII,

---

[9] See Henry George, *The Condition of Labor, An Open Letter to Pope Leo XIII* (1891).

[10] George, Jr., "Starting the Revolution in Great Britain," *Life of Henry George, Third Period, op. cit.,* George made similar assertions with respect to alleged statements by Cardinal Manning and William Jennings Bryan, claiming to have obtained endorsements of his theories, which Manning and Bryan both explicitly repudiated. See "Cardinal Manning on the Attitude of the Catholic Church," *The Milwaukee Journal*, December 14, 1886, 1; "Henry George's Theories. Cardinal Manning Tells of His Talk with George About Them." *The New York Times*, December 18, 1886; "A Denial from Bryan," *The Daily Star*, October 19, 1897, 1.

[11] "The Most Rev. Dr. Nulty," *New Zealand Tablet*, March 17, 1882, 13.

Nulty claimed his pastoral had been misinterpreted. He assured the pope of his complete loyalty both to the teachings and to the head of the Catholic Church.[12]

Davitt and the other leaders in the Land League had gone to great lengths to gain the support of the Irish Catholic hierarchy for the League's program. George's actions and Nulty's repudiation may have caused Davitt to have second thoughts about the wisdom of going along with George, particularly after George made disparaging comments about Parnell.[13]

Davitt's situation became worse when he went to the United States, arriving in New York on June 18, 1882. This was the same day the *New York Herald* published an interview in which Parnell expressed doubt that georgism could ever be politically practical in Ireland. Parnell added that the goal of widespread ownership had been agreed upon as League policy in a meeting between Davitt and himself and — as far as he knew — there had been no change.

This put Davitt on the defensive. On June 26, he made a speech in New York City in which he declared he had "made the crowning sacrifice in surrendering his cherished scheme of the nationalization of the land, in order that the Irish people would not be disunited."[14] Davitt returned to Ireland July 27, his credibility greatly diminished by "his inspired ineptitude in choosing this of all moments to launch his grand diversion [into georgist socialism]."[15]

Paradoxically, Davitt's conversion to the tenets of Henry George and the confusion it caused may have helped put

---

[12] "Bishop Nulty is Dead, An Irish Catholic Prelate Who Was Prominent in the Fight Against 'Landlordism'," *The New York Times*, December 25, 1898. If Nulty interpreted private property in land as an application of the principle of private property in his 1881 pastoral, he could maintain that abolishing private property in land did not violate the underlying principle — at least until 1891 when Leo XIII clarified the issue in *Rerum Novarum*, after which it was not possible for a Catholic to hold the georgist position.
[13] "Henry George and the Phoenix Park Murders," *The Age*, April 27, 1889.
[14] "Parnell and Davitt," *The True Witness and Catholic Chronicle*, June 28, 1882.
[15] Lyons, *Charles Stewart Parnell, op. cit.*, 234.

Parnell's career on the road to recovery. People saw Parnell as standing firm in support of the original goals of the Land League against Davitt's baffling changes of direction.

The Problem of Extremism

After the 1881 Land Act and the Kilmainham Treaty, Parnell had seemed confident that the focus could shift to Home Rule. In part as a result of Davitt's contradictory declarations, however, the need for an organization to replace the banned National Land League was now essential to retain and extend the gains that had been made in land reform, and to secure a voting bloc for future elections to support Home Rule. Davitt may have hastened the process by once again reversing himself and declaring his support for George's program of land nationalization, "provok[ing] hostility in many quarters."[16]

The Irish National League with the primary goals of Home Rule and peasant proprietorship was founded October 17, 1882, which "put Home Rule in the forefront of its programme and relegated 'land law reform' to second place."[17] The other goals of the National League, local self-government, extension of the voting franchise, and the development and encouragement of the labor and industrial interests of Ireland, were to build a base of support for Home Rule. Parnell had come down definitively on the side of constitutionalism.

Only two things interfered with the National League's constitutionalist approach. These were violence by extremists, and innovative economic and political theories of radicals. Of the two, the violence was more immediate, but the economic and political theories were, in the long run, more damaging.

Although the British authorities tended to lump all Fenian organizations together, especially in the United States, there was no monolithic Irish-American community, and certainly no single organization to speak for them. Most Americans of Irish birth or descent were essentially no different from anyone else.

---

[16] "Land Nationalization," *The Irish Canadian*, October 5, 1882, 4.
[17] Lyons, *Ireland Since the Famine, op. cit.*, 178.

Especially during the Great Depression of 1873-1878, people of Irish birth or descent were concerned with trying to make a living. For the most part faithful Catholics, and although they tended to the liberal, even radical in politics, most Irish-Americans had little time for secret societies and mass movements. They would contribute money — this was declining, but still significant — but that was the most Fenian leaders in the U.S. or Ireland could expect.

The problem was that both men and money for terrorism also came from America. Since 1875 there had been a "Skirmishing Fund" used to finance a campaign of direct action for those impatient with the constitutional process. Clan na Gael eventually took over the fund, but other sources of money were soon found.

Terrorism was significant neither as a gauge of Irish-American attitudes nor as a factor in the Home Rule and land reform campaigns. Its most important contribution to the Irish Question was to convince English conservatives and reactionaries (especially the Orange Lodges) that the Irish were inherently incapable as a people of taking their place among the nations of the world.

The Dynamite Campaign is a case in point. Between January 14, 1881 and January 24, 1885, there were a dozen bombings or attempted bombings, most of them in London. Dozens of people were injured, but the only three deaths were IRB men whose bomb exploded prematurely when they attempted to mine London Bridge on December 13, 1884. Tom Clarke, to be executed for his part in the 1916 Easter Rising, had been arrested for an attempt on the bridge in 1883.

Fabianism and the New Age

As deplorable as the dynamite campaign and similar efforts were, however, the new way of thinking and believing (the shift from the Intellect to the Will, or from reason to faith) was much worse, and far more devastating in its effects. The problem had been around for millennia; we have Aristotle's one-sided comments about the problems he encountered with the Sophists in this regard in the *Nicomachean Ethics* and the *Politics*.[18]

In the Middle Ages St. Thomas Aquinas temporarily defeated those who would base knowledge of God's existence and of the natural law on faith alone. They came back during the Reformation, however, reaching full flower in the spiritualist movement of the nineteenth century, providing the theoretical foundation of socialism, totalitarianism, and modernism.

After its invention by Madame Helena Petrovna Blavatsky (1831-1891), theosophy, the predominant form of spiritualism or spiritism, spread rapidly. Theosophy is the primary source of New Age thought,[19] especially Esoteric Buddhism, which must be distinguished from authentic Buddhism.[20]

The Fellowship of the New Life was founded in England in 1883, a part of the greater New Life movement within theosophy. The founding membership included the poet Edward Carpenter (1844-1929), novelist John Davidson (1858-1909), sexologist and eugenicist Henry Havelock Ellis (1859-1939), theosophist Annie Wood Besant (1847-1933), and writer Edward Reynolds Pease (1857-1955). Reflecting a distorted understanding of human nature,[21] the group sought to attain "the cultivation of a perfect character in each and all" in this life through pacifism, vegetarianism, and simple living.[22]

---

[18] See the analysis in Heinrich Rommen, *The Natural Law: A Study in Legal and Social History and Philosophy*. Indianapolis, Indiana: Liberty Fund Inc., 1998.
[19] Some commentators equate modernism and New Age thought. They are similar, and have influenced one another, but are not the same. See Pontifical Council for Culture and Pontifical Council for Interreligious Dialogue, *Jesus Christ the Bearer of the Water of Life: A Christian Reflection on the "New Age."* 2003, §§ 2.1, 4.
[20] *Ibid.,* § 3.2.
[21] "*New Age* is essentially Pelagian in its understanding of human nature." *Jesus Christ the Bearer of the Water of Life, op. cit.,* § 4; cf. Paul Heelas, *The New Age Movement: The Celebration of the Self and the Sacralization of Modernity*. Oxford, UK: Blackwell, 1996, 161.
[22] Colin Spencer, *The Heretic's Feast: A History of Vegetarianism*. London: Fourth Estate Classic Publisher, 1996, 283.

Soon after the founding of the Fellowship, heavily influenced by Henry George's theories, but expanding them to all forms of capital,[23] members wanted to use the power of the State to convert society. On January 4, 1884 they founded the Fabian Society as their political arm.[24]

As the political philosopher George Holland Sabine (1880-1961) commented,

> Fabian economics was for the most part not Marxian but an extension of the theory of economic rent to the accumulation of capital, on lines already suggested by Henry George. Fabian policy was based on the justice and the desirability of recapturing unearned increment [*i.e.*, non-labor income] for social purposes.[25]

New Age thought and the overly romantic versions of Irish myth, folklore, and history fostered by the Young Ireland movement merged in the Celtic Revival. Anxious to instill pride in being Irish, and ignoring the fact that within historical times there were only cultural differences between them, intellectuals and patriots created an artificial dichotomy between the presumably materialistic Teuton and Anglo-Saxon, and the allegedly mystical and other-worldly Celt.

Based on this, the Anglo-Saxon was believed to have an inherent aptitude for capitalism, while the Celt was considered a natural socialist. Few, if any, realized that both capitalism and socialism are unnatural, although socialism, as it negates human nature, is worse than capitalism, which merely corrupts it.

Infused with a false mysticism, Nationalist intellectuals and the artists and writers of the Celtic Revival tended to develop what Monsignor Ronald Arbuthnott Knox (1888-1957) called enthusiasm or ultrasupernaturalism. Knox defined enthusiasm as "an excess of charity [that] threatens

---

[23] George H. Sabine, *A History of Political Theory, Third Edition*. New York: Holt, Rinehart and Winston, 1961, 693.
[24] Edward R. Pease, *A History of the Fabian Society*. New York: E.P. Dutton & Co., 1916.
[25] Sabine, *A History of Political Theory, op. cit.*, 740.

unity."[26] For the Nationalists and artists of the Revival, the love was for Ireland — but an Ireland that existed in some cases only in their imaginations.

Combining with the Nationalist "us v. them" mindset, the laudable goals of the Revival tended to instill the impression that the Celt and the Anglo-Saxon were not merely products of different cultures and historical circumstances, but distinct and alien races. Some great and profoundly moving art resulted, but it was art that portrayed an unrealistic fantasy, not the real life and needs of the Irish people.

Gladstone's Conversion

It is extremely doubtful that Home Rule would have gotten as far as it did without the efforts of Gladstone. At the same time, Gladstone's understanding of Ireland and the Irish was filtered through English prejudice, nationalism, and an art that prevented him from getting an accurate idea of the needs and wants of the people of Ireland. He understood those of the English, the leading Nationalists, and artists, certainly, but these were themselves not completely in tune with the Irish people.

This made the mundane and pragmatic Parnell invaluable to Gladstone. Parnell's personal morality was hardly conventional, and in the end would destroy him. His political sense and understanding of the basic needs of ordinary people who lived in a real country called Ireland, and not some pseudo mystical Celtic Twilight, however, was unparalleled.

Despite the fact that so many people today have been brainwashed to think otherwise, ordinary people ultimately want control over their own lives. National sovereignty is all very well, but if individual children, women, and men are not sovereign — if they do not have control over their own lives within the framework of a just social order — then sovereignty of the nation is a cruel joke. And if some can exercise sovereignty only at the expense of others, sovereignty becomes economic and political sadism.

Nor is personal sovereignty a form of anarchy. Man, as Aristotle explained, is by nature a *political* animal.[27] Human

---

[26] Ronald A. Knox, *Enthusiasm: A Chapter in the History of Religion, with Special Reference to the Seventeenth and Eighteenth Centuries.* New York: Oxford University Press, 1961, 1.

beings as a rule only conform to their own nature — "pursue happiness" — by exercising their natural rights to life, liberty, and private property within the institutional environment of the *pólis*, the organized community.

This is why those sovereign rights that individuals possess by nature, that is, absolutely and inalienably, can only be exercised within strictly defined limits. As a rule, the exercise of even absolute rights is limited by the duty not to harm others or the institutions of the common good.

The exercise of sovereignty — the reason human beings come together in organized communities — is only possible if one has power. Power, however, is inextricably linked to private property. If only a few own productive capital (capitalism), then only those few are sovereign. If only the State owns productive capital (socialism), then only the State is sovereign.

A just society, therefore, requires that productive capital be broadly owned. Both Gladstone and Parnell understood this, and made it the cornerstone of their philosophy of Home Rule — but unfortunately limited their understanding of productive capital to land.

Gladstone had been vaguely in favor of Home Rule prior to the general election of 1885, but had not considered it a practical solution to the Irish Question. On March 1, 1885, however, he claimed he had a revelation. In 1890 when asked if he could identify the "crucial moment" when he became convinced that Home Rule was essential, he replied,

> Yes; I had been reading a speech of Mr. William O'Brien, and I put it down and said to myself — what is there in this speech that I must get to realise before I put it aside? And I saw then that there never was and never could be any moral obligation to the Irish race in the Act of Union.[28]

The problem was that Gladstone failed to take Parnell into his confidence, and Parnell had been busy with other arrangements in the face of what he considered the Liberals' betrayal. It was, after all, Conservatives who passed the Pur-

---

[27] *Politics*, 1253a.
[28] James Loughlin, *Gladstone: Home Rule and the Ulster Question 1882-93*. Dublin, Éire: Gill and Macmillan, 1986, 36.

chase of Land (Ireland) Act 1885, known as the Ashbourne Act . . . in an effort to undermine the Home Rule movement.

The Act established a £5 million fund — increased by amendment to £10 million in 1888 — by means of which tenants could borrow the full purchase price from the government, to be repaid at 4% interest over forty-nine years. Approximately 25,000 tenants became freeholders.

Parnell met secretly with Henry Howard Molyneux Herbert (1831-1890), Fourth Earl of Carnarvon, Lord Lieutenant of Ireland, in August 1885, and received distinct hints that a Conservative government would look favorably on Home Rule. Parnell did not know that Robert Arthur Talbot Gascoyne-Cecil (1830-1903), Third Marquess of Salisbury — who as prime minister knew of the meeting and Carnarvon's semi-promises — would repudiate the Lord Lieutenant.[29]

Consequently, on November 21, 1885, three days before the general election, Parnell issued his "Manifesto to the Irish in Britain." Claiming that the Liberal Party had no intention of keeping its promises to the Irish, Parnell said that the Irish should vote for Conservative candidates.

Government of Ireland Act 1886

Due in part to the reforms of 1884-1885 that tripled the Irish electorate, Parnell's Irish Parliamentary Party won 85 of 103 Irish seats in the general election of 1885. This made it impossible for either the Liberals or the Conservatives to form a government without Parnell.

This no doubt helped confirm Gladstone in his commitment to Home Rule, as did Parnell's actions in cracking down on branches of the National League that got out of bounds.[30] As almost his first act after forming a government, Gladstone announced on February 1, 1886 that one of his primary objectives was to find some way other than coercion to deal with Ireland.

At the same time, Irish landlords were indicating to Gladstone that they were open to substantial reforms, including

---

[29] J.L. Hammond and M.R.D. Foot, *Gladstone and Liberalism*. New York: Collier Books, 1966, 133-134.
[30] Loughlin, *Gladstone: Home Rule and the Ulster Question, op. cit.*, 47.

sale of their land to the tenantry on fair terms. Possibly a realization that their political power was fading as fast as their economic power as advancing technology overtook land as the predominant non-human factor of production, this was what Gladstone — and Parnell — needed to hear. Gladstone gave a three-hour speech in which he claimed it would be better to grant Home Rule now in honor, than later in humiliation.

From the Nationalist point of view, the problem with the Ashbourne Act, while a good start, was that it made the British government the mortgage holder. Gladstone made the transfer of the liability to an Irish government by means of his own land bill a cornerstone of his Home Rule Bill.

Parnell's — and thus Gladstone's — hand was greatly strengthened when, on February 16, the Irish Catholic hierarchy came out in favor of Home Rule. The reason was straightforward: "[I]t is our firm and conscientious conviction that [Home Rule] alone can satisfy . . . the legitimate aspirations of the Irish people."[31]

A number of British Liberals bolted the party, the most prominent being the noted constitutionalist and opponent of Bagehot, Albert Venn Dicey (1835-1922). Dicey's argument rested on two points. One, that the supremacy of the whole State must be maintained. This is because, two, only through unity can the State protect those rights of liberty and property it has granted to the citizens.[32]

We can only assume that Dicey let his natural loyalty to England overcome his common sense. A great admirer of the United States Constitution, Dicey was fully aware that Ro-

---

[31] *Addresses of the Most Reverence Dr. Walsh, Archbishop of Dublin*, app. BII, 462-463, quoted in O'Brien, *Parnell and His Party, op. cit.*, 184.
[32] Albert Venn Dicey, *Why England Maintains the Union: A Popular Rendering of England's Case Against Home Rule*. London: John Murray, 1887, 63-64. See also Dicey's *A Leap in the Dark: A Criticism of the Principles of Home Rule as Illustrated by the Bill of 1893*. London: John Murray, 1911, and *A Fool's Paradise: Being a Constitutionalist's Criticism of the Home Rule Bill of 1912*. London: John Murray, 1913, which restate the arguments for each subsequent Home Rule Bill.

man law and English Common Law vest political sovereignty in the citizens — individually, not the collective.

As Dicey explained in *The Law of the Constitution*, first published in 1885, "We, the People" as *politically* sovereign individuals, not the collective, delegate *legal* sovereignty via revocable grant to the legislature that represents them.[33] Rights are therefore a grant from the people to the State, not the other way around.

Parnell and his party accepted Gladstone's bill with certain reservations, the most serious of which was that they feared extremists in Ireland and the United States would oppose it. Oddly, the most immoderate criticisms came from moderates, while extremists, especially in America, were almost unanimous in their (qualified) approval, calling it "a great step in the right direction."[34]

Riots in Belfast when the bill passed the first reading split the Liberal Party. The Liberal Unionist Association (1886-1912) then joined with the Conservative Party to oppose Home Rule. Despite Parnell giving "one of the most masterly speeches that ever fell from him,"[35] however, the Bill was defeated on its second reading, 343 to 313. As the land bill depended on the passage of the Home Rule Bill, the former became a nullity.

Gladstone dissolved parliament in the hope of drumming up support for another Home Rule bill. It was to no avail, and he resigned in July after serving as prime minister for barely half a year. Robert Gascoyne-Cecil (1830-1903), Third Marquess of Salisbury replaced him.

The Plan of Campaign

With the failure of Gladstone's Home Rule initiative and the land bill, the only possible response that would satisfy extremists was reopening the Land War. With a drastic fall in agricultural prices, evictions had increased. Parnell failed to interest parliament in a tenants relief bill, and the situation deteriorated rapidly.

---

[33] A.V. Dicey, *Introduction to the Study of the Law of the Constitution*. Indianapolis, Indiana: Liberty Fund, Inc., 1982, 285.
[34] Alexander Sullivan, quoted in O'Brien, *Parnell and His Party, op. cit.*, 187.
[35] O'Brien, *Parnell and His Party, op. cit.*, 190.

In response — and without the concurrence of Parnell — Dillon (recently returned from America, where he had gone to his brother's home in Colorado to recover his health), O'Brien, and Timothy Charles Harrington (1851-1910) — but mostly Harrington — developed "the Plan of Campaign." O'Brien published the proposal in *United Ireland* on October 23, 1886.

The idea was a variation on the No Rent Manifesto. If a landlord refused to lower rents voluntarily, tenants were to organize and offer him a reduced rent that they considered fair. If this was refused, the money was to be put into a fund to take care of people who were evicted. Grabbers were to be boycotted.

Some leaders in the Campaign declared that, "Parnell was dead against it."[36] O'Brien maintained that Parnell was unwilling to take part in any agitation, but he was "in absolute agreement with the men who might be prepared to suffer the penalties, provided always that crime or any extreme courses that would paralyse Gladstone in his crusade in Britain could be avoided."[37]

Whatever the truth of the matter, Parnell's condemnations of violence kept the Campaign virtually crime free, except for the limited evils of non-payment of rent and boycotting. Still, the conflict destroyed the health of Sir Michael Hicks Beach (1837-1916), First Earl St Aldwyn, Chief Secretary for Ireland, and gave his successor, Arthur James "Bloody" Balfour (1848-1930), First Earl of Balfour, the chance to make his reputation in Unionist circles through his "exceptionally ruthless and consistent use of coercion."[38]

In combatting the Plan of Campaign Balfour relied heavily on the efforts of a young Crown Prosecutor who later earned his own share of notoriety: Edward Carson. The Irish Volunteers and the Irish Citizen Army of 1916 vividly recalled Carson's role in Balfour's program of repression when they decided that armed revolt was necessary and inevitable.

While condemning tenants for organizing against landlords, the government in the person of Balfour assisted land-

---

[36] *Ibid.*, 202.
[37] *Ibid.*, 203.
[38] Lyons, *Ireland Since the Famine, op. cit.*, 189.

lords in organizing against tenants. Paradoxically, even though the agitation was nowhere near as widespread as in the first phase of the Land War, and even though the great majority of conflicts were settled more or less amicably without recourse to violence or the boycott, the media — and Conservative politicians — made as much hay as possible out of the situation to strengthen the case against Home Rule.

Papal Condemnation

Even the Catholic clergy and hierarchy divided on the issue. While many bishops and priests gave the Campaign their support, others did not. At least two bishops joined the government in complaining to the Vatican about the involvement of parish priests in political matters.

This was not without effect. In 1887 Leo XIII sent Archbishop Ignatius Camillus William Mary Peter Persico (1823-1896) to investigate. Persico's report to the pope was sympathetic to the goals of the Campaign, but concluded that the tactics of withholding rent and boycotting were not consistent with Catholic teaching.

In 1887 Leo XIII therefore issued a rescript, followed by an encyclical in 1888, condemning the Campaign and, especially, boycotting as offenses against the moral law as they incited violence. The Irish hierarchy submitted, but made it clear that they in no way condemned the tenants rights movement, only the methods being employed.

This is perfectly consistent with Catholic moral teaching. Under the principle of double effect, people are permitted to carry out actions that are not evil in and of themselves, but that have unintended evil consequences, as long as the intended good outweighs the unintended evil.

People are not, however, permitted to carry out acts that are evil in and of themselves even to obtain the greatest good; it is not expedient "that one man should die for the people and that the whole nation perish not."[39] Non-payment of rent is objectively evil, as is treating people as if they do not exist. As Leo XIII explained in § 5 of *Saepe Nos*, his 1888 encyclical on boycotting addressed to the bishops of Ireland,

---

[39] John 11:50.

We yield to no one in the intensity of Our feeling for the condition of the Irish people, and We have no more earnest desire than to see them at length in the enjoyment of that peace and prosperity which they have so well deserved. We have never opposed their struggling for a better state of things, but can it be regarded as admissible that in the carrying on of that struggle a way should be thrown open which might lead to evil deeds? Rather, indeed, for the very reason that, under the influence of passion and political partisanship, things lawful and unlawful are to be found mingled in the same cause, it has been Our constant effort to mark off what was right from what was wrong, and to withhold Catholics from everything not sanctioned by the Christian rules of morals.

Despite the morality of the Church's condemnation of the Campaign, it provoked a storm of protest. There was, admittedly, some justification for this, although it was carried to unnecessary extremes. It is all very well for the Church to condemn immoral behavior, but it is better to suggest ways to achieve goals without immoral actions than to stop at a condemnation. Leo XIII would suggest peaceful alternatives four years later in *Rerum Novarum*, while Pius XI would present his completed social doctrine and the act of social justice in 1931, but that was little help in the 1880s.

Once again Parnell was edged out of center stage. Dillon, O'Brien, and Harrington seized the limelight. Their willingness to defy religious and civil authority, risk imprisonment, even their lives, increased their popularity as Balfour's application of coercion grew increasingly relentless and inflexible, and incidents of police brutality multiplied.

Henry George v. the Catholic Church

Henry George had been very successful in his efforts to link the Nationalist movement to his brand of socialism in the minds of many Irish-Americans. In January 1887, Bernard John McQuaid (1823-1909) Bishop of Rochester, New York, had written to Michael Augustine Corrigan (1839-1902), Archbishop of New York, warning him that "the Fenian element" would "do their best to stir up trouble."[40]

This was a serious problem. As Canon Sheehan noted years later about the drift into socialism at this time, "We

---

[40] Letter of January 20, 1887 from McQuaid to Corrigan, University of Notre Dame Archives.

obtained the Ashbourne Act, and just as it was about to emancipate the Irish peasant forever, we flung it aside for the phantom of land nationalisation."[41]

George had recently been defeated in his bid for the mayoralty of New York. He came in a close second to the Democratic candidate, Abram Stevens Hewitt (1822-1903), an honest but inadequate reformer selected to clean up Tammany Hall after the depredations of William Magear "Boss" Tweed (1823-1878). George soundly defeated the Republican candidate, a relative political newcomer named Theodore Roosevelt.

The situation in New York was extremely volatile due to George's having locked horns with the Catholic Church during the 1886 race while courting the Irish vote. In company with his local champion, a dissident priest named Father Edward McGlynn (1837-1900), George — a Protestant — had declared that the hierarchy, including Archbishop Corrigan and Pope Leo XIII, didn't understand Catholic social teaching.

According to George, the correct understanding of Catholic teaching just happened to be the program he detailed in his book, *Progress and Poverty*. As far as George was concerned, the Catholic Church was wrong not merely on the application of a principle, but on the principle itself, and George was the authority.

Worried about George's growing popularity, Tammany Hall requested an opinion as to the orthodoxy of his proposals. The spokesman for the Archdiocese, Father Thomas Scott Preston (1824-1891), Protonotary Apostolic and Corrigan's Vicar-General, explained that they appeared to contradict the Church's teachings. As Preston said, "The various theories embraced under the general name of communism or socialism are, in the opinion of the Catholic Church, not only contrary to the law of God, but destructive of the best interests of society."[42] Corrigan followed this up after the election

---

[41] Herman J. Heuser, *Canon Sheehan of Doneraile*. London: Longmans, Green and Co., 1917, 227.
[42] Rev. Thomas S. Preston, "Socialism and the Church," *The Forum*, Vol. V, No. 2, April 1888.

with a pastoral letter in November 1886 condemning socialism.

Blaming the Catholic Church in general, and Corrigan in particular for his defeat, George attacked the hierarchy, alienating many Catholics, Protestants, and even some anti-Catholics appalled at the obvious injustice. McGlynn was summoned to Rome to explain his actions, but George talked him out of going, and McGlynn feigned an illness.

Forgetting that Henry Edward Cardinal Manning (1808-1892) had recently noted that some of George's statements about Catholic teachings were not true,[43] and Nulty had repudiated the connection, George unwisely claimed to have received the endorsements of both. As McQuaid wrote to Corrigan,

> It is hard for me to give an opinion on the prudence of your communication regarding Father McGlynn. McGlynn's defense that his doctor forbade him to go to Rome comes too late. The Holy Father will probably issue a dogmatic decision on the question.[44] The worse George writes against you, the better for you. Many of their poor people have been led astray by the use of the names of Cardinal Manning and Bishop Nulty.[45]

McGlynn was summoned repeatedly to Rome, but George kept persuading him not to go. Dismayed at his friend's action, Davitt declared that George had irreparably harmed his own cause by setting himself against the Catholic Church. As Davitt declared in a speech he gave in Glasgow, Scotland, Saturday, January 15, 1887, the week following the first issue of George's newspaper, the *Standard*,

---

[43] "I saw a telegram some time ago that George had said the Catholic Church had never confirmed the principle of property in lands. This is not true. Exactly the reverse is the fact. The Church has from the beginning taught the right of property in lands." — Cardinal Manning, quoted in "Father McGlynn: Cardinal Manning's Opinion of Henry George's Theories," *San José Daily News*, December 14, 1886.

[44] This appears to be a hint of *Rerum Novarum* issued a few years later.

[45] Letter of January 22, 1887 from McQuaid to Corrigan. University of Notre Dame Archives.

Mr George's newspaper is the organ of the new labour movement, yet it chiefly attacks the Church, which cannot be the object of the labour party. Mr George gives Father M'Glynn bad advice in telling him not to visit Rome to defend himself."[46]

O'Brien in New York

McGlynn was given a final summons in May 1887 to appear in Rome within forty days under pain of excommunication. It was in this highly charged atmosphere that O'Brien came to New York in June to promote the Nationalist causes of Home Rule and land reform — and to ensure that American funds for the effort did not dry up in light of the papal rescript condemning the Plan of Campaign.

Seeing an opportunity, Henry George had O'Brien invited to address a georgist rally in New York City. George's advances to O'Brien at this time are not without the suspicion that he hoped to swing O'Brien to side with him in his (George's) quarrel with the Catholic Church as well as gain a powerful political endorsement.

O'Brien, however, politely declined to appear at the rally. He gave as his reason the fact that he was in New York to promote Irish nationalism, not Henry George.

O'Brien also had to be careful not to alienate Catholics. His and others' stance on the papal condemnation was that they disagreed with a specific prudential application of a Church teaching, and in no way dissented from the underlying teaching itself or questioned the Church's authority in matters of faith and morals — just politics.[47]

For refusing to "boom" for George, as one individual put it,[48] George's supporters and McGlynn's followers harshly criticized O'Brien. What astounded George and his diehard disciples, however, was the public outcry against George and McGlynn. Many prominent individuals and groups, Catholic and non-Catholic, Irish and non-Irish, including the Sixty-

---

[46] "Mr Davitt and Mr Henry George," *The Glasgow Herald*, Tuesday, January 18, 1887, 5.
[47] Lyons, *Ireland Since the Famine, op. cit.*, 190-191.
[48] "Mr. O'Brien Commended: All But the George People Say He Did Well," *The New York Times*, June 7, 1887.

Ninth New York Regiment Association, were disgusted. A significant number of people left George's organization.[49]

McGlynn was excommunicated for disobedience on July 5, 1887. He was reinstated December 24, 1892[50] after he apologized for his insults and intemperate language, accepted *Rerum Novarum* without reservation, and went to Rome to present his case to the authorities. He fully recanted his georgist views in December 1894, and was assigned a parish.[51]

In 1897 George again ran for mayor of New York. When reporters tasked him with his attacks on the Irish and the Catholic Church a decade earlier, he hysterically denied that he had ever done any such thing, suffered a stroke (his second), and died on October 29, 1897, four days before the election.

"Parnellism and Crime"

Worried about the effect on English public opinion — and thus on Gladstone's chances of returning to power — Parnell (as usual) counseled moderation. In December 1886 he cautioned O'Brien not to extend the Campaign into new areas, and to have the core group refrain from making violent speeches.

A year and a half later, Parnell reminded people that, whatever their feelings about the papal rescript, the encyclical, the Campaign, or the provocation offered by the government, they mustn't lose sight of the goal: economic justice as a foundation for the political goal of Home Rule. A good foundation had already been laid for lasting land reform and the creation of a peasant proprietorship.

It was important, however, that the gains they had made not be lost. Once Home Rule had been achieved, land reform could be extended far beyond Ashbourne's Act — but they had to hold on to the economic gains they had made before they could even think of the political goal of Home Rule.

---

[49] *Ibid.*

[50] "M'Glynn Makes His Peace: The Noted Recalcitrant Priest Has His Authority Restored," *Aurora Daily Express* (Aurora, Illinois), Saturday, December 24, 1892.

[51] "Parish for M'Glynn: He Recants and Will Soon Be Completely Forgiven," *Meriden Daily Republican* (Connecticut), Wednesday, December 19, 1894, 3.

As soon as parliament opened on January 28, 1887 Parnell exerted himself to mend fences with the Liberal Party, stressing his opinion that the solution to the Irish Question and attainment of Home Rule lay in reform (primarily land reform), not coercion. Balfour, however, now Chief Secretary for Ireland, introduced a new Coercion Bill on March 28, the immediate effect of which was to solidify English and Irish public opinion behind the Plan of Campaign and the Home Rule movement.

The popularity of the National League leadership soared, especially anyone who had been in prison. These became greatly in demand as speakers at Liberal meetings. It was at this point that the *Times* of London began publishing its series "Parnellism and Crime" in a blatant attempt to influence the vote on the Coercion Bill.

The articles, however, were based on a letter of extremely doubtful authenticity that the *Times* had acquired under suspicious circumstances. Parnell immediately declared the letter a "felonious and bare-faced forgery."

That was, in fact, the case. The Coercion Bill passed anyway, however, a number of Home Rule leaders were imprisoned, and the faith of many Liberal supporters of Home Rule was badly shaken, especially after the *Times* published more letters.

Two years later during hearings of the commission established to enquire into the matter, the forger, a Dublin journalist named Richard Pigott (1835-1889), broke down under examination and admitted everything. He fled to Madrid, where he committed suicide. Parnell sued the *Times* for libel, receiving £5,000 in an out of court settlement, and £200,000 for legal costs.

The 1887 Land Bill and After

Having gotten their Coercion Bill, the Conservatives followed their usual pattern of iron fist first, then velvet glove, and introduced a new land bill. Balfour's fixed belief was that having established dominance, a show of generosity would resolve the Irish Question and all opposition would evaporate. On August 23, 1887, the Commons passed the Land Law (Ireland) Act, amending the 1881 act, extending its provisions to all leaseholders.

If Parnell had overestimated the negative effect of the Campaign on English public opinion, Balfour grossly overestimated both the utility and political wisdom of what was, in effect, a reign of terror. Balfour's ruthless countermeasures were far more effective in building public support in both England and Ireland for the National League and the Campaign than in suppressing disorder.

In particular there was the September 1887 "Mitchelstown Massacre," in which three people were killed and two others wounded when the police opened fire on a large crowd. An attempted cover-up by Balfour only gave Gladstone ammunition in his campaign to expose the lawlessness of the Chief Secretary.

The incident generated an immense amount of sympathy in the Liberal Party and ordinary English men and women for the Irish, particularly the tenantry who were being denied the right to organize that the trade union movement had recently won for English workers.

The Nationalist-Liberal Home Rule alliance was now at the height of its power under the dual leadership of Gladstone and Parnell. To try and drive a wedge between them — and undermine Home Rule — Balfour decided to raise again the sensitive issue of a Catholic university for Ireland, and an improved land bill.

The Liberals opposed all religious education at State expense, and Gladstone adhered to the party line. The Catholic hierarchy was in favor of it, and they supported Parnell. The Ashbourne Act, a Conservative initiative, had come close to dissolving the alliance, but the combination of coercion and the Conservative opposition to Home Rule mended matters.

Parnell, a Protestant, simply said that anyone was entitled to vote against the university, but that the Irish would not turn it down if it were offered. He hinted that even if the Conservatives passed a university bill, he personally did not expect them actually to do anything.

The issue did, in fact, threaten to divide Home Rulers, but then the "No Popery" Conservatives — who had furnished the votes for the victory in the 1886 general election that followed the collapse of Gladstone's government — expressed outrage. In response to the creaking "Home Rule is Rome

Rule" dogma, Balfour was forced to declare that he had never meant to propose a Catholic university; it had all been a misunderstanding.

The land bill fared no better. Parnell described it as "absurd and objectionable," as it appeared intended to induce tenants to buy holdings at inflated prices based on grossly excessive rents. He proposed as an amendment that no purchases should take place until "judicial rents" (rents set by the Land Commission instead of by the landlord) had been reduced by at least 30%.

The bill was withdrawn in July 1890. Balfour planned on reintroducing it in the Autumn in an effort to "kill Home Rule with kindness." Parnell said he would support it if amended.

The Fall of Parnell

While Parnell and Gladstone sparred with Balfour, however, Captain O'Shea was pursuing a divorce from his wife, Parnell's mistress. His motives for taking action after ten years during which he was fully aware that the couple were living as man and wife are unclear, but it has been suggested that he had recently discovered that an inheritance from his wife's aunt, and on which he had been counting, had been left in such a way as to keep it out of his hands.

Further, Parnell was no longer politically useful to O'Shea. He had gained a seat in parliament under Parnell's sponsorship, but then deserted the Home Rule-Liberal alliance. The timing of the filing of the lawsuit on December 24, 1889 suggests that Captain O'Shea might have been given vague promises of preferment if he helped bring down Parnell.

In any event, nothing happened until the case came to court on November 15-17, 1890. The judgment went against Parnell and Mrs. O'Shea. The scandal, combined with Parnell's refusal to resign, forced first Gladstone, then the Americans, the Catholic hierarchy, and most of the Irish party to repudiate Parnell's leadership. The movement split into pro- and anti-Parnell factions.

One thing more needs to be said about the disaster, other than it is a graphic example of the need to "cut square corners" when one is engaged in any revolutionary enterprise.

"Everybody knows" that the Catholic bishops and puritanical Nationalists broke Parnell.

What "everybody knows," however, is wrong. As Conor Cruise O'Brien pointed out in *Parnell and His Party*, the Irish bishops, while disapproving, stayed out of the matter in obedience to the spirit of *Saepe Nos*. Among prominent Nationalists, only Davitt, with his own ax to grind over the issue of land nationalization, demanded Parnell's resignation.

It was Gladstone's own strict religious and moral principles and his supporters that made it clear Parnell was no longer acceptable. Gladstone's choice was Parnell or Home Rule, and he made the only decision possible. The bishops and the party believed they needed Liberal support for Home Rule, and did the same. The majority anti-Parnellite League members formed the Irish National Federation, headed by John Dillon, while John Redmond assumed leadership of the Parnellite minority that remained.

The Celtic Twilight

Parnell died in October 1891. He left behind a divided and demoralized land reform and Home Rule movement, more intent on fighting amongst themselves than in furthering land ownership or nationalism. This left the Nationalists of the Celtic Revival as the most influential and organized faction of the cause.

The Revival — also known as the Celtic Twilight — was (and remains) an essential element in building a spirit of nationalism and creating a proper pride in being Irish. It was also an international movement, promoting solidarity not only among people of Irish birth and descent, but also other Celtic peoples throughout the world, Scots, Welsh, Manx, Cornish, and Breton, to say nothing of countering stereotypes such as the "stage Irishman."

The problem was that the Revival relied heavily on the romanticized version of Irish history fostered by the Young Ireland movement. It tended to replace negative and historically inaccurate typecasts, with positive but equally inaccurate fantasies, such as the brooding mystic and the noble savage.

Adherents of alternative spiritualities such as theosophy found it easy to integrate esoteric thought into the Revival.

This provided fertile ground for the spread of socialist concepts and ideology, particularly as found in Fabian socialism, as well as a mysticism in conflict with western tradition, religious faith, and cultural reality.

The Sun Never Sets

With Parnell out of the way, Balfour was able to advance his program of land reform as an alternative to Home Rule instead of as a necessary precondition to national sovereignty. Accounting for the utter astonishment and lack of comprehension of what was happening, Balfour's program would guide British policy in Ireland and understanding of the situation up to the very day of the Easter Rising, and in large measure afterwards.

As a result, what formed the Ireland of the late nineteenth and early twentieth centuries was not the nationalism of Parnell or even the Revival, but the imperial vision of British conservatism. This was dedicated to the preservation and expansion of the Empire, and the uplifting of native peoples on alien terms — "the White Man's Burden." Balfour did not consider coercion an end in itself, but a means of establishing and maintaining a just and orderly society under the imperial umbrella.

The Purchase of Land (Ireland) Act 1891 therefore had the goal not merely of creating more peasant proprietors, but of doing so in such a way as to alleviate poverty by making more land available. This was a problem especially in the south and west, where far too many people were crowded on to sub-economic plots, while large tracts lay fallow.

The Act provided more funds than any previous effort (£33 million) and created nearly 50,000 new owners. More would have been participated, but the regulations were complicated and discouraged many people from applying.

Further, landlords were not paid in cash, but in special shares of "land stock" that fluctuated in value. This discouraged sales as well as investment of the proceeds in other forms of capital. Industrial and commercial development suffered as a result, what little there was being concentrated in even fewer hands than land had been in the early nineteenth century.

The Conservatives won the single largest bloc of seats in the 1892 general election, but not enough for an overall majority, especially after the Liberal Unionists who had supported them lost seats. Gladstone's Liberals won more seats than they had in 1886, while Dillon's anti-Parnellite Home Rulers and Redmond's Parnellite Home Rulers joined forces and retained all their seats, giving Gladstone a majority.

After forming a government Gladstone announced his goals as Home Rule for Ireland, and the disestablishment of the Welsh and Scottish churches. He introduced the Government of Ireland Bill 1893 in February. It passed the House of Commons on September 1, but was thrown out by the House of Lords within a week.

Gladstone resigned as prime minister on March 2, 1894 in protest over amendment of the Local Government Act 1894 by the House of Lords, but retained his seat for another year. Considered one of the United Kingdom's greatest prime ministers, he died on May 19, 1898.

In 1895 Gerald William Balfour (1853-1945), Second Earl of Balfour, succeeded his brother Arthur as Chief Secretary for Ireland. He amended the 1891 Land Purchase Act, removing many of the complications that had discouraged people from taking advantage of it, and increased the amount of land available. The approach was still piecemeal, however, and did not address the greater problem of growing concentration of ownership of commercial and industrial capital.

George Wyndham (1863-1913) replaced Gerald Balfour as Chief Secretary in 1900. A great-grandson of Lord Edward FitzGerald, he sponsored a Land Conference in December 1902 that worked out a proposal for a more extensive program for tenant land purchase than had previously been implemented. This resulted in the Wyndham Land (Purchase) Act of 1903. Augustine Birrell extended the provisions of the act by allowing for compulsory sale in his Land Purchase (Ireland) Act of 1909.

The overall effect of land reform in Ireland from 1870 to 1921 was to turn more than 300,000 tenants into owners of the land they farmed, more than 10% of all households. Unfortunately, it was not enough, as even in Ireland land was becoming less important than advancing technology as the source of marketable goods and services.

Growing Unrest

Despite the ostensible success of land reform and much to the consternation of the government, the effort to "kill Home Rule with kindness" did not end Nationalist agitation. It simply transformed the agrarian-nationalist alliance into an industrial/commercial-nationalist alliance as the needs of propertyless workers continued to deteriorate in the face of growing concentration of ownership and an increasing income gap in sectors other than agriculture.

In a baffling paradox, while widespread ownership of land had been understood as the solution to agrarian agitation throughout the nineteenth century, no one connected the growing unrest with the lack of capital ownership among the workers in commerce and industry. When reformers and politicians spoke of industrial and commercial development in Ireland, it was always in terms of the jobs it would create, not ownership opportunities for the propertyless workers.

Home Rule had not been "killed with kindness" — nor had opposition. The Unionist position, especially the Orangist, instead of fading as living standards rose and conditions improved for the rural Irish, became increasingly radical.

This may have been due in part to what we can call the "limited wealth" or "past savings assumption." If the only way to finance new capital formation, and thus increase wealth, is to restrict consumption and accumulate money savings, then the only way to have widespread ownership of capital or even create significant numbers of jobs is to take capital or jobs away from those who have them, and give them to those who do not.

As the largely Orange north of Ireland was also the most industrialized, "Home Rule" did not mean merely a threat to the Empire and the imposition of Catholicism. A Dublin parliament would take jobs and income away from loyal Unionists for the benefit of traitorous Nationalists.

That neither of these events was in any way likely even under the past savings assumption is irrelevant. Unionists feared them, and that was what the politicians opposed to Home Rule needed to enable them to build a pro-Union support base, the more fanatical, the better.

Ironically, the effort to kill Home Rule with kindness had undermined the economic (and thus political) power of the southern Unionists based on land, and at the same time increased that of the northern Unionists based on commerce and industry. This exacerbated existing differences between the two groups.

Southern Unionists were generally well-integrated into British conservatism, often with social and professional positions in both England and Ireland. Northern Unionists, however, as a group tended to be viewed almost as aliens by their British counterparts, more so in some cases than other Irish, much more concerned with maintaining the status quo — and more apt to perceive threats and react to them.

The Parliament Act of 1911 was one such threat. Prior to its passage, the House of Lords had a permanent veto on any legislation, which it had used to good effect in throwing out the 1893 Home Rule bill. The Act replaced the Lords' veto with a maximum delay of two years before receiving the Royal Assent, clearing the way for a new Home Rule bill and Asquith's 1912 "Home Rule All Round" campaign that aimed at some form of autonomy for Scotland and Wales as well as Ireland.

With the passage of the Parliament Act, Carson, Arthur Balfour's protégé (Balfour being at this time Leader of the Opposition), guided — some would say manipulated — by James Craig, began agitating against Home Rule. Soon after, the ruthless and unscrupulous Bonar Law, a Canadian-born Ulster industrial magnate, replaced Balfour as Leader of the Opposition.

Rhetoric not untinged with hysteria against a new Home Rule bill reached epic proportions. When in 1912 Asquith, who had become prime minister in 1908, introduced what became the Government of Ireland Act 1914, however, it seemed to have been a great deal of fuss over nothing. The Act was, at best, tokenism, granting Ireland a parliament with less power than many city councils.

The bill's real importance lay in the fact that it was clearly inadequate and could only be regarded as provisional, a stepping stone to something more. It was for this reason that Redmond could accept, and Carson violently oppose, what would otherwise be nothing more than a meaningless gesture.

In short, it was not what Home Rule actually was in 1914, but what it had the potential to become that led to the conflicts culminating in the Easter Rising. Similarly, today it is not what Ireland — or any other country — is that ultimately matters, but what it can become by following a just, third way.

Chapter 8: Caldwell's Statement

ROINN COSANTA
Bureau of Military History, 1913-21.
Buro Staire Millata 1913-21
Statement by Witness
No. W.S. 638, Document No. W.S. 638
Witness: Patrick Caldwell,
54 Croydon Green, Fairview, Dublin.
Identity: Member of Irish Volunteers, Liverpool, 1914-; Member of Kimmage Garrison, 1916.
Subject.
(a) National activities 1914-1921;
(b) G.P.O., Dublin, Easter Week 1916;
(c) I.R.A. Intelligence, 1919-1921.
Conditions, if any, Stipulated by Witness: Nil
File No. 8.1857, Form BSM 2

CONTENTS.

		Page
1.	Liverpool Volunteer Company	1
2.	The Kimmage Garrison	2
3.	Easter Week, 1916	4
4.	Deported to English Gaols	12
5.	Volunteers Reorganized	16
6.	I.R.B.	17
7.	G.H.Q. Intelligence	20
8.	British Intelligence Officer Barnes	21
9.	Molloy — British Agent	21
10.	Alan Bell — British Financial Agent	23
11.	District Inspector Roberts	23
12.	Intelligence Reports on Managers of G.W. and G.S. Railways	25
13.	Captain Hardy	26
14.	General Tudor — Intelligence Reports on his movements	29
15.	The Igoe Gang	31
16.	An tÓglach	31

[1]
ORIGINAL

Bureau of Military History 1913-21
Buro Staire Millata 1913-21

Statement by Patrick Caldwell
54, Croydon Green, Fairview, Dublin.

Liverpool Volunteer Company
About the month of August, 1914, I went to England and took up employment in the city of Liverpool. Following the split in the Volunteer Movement as a result of John Redmond's recruiting speech at Woodenbridge, I read in a paper called *The Irish Volunteer*, which was in circulation in Liverpool at the time, a telegram congratulating the Dublin Executive on their action in repudiating Redmond's recruiting speech. About the 1st October of that year I joined the Company of the Liverpool Volunteers at Duke Street in a house, part of which was used by the Volunteers for drilling and lectures. Frank Thornton was then in charge of the Company and Thomas Craven was Lieutenant.

All though 1914 and 1915 the only activities undertaken by the Company were drills and route marches through the suburbs.

In the summer of 1915 Thomas Craven, 1st Lieutenant of the Company, was replaced by John P. O'Hickey who came over from Dublin. Craven reverted to 2nd Lieutenant as a result of a Company election. A second Company of the Volunteers existed in Bootle. I cannot say very much about that Company as we had little intercourse with it. However, I knew some of its officers including Captain Seán Hennessy, whom I had met at social functions.

When the landlord of the premises which we occupied in Duke Street got to know that drilling was taking place in the hall he approached the Gaelic

[2]
League which was the body he had it let to and asked them to take steps to have this drilling stopped. The result was

that we moved from there to a basement in the premises of a Mr. P. Cahill, Scotland Road, Liverpool.

Early in the year 1916 a mobilisation parade of the entire Company was ordered for a suburb — at Birkenhead, Cheshire. The mobilisation orders were supposed to have been signed by Seán MacDermott. The Company turned out in strength and partook of a route march. Following this mobilisation parade a controversy took place between the officers as to the authenticity of the signature of Seán MacDermott in the mobilisation order. This resulted in a disagreement that eventually led to the resignation of the three officers of the Company. A special meeting was then held to fill the three commissioned positions. Thomas Craven became Company Captain with William McNeive and Seamus Donegan as Lieutenants. I should have mentioned that about the spring of 1916 a number of the members of the Company had been issued with .32 revolvers and a small quantity of ammunition. The rank and file of the Company were very annoyed over the disagreement amongst the officers as we felt that at that particular time more unity than ever was required in view of the Conscription Act which had gone through the House of Commons.

The Kimmage Garrison:

The Company Commander, Tom Craven, became uneasy about the position of his men in England should Conscription be immediately enforced. He seemed to come to a very quick decision and ordered the entire Company to be ready for transfer to Dublin. I was

[3]

ordered to proceed to Dublin at once and on arriving there accompanied by Mr. P. Supple, who was a member of the Bootle Company, reported to William McNieve, one of my Company Officers who had gone to Dublin in advance to make necessary arrangements for the transfer of the entire Company. On the instructions of G.H.Q. we were located in a Mill belonging to Count Plunkett at Kimmage. The remainder of the Company were sent over in small groups. The command of the Company was given to George Plunkett by G.H.Q.; Captain Craven resented this. The maintenance of the Company now began to cause a certain amount of trouble but the people behind in Liverpool subscribed sufficiently generously to keep the Camp going, supplemented presumably by grants from G.H.Q. The chief actor in the Liverpool side keeping these funds going was Neil Kerr.

When I came over I was immediately appointed Quartermaster by Lieutenant McNieve. We were all maintaining ourselves out of our own resources in the initial stages. We were soon joined by the King brothers — John and Patrick — from Liverpool. John succeeded me as Camp Quartermaster by mutual agreement. In the meantime some of us endeavoured to relieve the financial position of the upkeep of the Camp by trying to get civilian employment. Five of us decided to take up employment in the De Selby Quarries at Jobstown, County Dublin. Before leaving the Camp to take up employment Captain Plunkett paraded us before Seán MacDermott, saying, "These are the men who have decided to leave for work in the Quarries". Next morning George Plunkett told us that it was alright for us to go. Apparently there was some doubt as to the advisability of our taking up employment. By the

[4]

time we left the Camp the Kimmage garrison was full time employed by Captain Plunkett on the filling of cartridges with buckshot and also the making of crude bayonets and home-made bombs. My employment with the Selby Quarries was approximately of six weeks' duration from the 1st February to about the middle of March when Craven and myself returned to the Camp.

On our return to the Camp it was obvious to me that its members had increased considerably. In addition to the Liverpool Company, the Bootle Company had arrived together with men from Glasgow, Manchester and London. The last additions to the garrison were Seamus Brennan and Peter Bracken who arrived there the morning following a shooting affray with R.I.C. at Tullamore.

Easter Week 1916:
While we were not aware at Kimmage that a Rising had been definitely decided on we, nevertheless, felt that a clash would soon take place. We knew that we were arming for some purpose.

On Easter Sunday morning very early, about 6 or 7 o'clock, Thomas Craven came into the Camp after an all night meeting in Liberty Hall, and told me to get dressed and come along with him as we were going out to the De Selby Quarries to commandeer gelignite there and take it to Liberty Hall. The two of us accompanied by a Glasgow man named Sandy Carmichael went to a taxi which was waiting. As we were going to the car I met Captain Plunkett and told him the mission we were on at the same time asking for his consent, which he gave. In the car with Thomas Craven were two brothers named Golden from 2nd Battalion. We ordered the driver of the car to take us to the Quarries at Jobstown. On

[5]

arriving there we met two of our men who had been living in a hut there — Martin Walsh and Patrick McDermott. After a strenuous couple of hours' work we got as many boxes of gelignite loaded into the car as it would carry. I was then left behind to prevent the alarm being given for at least an hour. I was told later that the gelignite was, in fact, delivered to Liberty Hall. I walked back to Kimmage having heard Mass at Saggart. On arrival there about 12 o'clock it was announced that the parade which had been ordered for 12 o'clock was off. I could hear the men around me grousing and passing remarks to the effect that, "They have funked it". For the remainder of the day a certain number of men were confined to the camp, including myself.

At about 11 a.m. on Easter Monday, Captain Plunkett again instructed us to parade under arms with two days' supplies of provisions. Our arms consisted of a shotgun and pike to each man. Pikes, incidentally, were also made at Kimmage. I think it was 100 rounds of shotgun ammunition we were given, and a certain number of us had revolvers. When the Company paraded it was about 60 strong. When the Company "fell in" George Plunkett appointed two Section Commanders. We moved out of Kimmage in from about 15 to 20 minutes from the time we "fell in", and marched down in fours to Harolds Cross Road where we boarded two trams and proceeded into the City. Captain Plunkett paid the tram fares. Arriving at O'Connell Bridge we dismounted from the trams and marched to Liberty Hall. We were kept standing to attention there for some time. Finally we marched up Abbey Street. I was in the second section under Joe Gahan.

[6]

When we marched into O'Connell Street [sic] our section commander, Joe Gahan, shouted, "Military coming; man the barricades". Why he shouted this direction I cannot say as, in fact, there were no barricades erected at the time. I think what he meant was to put up barricades.

Up to this time no statement had been made to us that a Rising was about to take place. When I heard the order about the barricades it recalled to my mind a lecture that had been given in Kimmage previously by P.H. Pearse on street fights and barricades. Evidently Joe Gahan was thinking of this at the time he referred to the barricades. We did not, in fact, erect barricades in O'Connell [Sackville] Street. The section Commander led us to Mooney's public house in Abbey Street which we tried to occupy but the Manager had banged the hall door against us and we could not get entrance to the upper part of it. Martin Gleeson, who was with us, fired a shot at the lock but it failed to make any impression and then we moved a couple of doors further down Abbey Street and occupied the Ship Hotel. We got to work immediately in barricading the windows. We were expecting to be attacked at any time although we did not know what we were supposed to do, but as nothing happened the section commander said he would go outside and contact somebody for definite instructions. He returned in a short time, ordered us to evacuate the building and led us out the back way up as far as Talbot Street and then across to the G.P.O. I then saw a green flag, with the words, "Irish Republic" printed across it in white, flying from the flag staff of the G.P.O. My impression of the exact position of the flag is not very definite but I seem to recollect that it was flying nearer to the Henry Street side of the G.P.O.

[7]

than to Princes Street end. The fact that the Irish Flag was flying on this particular building was the first clear indication I had that a Rising was in progress. The main door of the G.P.O. was open and we marched in. On entering the building one of the first men of prominence that I saw was Tom Clarke. He said, "There are rifles here if any of you want them, but there is no ammunition for them". I looked at them and decided that it was better to use the shotgun with which I was more familiar.

We were broken up into small groups and allocated positions in various rooms throughout the G.P.O. I was sent to a corner room on the second floor overlooking O'Connell Street and Henry Street. On entering the room we found it contained a small number of postal packets. John King, who, I think, had been a section commander for some time with the Kimmage garrison, entered the room and gave instructions that the windows were to be barricaded, *etc*. At this time there were about five or six armed men in the room. On that afternoon (Monday) we saw a detachment of British cavalry coming up O'Connell Street from the direction of the Rotunda. As the detachment came near Nelson Pillar it was brought to a halt. Simultaneously with this, fire was opened on it from the various rooms in the G.P.O. including the room I was in. The cavalry detachment did not return the fire but retreated. The only casualty I observed was one dead horse. Later that evening, Monday, a Captain Cullen took charge of all Volunteers in that room. He ordered two of us to transfer to another room overlooking Henry Place. This room contained a large water tank and I was instructed to ensure that it was kept full at all

[8]

times. In addition to keeping the water tank full two of us — Dave Begley and myself — had to do guard duty at the window overlooking Henry Place. We took it in turns to watch this window and it was not until Wednesday that a third man belonging to a Maynooth detachment came to our assistance. Except for occasional shots which seemed to enter this room we were not otherwise under any fire. On entering the room that I had first occupied on Monday I observed the ceiling showing signs of fire and on going upstairs to the room above it I saw Captain Cullen directing a number of Volunteers in an endeavour to combat the flames. The British had been shelling the G.P.O. for some time before this. Their efforts to combat the flames were unsuccessful and the entire roof gradually became enveloped in flames. Up to this [time] the downstairs rooms showed little signs of the fire and everything proceeded as usual until about 9 or 10 o'clock on Friday night when we were all ordered to a large main room on the ground floor. The entire garrison was mobilised there and addressed by Commandant-General Pearse. I cannot remember his exact words but I know that he informed us that we were to prepare to evacuate the G.P.O. as he considered it no longer tenable. Jim Connolly was on an iron bed with his foot bandaged. Some members of the Cumann na mBan were attending to him. I was told to stand by the bed to assist in carrying him. While standing there a man with whom I had been intimate, named Andrew Furlong, was wounded in the knee. I cannot say where the shot came from. I went to his assistance and he gave me his gun. When I returned back to Connolly's bedside some of the members of Cumann na mBan said I was carrying too much equipment and somebody else was selected in my

[9]

place to carry the bed. I returned to Andy Furlong. Myself, Alexander Carmichael, Andrew Friel — members of the Kimmage garrison — were told by somebody, whose name I can't remember, to take him down to Jervis Street Hospital. A guide came along and directed us through holes in the wall to the next house and so on. I don't know how far we were able to take our wounded man — probably a distance of about four houses. The officer in charge at that particular time was M.W. O'Reilly, now of the New Ireland Assurance Company. When we got about five houses away Captain William Pearse overtook us and ordered us back to the G.P.O. A disagreement arose about this order between W.M. O'Reilly and Willie Pearse. O'Reilly wanted us to go ahead as he maintained we were very near Jervis Street Hospital and Pease said no, that we were to return to the G.P.O. I then intervened, saying to O'Reilly, "Willie Pearse is a senior Captain and, therefore, we must obey his orders." Finally Captain O'Reilly gave way and on the return journey we found, by experience, that it was easier on the wounded man to be carried by two men than by three. Volunteer Carmichael and Friel carried Furlong back to the Post Office while M.W. O'Reilly and myself followed them. When we got back to the Post Office we found that it was for all practicable purposes completely evacuated by the Volunteer garrison. William Pearse brought us to an exit door facing Henry Place and

Patrick Pearse was standing at this door at the time and he instructed us to make a run for it into Henry Place. The wounded man was taken across first. Patrick Pearse went across soon after and I followed immediately behind him and joined two Volunteers who were behind a barricade in Henry Place.

I have heard arguments from time to time as to

[10]

who was the last man to leave the G.P.O. on the day of its evacuation. My recollection is that it was either Willie Pearse or M.W. O'Reilly. When I was making for the barricade these two men were standing at the door-case of the exist door facing Henry Place. I am positive that no other Volunteers were in the building at that particular time.

Commandant Johnie [sic] McLoughlin, a Fianna boy, gave us instructions to evacuate the barricade and move up Henry Place towards Moore Street. At this time he was carrying a sword in his hand. As we passed Moore Lane we came under British rifle fire for a short time but got safely through to a house at the corner of Moore Street. We entered this house and found that a number of houses running down Moore Street had been bored through to provide a line of retreat. Sometime on Friday night Harry Walpole came into the house that I was in and looked for a party of Volunteers to deal with a supposed enemy patrol in Moore Lane at a point immediately in [the] rear of our houses. I asked him was he sure they were enemy, adding that he would want to be very careful as some of our men who formed the Kimmage garrison also spoke with a cockney accent. He there and then agreed to drop the idea of bringing out a patrol. In the particular house which I was in on the Friday night Tom Clarke was there also. He was seated on a chair and when I spoke to him he said he was felling out of sorts and asked me could I get him a cup of tea. I obliged him and when he had partaken of the tea he said it had done him a lot of good.

It was ominously quiet on Friday night and Saturday morning and we were wondering what was the cause of it. Sometime on Saturday evening all

[11]

Volunteers who were in occupation of houses in Moore Street were ordered out into the Street. We were there addressed by Captain Frank Henderson. With him was Joseph Mary Plunkett. He informed us that we were to surrender. We were told that we would have to pile our arms in O'Connell Street. Then we were given a "Right Turn" and marched into O'Connell Street. At this time we were guided by British soldiers stationed along the route at intervals. We threw the arms in a heap in O'Connell Street and then formed up in either single or double line in O'Connell Street. Tom Craven and Seán MacDermott were standing beside me. I remember an altercation between Seán MacDermott and the British Officer in charge, namely Captain Lee Wilson. What gave rise to it I cannot say, but I can recall MacDermott saying, "We can still go back to our positions" and Lee Wilson rejoined, "You have no damn' positions to go back to". Seán MacDermott's comment was, "We can see about that". A rather amusing incident occurred at this time. A British officer who had been examining the ammunition that we had deposited in O'Connell Street opened a shotgun cartridge and shouted to Captain Lee Wilson. "Look at this bally cartridge; it has five bullets, each of which would kill a bally elephant".

That evening we were marched to the Rotunda and remained in the green plot of grass overnight until the following morning. While there I saw Tom Clarke being called out and taken over to a special place. Joseph Mary Plunkett was also taken out. These men were searched according as they were called out. Captain Lee Wilson found a letter in the back pocket of Joseph Mary Plunkett's clothes and he shouted around, "This bally fellow thinks he's going to be shot", and

[12]

then, as an afterthought, he handed the letter back to Plunkett, saying, "Keep it, you will be shot". Several others were called out from time to time whom I cannot recall at the moment. I do, however, remember Michael Collins being called out and Lee Wilson saying across to some other officers to search his so-and-so boots", adding, "I wouldn't trust that so-and-so". I could not understand why Collins was called out from the many prisoners who were there as he was not a prominent man at that time. My guess is that his name was confused with another Collins whose papers had been confiscated by the British Government sometime previously.

Deported to English Gaols

On Sunday morning the prisoners were formed up in four[s] and marched under heavy escort to Richmond Barracks. We were not long there when we were put into a large room, and members of the Detective Division were brought in who picked out men that were subsequently court martialled. On the following even the remainder of the prisoners were marched down the Quay for deportation to gaols in England. After a rough crossing and a tedious train journey I found myself with a good many of my comrades in Knutsford gaol. This was a military prison and the discipline was very rigid. The first five weeks there we were kept in solitary confinement and food supplies were very meagre and scanty. At the end of five weeks conditions improved somewhat. We were allowed visitors and the discipline was relaxed. We were then allowed to mix and talk to one another. This was a great privilege. Up to this we had to march round in single file and were allowed no intercourse or communication with each other. We were also

[13]

deprived of hearing Mass for a number of Sundays and then at the first Mass we attended the Chaplain explained that he had interceded on our behalf that we might avail of the privilege of attending Mass. He also informed us that we might have no qualms about eating meat on Fridays. Alfie Byrne was one of our first visitors. I did not know him then but some of my comrades told me who he was. From the first free Sunday we began mingling with each other. From then on visitors came from all over England and even from Ireland every Sunday. The presents of food they brought were very welcome and added considerably to the prison menu. On the Sunday that the first visitors came I was taken from my cell and brought to an interview room. I found that Thomas Craven had also been brought there and a stranger, dressed in civilian attire accompanying the Camp Commandant, inspected both Craven and myself. He then questioned us on our movements on Easter Sunday. We denied all knowledge of the raid on the quarry. After a short interrogation I told him I refused to answer any further questions. He had the driver of the taxi with him but the driver did not identify us. Some of the Dublin prisoners told me afterwards that this man was Sergeant Maye of the R.I.C. at Tallaght. It was obvious that he wanted to associate me with the capture of the gelignite from the De Selby quarries. A second attempt was made later on to identify us with this incident. This time the two quarry foremen were brought over and I was again paraded before them in company with Tom Craven. They did not, however, identify me.

About August practically all the prisoners were transferred to Frongoch. I was amongst the last to leave Knutsford for that place. Two of my hut-mates [at]

[14]

Frongoch were Dick McKee and Joe Trimble. We were located in the North Camp. A couple of weeks later I was taken to London to appear before the Sankey Commission which was considering the case of each prisoner with a view to his release or further detention.

While in London awaiting a call from the Sankey Commission we were accommodated in Wandsworth Prison. When I was called before it I was questioned as to my activity on Easter Sunday. I did not give a truthful account of my activities on that day. This was not a sworn statement. Following my appearance before the Commission I was sent back to Frongoch with the other prisoners. When the Commission had finished its hearing some prisoners were released, but I was detained. Owing to the continued release of prisoners during the summer and autumn the North Camp was closed and all the prisoners in it were transferred to the South Camp which was a disused distillery.

About October of that year, 1916, an attempt was made to conscript for British military service certain prisoners who were detained in Frongoch. The King brothers, Patrick and John, and the Noonan brothers, Jack and Ernest, were taken out, and forced to join some regiment. I believe that they refused to take the Oath of Allegiance subsequently. A second attempt was made to conscript one other prisoner, Hugh Thornton. In this case the prisoners sensed what was intended for the individual and advised him not to answer his name. A general roll call then of all the prisoners was ordered and the majority of them refused to answer their names. However, as Thornton feared that the other prisoners might be unduly punished he came forward voluntarily

[15]

and surrendered. Those who answered their names were transferred back to the North Camp where they continued to enjoy the recognised privileges such as letters from home *etc.* This arrangement worked very well for us as the prisoners in the North Camp were able to receive parcels of cigarettes *etc.* and smuggle a quantity of them to the South Camp by the fatigue parties.

As a protest to Hugh Thornton being taken away for military service a short hunger strike took place in the lower camp. It only lasted three days as Father Stafford, the prison Chaplain, succeeded in settling it. I should mention that this hunger strike was not highly organized. It was merely a spontaneous protest on the part of the prisoners. After that things settled down and the normal routine of the Camp continued until Christmas Eve when we were notified that a General Release had been ordered. We were released that evening and travelled during the night by a special train and boat to the North Wall, arriving in Dublin on Christmas morning. Breakfast was provided for us at Fleming's Hotel in Gardiner Street. John O'Mahoney was the proprietor of it at that time. While the city prisoners returned to their homes those of us who resided in the country were accommodated in different places in the city. I and a few others spent a few days at St. Enda's Schools, Oakley Road, Ranelagh, where Mrs. Pearse catered for our requirements. I did not leave the city at all and accommodation was provided for me later at the house of Mrs. Malone whose son, Lieutenant Michael Malone, had been killed at Mount Street Bridge during the insurrection. After about three months I obtained employment in the Dublin Corporation through

[16]

the influence of Alderman Tom Kelly. Two very prominent officers in similar employment with me at the time were Commandant Joseph O'Connor of the 3rd Battalion and Commandant Thomas Byrne of the 1st Battalion.

Volunteers Re-organised:

We were not long back from prison when we were informed that the Volunteers had again been reorganised by men who were released earlier from Frongoch and other prison camps. I think instructions were issued that all prisoners should return to their units. That raised a question for me as to what unit I should join as the Kimmage garrison no longer existed. George Plunkett held a meeting of the Kimmage garrison and informed all present that it could not be reorganised as a separate unit and that Volunteers, if they wished to continue their service, should be attached to one of the Battalions of the Dublin Brigade. Although residing in the south side of the city I joined "F" Company of the 1st Battalion which was a north city unit. It was through Michael Collins's influence that I joined this particular Company as he pointed out to me that the Company had been greatly reduced in strength due to a number of important men who served in it being transferred to Headquarters. Tom Byrne was the Battalion Commandant and my Company Officer was John O'Connor who is now a Solicitor. O'Connor resigned the captaincy after about a month in order to continue his studies for the Bar. His place was taken by Frank McCabe. At that time the Quartermaster was, I think, Michael Kelly, a brother of the President.

Early in 1917 a Sappers' Company was formed within the Brigade. This Company was, I think,

[17]

representative of all Companies of the Dublin Brigade. I think that approximately two to four men from each Company were selected to form it. I was one of the selections from my Company and the instructors were Andy Fitzpatrick and Seán Ó Broin. This latter is now in the Post Office Service. Lectures were given to us on the operation of field telephones and instructions on how the telephones throughout the city and suburbs were planned. We were taken round the city in small groups and show the underground system of telephonic communication as well as the overhead systems. Our chief instruction concerned the methods to be adopted to put these systems out of order if and when required for future military operations. Most of the lectures were given in Columcille Hall, Blackhall Place. As the organising of the Dublin Brigade progressed, an Engineer Battalion was subsequently formed and the Sappers' Company was incorporated in it.

I.R.B.

During the summer of 1919 Michael Collins approached me and asked me would I go to Cavan to reorganise the Irish Republican Brotherhood there. I should have mentioned that when in Liverpool in 1915 Thomas Craven had been asking me a number of questions about my previous life which caused me to wonder at the time. When on an outing at a place called Eastham in Cheshire, one Sunday, Stephen Lannigan, late of the Revenue Commissioners' Office, mentioned the matter of my joining the I.R.B. and I told him that Mr. Craven had been asking me some questions which rather puzzled me. He then broke off the conversation stating that he would leave the matter

[18]

to Mr. Craven. As a matter of fact, it was not until we were working at the De Selby quarries that Craven actually swore me into the Irish Republican Brotherhood. The organisation was reorganised in Frongoch internment camp. A man named Tobin of Wexford reorganised as many of the Kimmage garrison as possible in one unit. This remained intact after our release. At one of the earlier meetings of our group, which was held at Parnell Square (the Keating Branch of the Gaelic League premises), our group was christened "The Seán MacDermott Circle" and Michael Collins was the Centre. I was elected Secretary. Meetings were held monthly and activities were confined to the introduction of new members. Collins was at this time appointed Volunteer organiser. Very often the question of suitability of officers for Volunteer Companies was discussed at these meetings. The Volunteer units at the time were electing their own officers and efforts were made to install the most suitable type of man for commissioned rank. It was at one of these meetings that Michael Collins told me to report to Seán Ó Muirthille regarding the reorganisation of the I.R.B. in County Cavan. My work in Cavan consisted of travelling from parish to parish and contacting the men who had already been in the I.R.B. The chief centre of both I.R.A. and I.R.B. activities in the County Cavan at that time was in the village of Ballinagh. The Centre there was Peter Conaty who later became Chief Centre for the whole of Cavan. We organised new Circles in areas hitherto untouched. We went, I think, from Swanlinbar in the west to Bailieboro in the east. When a general meeting was held and a County Board had been elected, I was transferred to the County Monaghan

[19]

where I reported to Eoin O'Duffy who was then County Engineer, I think, and had as his assistant Dan Hogan. O'Duffy had Monaghan fairly well organised and I was chiefly used by him to visit areas where he did not wish to identify himself with I.R.B. activities. At this time O'Duffy explained to me that he had been using the I.R.B. as an Intelligence Organisation for the Volunteers and that he was working on a scheme to have all communications between Belfast and Dublin carried by Volunteer and, if possible, I.R.B. members only. We got this route extended from Clones in the County Monaghan as far as Mount Nugent in Cavan, but we never got the Meath end of it fixed up.

I then returned to Dublin and after a short time I was sent by Seán Muithille this time to Tipperary to try to reorganise that County. My chief contacts in Tipperary were Ramon O'Dwyer of Gooldscross, Frank Drohan of Conmel and Seán Duffy of Clonmel, Seán Duffy also of Tipperary town and Éamon O'Neill of Cashel who was a teacher in Rockwell College. I think the latter was looked on as the Centre for Tipperary. I found these men very enthusiastic but rather hesitant in embarking on any activities. From a remark that one of them dropped I came to the conclusion that they did not trust me. I went back to Dublin and reported my impression to Seán O'Muirthille. About a couple of weeks later the latter sent for me one Saturday evening and told me to meet him on O'Connell Bridge at, I think, 7 o'clock, on Sunday morning and we went to a Convention which he had arranged in some country part of Tipperary somewhere near Rearcross. We were driven in a taxi by Joe Hyland and a Convention of the Tipperary men

[20]

was held at which Mr. Seán Ó Muirthille explained the entire situation. He assured them that there was no conflict of interest between the I.R.B. and the I.R.A. that both organisations were out to achieve the same end. I think this conflict arose over the Tipperary men's inclination to follow the advice of Cathal Brugha that the I.R.B. was no longer necessary. I believe Ó Muirthille stated that Cathal Burgha had taken him into the I.R.B. in the first instance, but that he did not recognise the right of any man to take him out of it again, and as a result of his appeal the Tipperary County Board was re-formed. During my travels throughout the country on I.R.B. organisational work I also visited Frank Barrett, O.C. West Clare Brigade. He had an office in the family hotel in Ennis. I found that his policy was similar to O'Duffy's in Monaghan, that is using the I.R.B. as an Intelligence Organisation for the Volunteers.

G.H.Q. Intelligence:

In the autumn of 1919 Dick McKee spoke to me in the shop of Seamus Donegan, 10A Aungier Street, where he was printing *An t-Oglach* and told me to report to Liam Tobin. I reported to the latter in Crowe Street, I think. At the time I did not know what appointment Tobin held but I sensed, however, that it had something to do with Intelligence. He did not enlighten me during my first interview with him; he simply told me that I had been recommended by Dick McKee. He accordingly told me that I was to go to South Anne Street and watch a certain house there and report if I saw any plain-clothes policemen frequent it. I kept the place under observation for about three days and only observed two plain-clothes men on one occasion

[21]

entering it. I reported to the office in Crowe Street every morning and evening and soon found myself meeting other members there who were engaged on similar work.

He explained to me what the Intelligence work consisted of and gave me a rough idea of what my duties were likely to be. From then on my duties as a member of the Intelligence Staff mainly consisted of observing and reporting on the movements of persons whose names and addresses were given to me by Liam Tobin or Tom Cullen.

British Intelligence Officer:

A British Officer whose name, I think, was Barnes was, I believe, in charge of Military Intelligence, G.H.Q. Parkgate Barracks. Liam Tobin gave me his particulars and told me to watch and memorise the frequency of his movements in and out of barracks. I was told this officer generally drove in and out of barracks in a horse and trap and that he resided on the North Circular Road close to the Phoenix Park. For about four or five days I walked and dallied along the roadway from McKee Barracks round to the Phoenix Park, North Circular Road end but I never once saw him.

Molloy — British Agent:

About the middle of March, 1920, Joe Guilgoyle and myself were given the job of watching out for a British agent going under the name of Molloy. I think his real name was Bernie McNulty of Foxford, County Mayo. I think we picked him up in O'Connell Street. At the time he was talking to Liam Tobin and Tom

[22]

Cullen and when he left them we followed him around. He walked round for about an hour and he went into a shop apparently to buy cigarettes. While he was inside Guilfoyle left me. In the meantime Molloy came out of the shop again and I kept after him until he went into the Lower Castle Yard. There I left him and reported the matter next morning to Liam Tobin. The latter simply said, "That is correct". About a week later Joe Guilfoyle and myself were instructed to meet Tom Cullen and Liam Tobin in Grafton Street between 7 and 8 p.m. I met them at the appointed place and Tom Cullen brought me into a doorway and handed me a .45 Webley Revolver. Tobin told me that the job on hands [sic] was the execution of the British agent, Molloy, that it was to be done by members of the Squad and that we were to ensure that the Squad was not interfered with from any unexpected source. I think an appointment was made by Tobin and Collins to meet Molloy in Grafton Street. In any case I saw Molloy outside Neblett's at the junction of South King Street and Grafton Street. He walked down towards Wicklow Street but was followed closely by the two men who were to carry out the actual shooting. I think it was originally planned that this shooting should take place in Grafton Street but for some reason or other Molloy was allowed to go as far as Wicklow Street where he was shot in the vicinity of the National Bar. Following the shooting the crowd became threatening and wanted to hold the two members of the Squad concerned for the police, but these men drew their revolvers and got safely away. The public did not realise at that time who the shot man was, or the organisation responsible for his shooting.

[23]

Alan Bell — British Financial Agent:

Alan Bell was a British financial expert engaged in examining the various Banks' Accounts in this country with a view to locating or idenitying [sic] Dáil monies. A decision was arrived at that this man should be eliminated. I was present at Crowe Street when plans for his execution were discussed, and each man detailed to the part he was to play. About eight members of the Squad and Intelligence were to watch out for him on the morning, I think, of the 26th March, 1920. It was known that he would travel at a certain time on the Dun Laoghaire tram. A number of us were detailed to board the tram. Some of them were to enter the lower saloon and Joe Guilfoyle and myself were to go upstairs with others. The idea was that when the lower party would leave the tram to carry out the execution those of us upstairs would take steps to prevent the tram from moving off for some time and further prevent interference to members of the Squad who were carrying out the job. A cyclist was instructed to report whether or not Bell was on the tram. The party boarded the tram at Ailsebury Road at a signal from Tom Keogh who was the cyclist in this case. As I was going towards Ailesbury Road to carry out my instructions Tom Keogh saw me and indicated to me that the tram had gone. At this particular time I heard shots being fired which I learned later were by the men who shot Bell. I walked up a side-road which led to Donnybrook. A motor-cyclist with a sidecar passed me. He must have passed by the scene of the shooting because he reported the matter to the police at Donnybrook.

District Inspector Roberts:

I was sent to Amiens Street Station by Liam

[24]

Tobin to watch out for a man by the name of Roberts. He handed us a photograph of Roberts in the uniform of the Dublin Metropolitan Police. At certain times for a period of three or four days I remained on duty at Amiens Street Station without result. On one occasion I followed a man who looked very like him, but Tom Cullen had a good laugh about this as several had apparently made the same mistake. About a week after this more definite information was given to me that it had been ascertained definitely that Roberts would arrive at Amiens Street Station on a particular morning. I took up my position at the Station on the morning in question and saw him leaving the station and entering a car. I reported this to Liam Tobin and he instructed me to return the next morning and this time to go on to the platform and observe all movements from the time Roberts left his carriage until he drove away in the car. I did this for several mornings and noticed that each morning he had an escort of two plain-clothes policemen and a plain-clothes driver. My presence there on so many mornings must have given rise to suspicions as on one occasion I saw one of the two plain-clothes men talk to Roberts and look in my direction. The latter merely shook his head and entered the car as usual, while I followed at a distance and watched the car proceed through Stores Street to the Castle.

On the morning of the 22nd June, 1920, members of the Squad under Paddy Daly were detailed to shoot Roberts. As I was the Intelligence Officer who could identify him I was instructed to watch out for him and give warning of his arrival to the Squad. We took up positions near the railway bridge at the corner of Brooks Thomas, Abbey Street. I took up a vantage

[25]

point about [the] middle of the Custom House and when I saw the car coming from Amiens Street Station direction I gave the pre-arranged signal, that is to say I took out my handkerchief and brought it to my nose at the same time starting to walk away. I had not gone very far when the shooting started. When I turned round I saw one of the escort trying to get out of the car. He was pulled back by the second escort and the car then accelerated towards Butt Bridge. The car was attacked by grenade and revolver fire but Roberts was only wounded. He resigned from the Police and I don't think only [sic] further action was taken against him.

Intelligence Reports on Managers of G.W. and G.S. Railways:

Apart from British agents and spies my Intelligence duties were extended at one period to procuring as much information as I possibly could regarding the General Manager of the Midland Great Western Railway, namely J.F. Keogh, and also the Manager of the Great Southern Railway — E.A. Neale. This was the time when railway employees, engine-drivers and guards were being dismissed by the railway people for refusing to work trains conveying British troops and police. As regards Keogh of the Midland Great Western Railway, the information I collected about him was his place of private residence, the time he left for his office, the time he returned, the registration number of his motor car and where he parked it and the location of his office in the Broadstone Station. I obtained similar information though not as detailed about Neale of the Great Southern Railway. I passed the information to Liam Tobin but, so far as I know, no action was taken. I believe it was contemplated to have these men made

[26]

prisoners should they continue to dismiss railway employees who felt it their patriotic duty to have nothing to do with the movements of British Army forces.

Captain Hardy:

About the first week of September, 1920, I was sent down to Kingsbridge Station to look out for a car bearing the letters XA, I think, but I cannot remember the number that followed. The car that I was looking for was at the station but I noticed that a car bearing the same registration letters but a different number leave a military office in John's Road frequently and that its occupants were obviously plain-clothes policemen. I reported this to Liam Tobin but he did not seem to be interested. A few days later, however, he called me into his office and said, "That car number you gave me now transpires to be Tudor's car and I want you to get all the information you can about its movements". I kept the number of this car in my pocket in a notebook. A few days later Tobin sent me up to Harcourt Street to keep watch on a British Intelligence Officer by the name of Captain Hardy who he knew used to visit an hotel there. I kept up this watch at certain times for a period of a couple of days. One evening, about 6 o'clock, I saw a man with a limp go into the hotel having got out of a small van. At this time I was not sure whether this was Hardy or not but Joe Guilfoyle came along and I reported my suspicions to him. We both decided to watch and make sure if these were the men we were looking for. We left the spot where we were watching and went in the direction of Camden Street via Montague Place. When we reached an archway leading into this place a British Officer and two soldiers ordered us quietly to get inside a Crossley tender. The men who ordered

[27]

us into the van was Captain Hardy who, incidentally, was the man I had seen enter the hotel a short time before that. We were taken to Dublin Castle and questioned. From the questions we knew that they were endeavouring to link us with members of I.R.A. Intelligence. When I was being searched I had a notebook in my pocket containing the number of Tudor's car. Simultaneously with my being searched Joe Guilfoyle was also being searched and he had in his possession a letter from Liam Tobin to a Mr. McCabe of the Plasterers' Union, asking to get some members of his Union to supply information about the Castle which was then undergoing repairs by them. The officer who was searching Guilfoyle became quite excited when he found this note and said to Captain Hardy, who was searching me, "We have here a letter from the notorious Liam Tobin". With that Hardy forgot all about me and directed his attention to Guilfoyle. When I got a chance I was able to destroy the paper containing the number of Tudor's car by chewing it. A short time later we were taken to the Bridewell. About 3 o'clock in the morning Captain Hardy and a number of others whom I can't remember now came in and asked for Guilfoyle. They told him to get ready to leave. He had left his coat beside me and was allowed to return to it. He then told me that he was being asked to sign a statement to the effect that his personal effects had been given back to him. He asked my advice about giving his signature as we both felt that Hardy wanted it with a view to comparing it with that on other documents that had been captured from time to time. Another view we took of it was that the signature was for evidence that Guilfoyle had been released and that no blame could be attached to the military authorities if he

[28]

were found dead after alleged release. My advice was that he had no option but to sign. The party then left the Bridewell with Guilfoyle and about two hours later he returned. He told me that he had been taken out to some golf links at Dartry and there blindfolded. They threatened to shoot him if he did not tell them the whereabouts of his brother, Seán. He said that of course he did not give them any information. He added that Hardy did not give him any rough handling; in fact he spoke to him in confidence, advising him to tell where his brother was, that it was better for all concerned and that no harm would come to either of them as a result. Guilfoyle told me that Hardy further said to him, "You know we have full authority to shoot any I.R.A. man as we think fit, that we have been guaranteed immunity from any disciplinary action, no matter how extreme". Guilfoyle was returned to the cell none the worse of [sic] his adventure and the next day, about midday, an order came for his release. I was informed that I was being transferred to Mountjoy gaol. I was taken out to the back of the Bridewell where I was placed in an armoured car which conveyed me to Mountjoy prison where I was in the category of an untried prisoner for a period of about three months. Sometime in November, Captain Hardy swore a deposition against me that in searching the premises where I stayed he found a membership card of the Sinn Féin organisation. As a result I was tried by court martial and having waited a considerable time for the verdict I was told that the court martial was illegal and that I would have to be tried a second time. At the second trial I was sentenced to three months' imprisonment to date from the date of my arrest. I was released sometime in the beginning of December.

[29]

While in prison we heard the shooting in Croke Park on Bloody Sunday and we also knelt in prayer on the morning of Kevin Barry's execution. When I was notified of the date and place of my trial, which was Marlboro (now McKee) barracks, I was able to let a visitor know these particulars who conveyed them to Liam Tobin, but he afterwards explained they were unable to take any action.

After my release I walked round the streets in the vicinity of Crowe Street where I expected to meet some of my former Intelligence Officers. I forget which of them I met, but I was told to report at the office.

Shortly after my release Liam Tobin instructed me one morning to go to Kirwin's public house in Parnell Street where I would meet a man named D.P. Walsh. On arrival I found Michael Collins and Walsh in the premises. I was introduced to the latter and it was explained to me that he and I were to take two bicycles to Dun Laoghaire and hand them over to Dan Breen and another man who would accompany him by road to Tipperary. Dan Breen at this time was almost recovered from shotgun wounds received at Drumcondra sometime before that. We cycled out to Dun Laoghaire and met Breen and the other man there, handed the bicycles over to them and returned to the city.

General Tudor — Intelligence Reports on His Movements

While I was in prison the Intelligence staff was considerably increased. Frank Thornton had finally left his employment in the Insurance Company and was attached to the Intelligence Department permanently. From then on any instructions issued to me were, as a general rule, given by Thornton.

[30]

I was put back again on the tracking of General Tudor and another assignment I received was to watch out for Sergeant-Major Hepworth who was, so to speak, Captain Hardy's right-hand man. He was with Hardy when Guilfoyle and myself were arrested. Tom Cullen introduced me to a Sergeant named Harte of the Dublin Fuziliers [sic] who had something to do with food distribution in Dublin Castle. Obviously this man was doing Intelligence work for us. He gave us correct descriptive particulars of Hepworth and others whom we were looking for. It transpired, however, that these particulars would not help us in establishing their identity. We were never able to track down Hepworth. I believe he left Dublin shortly after that. In the meantime we had obtained full particulars of the exact route taken by General Tudor when travelling from John's Road to the Castle. It took me a considerable time to mark out this route as I had to take up positions at various street corners along the entire route in order to make sure that I would have him routed correctly. As a result plans were made to eliminate Tudor. The attack did not come off as for some reason or other he began to change his route and took a different one each day and his visits to the Castle became irregular. Further efforts were made to ascertain Tudor's movements, this time through the agency of a man named Gunner Doyle who was very friendly with Tudor's driver. It was usual for Doyle to approach the driver each day and judiciously and indirectly inquire where the car was going that day. However, nothing came of this as the driver himself was unaware of destinations or times of leaving the Castle until about an hour before leaving. This source of information also petered out because Doyle left the country and went to England.

[31]

The Igoe Gang

The Intelligence Department was making every effort to track down two squads of R.I.C. men operating under Sergeants Igoe and Killeen. In common with other members of the Intelligence Squad I spent a considerable amount of time observing and watching out for the movements of these Police Squads. On a few occasions I met up with them accidentally and reported the direction they were travelling back to headquarters.

An tOglach

Sometime in January, 1921, I was transferred from G.H.Q. Intelligence to the Adjutant-General's Branch. Liam Tobin instructed me to report to Gearóid O'Sullivan who was then Adjutant-General and had an office Ormond Quay. The latter put me in charge of the distribution of *An tOglach*.

An tOglach was printed at the back of the shop at 10A Aungier Street owned by the Gleeson family. It was customary for me when on the Intelligence to leave my revolver there when not actually required. I now began working in the office at the back of that shop on the distribution of An tOglach. The circulation was between four and five thousand copies every week. These had to be made into parcels of varying numbers and transmitted to the O.Cs. of Brigades throughout the country and I think to some in Great Britain. I was assisted in this work by a young man named Bennett. Each parcel had double wrappers, the outside one addressed to an accommodation address not suspected of being closely associated with I.R.A. activities and the inner one addressed to the O.C. concerned. Mr. Pierce Beasley was the editor and

[32]

the copy was carried from him to Aungier Street by a typist. The only one whose name I can now remember was a Miss Cooley. Joseph Cullen was the compositor and Charles Walker the machinist. The paper for the journal was supplied by Mr. Patrick Mahon of Yarnhall Street whose premises are now owned by James Ardiff. Mr. Ardiff used to relieve Joe Cullen when the latter was on holidays. When posting the parcels to the various accommodation addresses it was usual for me to divide them and post only a few in each Post Office. The stationery for the Adjutant-General's Department was printed at 10 Aundier Street, the paper for this purpose being supplied by Andy Hyland who managed a book binding establishment in Clarendon Street. I continued on this work up to the Truce on the 11th July, 1921.

Signature s/ Patrick Caldwell

Date 25th January 1952
Patrick Caldwell
Witness William Jerry Comdt.

Bureau of Military History 1913-21
Buro Staire Millata 1913-21
No. W.S. 638

Chapter 9: Ireland's Future, the Just Third Way[1]

Could the goals of the Easter Rising been achieved without violence? Trying to be as objective as possible, and noting that (as CESJ co-founder Father William J. Ferree, S.M., Ph.D. observed) in social justice terms, nothing is impossible, we would have to answer that question with a qualified "yes." As Ferree explained,

> Another characteristic of Social Justice . . . is that in Social Justice there is never any such thing as helplessness. No problem is ever too big or too complex, no field is ever too vast, for the methods of this Social Justice. Problems that were agonizing in the past and were simply dodged, even by serious and virtuous people, can now be solved with ease by any school child.[2]

Does this mean that those who sacrificed their lives to establish an independent Ireland based on respect for the dignity of the human person and equality of opportunity for all were wrong, or that they died in vain?

Absolutely not.

It is one thing to look back with all the advantages of hindsight and say what could, should, or would have been done "if only" — if only O'Connell hadn't yielded to threats, if only there hadn't been a Famine, if only Henry George hadn't interfered, if only Parnell hadn't fallen, if only the British government hadn't relied on coercion, if only the Curragh Mutiny hadn't occurred, if only Maxwell had acted rationally, if only, if only, if only . . . the list is potentially endless.

It is another thing altogether to know what can be done today, without being bound by any mistakes of the past — if they even were mistakes. We must learn from history, not be enslaved by it, or by anything else.

A Unique Opportunity

The Centenary of the Rising presents Ireland with the unique opportunity to become the global leader delivering

---

[1] Norman G. Kurland and Dawn K. Brohawn contributed significantly to this chapter.
[2] Ferree, *Introduction to Social Justice, op. cit.*, 47.

the first example of a Just Third Way vision of economic and social justice that is neither capitalism nor socialism to all the people of the world — and in a way that the people of Ireland benefit first, but at no one else's expense. The goals expressed in the Easter Proclamation — ownership, control of one's own destiny, equal rights and opportunities — all these and more can be achieved. They are within the reach not only of every child, woman, and man in Ireland, but as a model for every person in the world.

The Rising led the way for many of the political movements of the twentieth century. Now is the time for Ireland to lead the way economically and socially as well.

We can say what the men, woman, and yes, children of Easter Week should, in our opinion, have done or not done. That's easy.

What is not so easy is to say what *we* should — and can — do now. It is all very well to point out the mistakes of the past and show how *we* could have done much better. So could they have done much better — if they knew what we now know . . . and "if only" . . .

With that in mind, we will present a framework that we believe answers the question, Where do we — for we hold with Davitt that Ireland's cause is the cause of humanity — go from here? and does so in a just and practical manner. We will first present a brief overview of the Just Third Way, then set out the principles of economic justice, and then those of social justice. We will conclude by presenting an outline for a program that could be applied in Ireland — or anywhere else in the world.

Obviously, some of what we say might not apply in Ireland, or we might have missed something. With the right framework, however, it is a simple matter to add or subtract specifics to tailor a Just Third Way program to fit any situation.

The Four Pillars of the Just Third Way

As Parnell was fully aware, the answer to "the Irish Question" is widespread capital ownership. This was recognized before his time in the Virginia Declaration of Rights that listed access to the means of acquiring and possessing property as a natural right inhering in all people. In our day, Article 17(1) of the United Nations Universal Declaration of

Human Rights affirms that, "everyone has the right to own property alone as well as in association with others."

Unfortunately, Parnell made two mistakes — aside from failing to keep in mind that in the revolution, one cuts square corners personally as well as professionally. One, he limited his understanding of what was needed for every person to become an owner of land. Two, he didn't realize that relying on existing savings — whatever the source — is the least efficient way to finance new capital formation or turn people into owners of productive assets.

Catholic social teaching agrees with Parnell's general prescription. As Leo XIII noted, "We have seen that this great labor question cannot be solved save by assuming as a principle that private ownership must be held sacred and inviolable. The law, therefore, should favor ownership, and its policy should be to induce as many as possible of the people to become owners."[3]

The overall program can be summarized in what CESJ calls "the Four Pillars of a Just Market Society":

- **A limited economic role for the State**: "There is no need to bring in the State. Man precedes the State, and possesses, prior to the formation of any State, the right of providing for the substance of his body."[4]

- **Free, non-monopolistic, and open markets** within an understandable and fair system of laws as the most objective and democratic means for determining just prices, just wages and just profits — the residual after all goods or services are sold: "Let the working man and the employer make free agreements, and in particular let them agree freely as to the wages; nevertheless, there underlies a dictate of natural justice more imperious and ancient than any bargain between man and man."[5]

- **Restoration of private property**, especially in corporate equity and other forms of business organization: "A working man's little estate thus purchased should be as

---

[3] *Rerum Novarum*, § 46.
[4] *Ibid.*, § 7.
[5] *Ibid.*, § 45.

completely at his full disposal as are the wages he receives for his labor. But it is precisely in such power of disposal that ownership obtains, whether the property consist of land or chattels."[6]

- **Widespread capital ownership**, individually or in free association with others: "The law . . . should favor ownership, and its policy should be to induce as many as possible of the people to become owners."[7]

The Principles of Economic Justice

The four pillars are applications of the three principles of economic justice worked out by Louis O. Kelso and Mortimer J. Adler, and refined by CESJ. Significantly, like the legs of a tripod, if even one principle is missing, the whole structure collapses. Just as a tripod is the strongest and most stable type of structure, however, the three principles of economic justice taken together provide the moral framework for building a more just and stable form of sustainable and non-inflationary development:

1. **Participative Justice**. This is how every person can make input to the economic process in order to earn a decent living. It requires equal opportunity in gaining access to private property in productive assets as well as equality of opportunity to engage in productive work. Participative justice does not guarantee equal results, but requires that every person be guaranteed by society's institutions the equal human right to make a productive contribution to the economy, both through one's labor (as a worker) and through one's productive capital (as an owner). Thus, this principle rejects monopolies, special privileges, and other exclusionary social barriers to economic self-reliance and personal freedom.[8]

2. **Distributive Justice**.[9] This is the out-take principle based on the exchange or market value of one's economic con-

---

[6] *Ibid.*, § 5.
[7] *Ibid.*, § 46.
[8] Norman G. Kurland, Dawn K. Brohawn, Michael D. Greaney, *Capital Homesteading for Every Citizen: A Just Free Market Solution for Saving Social Security*. Arlington, Virginia: Economic Justice Media, 2004, 131, 202.
[9] This is not "distributive justice" as redefined by Msgr. John A. Ryan of the Catholic University of America who was harshly critical

tributions. This is the principle that all people have a right to receive a proportionate, market-determined share of the value of the marketable goods and services they produce with their labor contributions, their capital contributions, or both. In contrast to a controlled or command economy, this increases respect for human dignity by making each person's economic vote count.[10]

3. **Social Justice.**[11] This is the feedback principle that results in harmony. Social justice rebalances participative justice (productive input) and distributive justice (consumption choices) when the system violates either essential principle. Social justice includes a concept of limitation that discourages personal greed and prevents social and economic monopolies.[12]

In general, social justice holds that every person has a personal responsibility to organize with others to achieve that threshold of "We, the People" power to correct their organizations, institutions, laws and the social order itself at every level whenever the principles of participative justice or distributive justice are violated or not operating properly.[13] The application of social justice to the common good of specific economic institutions brings those institutions into conformity with the demands of the common good of all society.[14]

---

of the Easter Rising. Ryan's concept, found in his two major works, *A Living Wage* (1906) and *Distributive Justice* (1916) should more accurately be described as "redistributive pseudo charity," as it relies on coerced redistribution by the State to achieve an expanded georgist socialism. Ferree listed Ryan among dissenting writers on the subject of social justice. Rev. William Ferree, S.M., Ph.D., *The Act of Social Justice*. Washington, DC: The Catholic University of America Press, 1943, 87.

[10] Kurland, *et al.*, *Capital Homesteading for Every Citizen, op. cit.*, 203.

[11] Kelso and Adler termed this the principle of limitation, which we consider too limited.

[12] Kurland, *et al.*, *Capital Homesteading for Every Citizen, op. cit.*, 203.

[13] *Ibid.*

[14] *Ibid.*, 131, 202.

Defining Social Justice

When dealing with social justice issues, few people seem to stop and think what the term really means. This creates a problem, for if you can't define "social justice," you won't be able to apply the principles of social justice properly.

According to Ferree, the general virtue of legal justice and the particular virtue of social justice both have the common good as their object — the common good being that vast network of institutions within which people can realize their fullest development or "individual good." Social justice, however, has a particular (direct) act, while legal justice does not.

To explain, Aristotle loosely defined legal justice as "virtue entire."[15] "The Philosopher" divided legal justice into matters affecting the life of the individual ("all the things with which the good person is concerned"[16]), and matters affecting the life of the individual as a member of society ("all the acts of virtue commanded by law"[17]). He believed this can lead to a conflict between being a good person, and being a good citizen.

Socialists attempt to resolve this conflict by asserting the primacy of social virtue over individual virtue — the State or collective over the individual — capitalists by claiming that of individual virtue over social virtue: the individual over the collective. According to Ferree, however, only the act of social justice can resolve the conflict, and make it possible to be both a good person and a good citizen by bringing the structuring of institutions and laws in line with moral principles.

Legal justice can consequently only affect the common good through the indirect effect that acts of individual virtue have on the social order. In contrast, the act of social justice enables people as members of organized groups to join in solidarity to influence, build and correct unjust social institutions — thereby acting directly on the common good itself.

Acts of social justice, while a moral obligation, must not be coerced. Individuals organizing for social change must do so on a purely voluntary and peaceful basis, relying on the nat-

---

[15] *Ethics*, 1130a10.
[16] *Ibid.*, 1130b4.
[17] *Ibid.*, 1130b24, 1129b23.

ural right of free association (liberty/contract) for their effectiveness.[18]

The Laws of Social Justice

Like any other human activity, social justice must operate within certain parameters. If it does not adhere to the "laws" of social justice or conform to its characteristics, it is not social justice. Ferree discerned seven "laws" of social justice that we must keep in mind if we want to act in a socially just manner. As described in his pamphlet, *Introduction to Social Justice*,[19] the "laws" are:

I. That the Common Good Be Kept Inviolate. In all private dealings, in all exercise of individual justice, the common good must be a primary object of solicitude. To attack or to endanger the common good in order to attain some private end, no matter how good or how necessary this latter may be in its own order, is social injustice and is wrong.[20]

II. Cooperation, Not Conflict. Given the uniqueness of each human person, the particular good of each individual is different. Any particular good that is falsely made into an ultimate principle must necessarily be *in conflict* with every other particular good. Only cooperation, organization for the common good, can make a real society. This does not mean overriding or ignoring individual goods, but integrating them into the whole effort.[21]

III. One's First Particular Good is One's Own Place in the Common Good. The *first* particular good of every individual or group is that that individual or group find its proper place in the common good. As Ferree put it, "It must be admitted that this is not the way most of us think at the present time, but that is because we have been badly educated. It must be admitted also that to carry out such a principle in practice looks like too big a job for human nature as we know it; but that is because we are individualists and have missed the point. Of course it is too big a job if each one of us

---

[18] *Quadragesimo Anno*, § 87.
[19] The following cites are from the Just Third Way (JTW) edition of Father Ferree's pamphlet, available as a free download from the CESJ website, http://www.cesj.org/resources/articles-index/.
[20] Ferree, *Introduction to Social Justice*, op. cit., 35-36.
[21] *Ibid.*, 36.

and each of our groups is individually and separately responsible for the welfare of the human race as a whole. But the point is that the human race as a whole is *social*."[22]

IV. Each Directly Responsible. Every individual, regardless of his age or occupation or state of life, is *directly* responsible for the common good, because *the common good is built up in a hierarchical order*. That is, every great human institution consists of subordinate institutions, which themselves consist of subordinate institutions, on down to the individuals who compose the lowest and most fleeting of human institutions. Since every one of these institutions is directly responsible for the general welfare of the one above it, it follows that every individual is directly responsible for the lower institutions which immediately surround his life, and indirectly responsible for the general welfare of his whole country and the whole world.[23]

V. High Institutions Must Never Displace Lower Ones. No institution in the vast hierarchy that we have seen can take over the particular actions of an institution or person below it.[24]

VI. Freedom of Association. If every natural group of individuals has a right to its own common good and a duty towards the next highest common good, it is evident that such a group has the right to organize itself formally in view of the common good.[25]

VII. All Vital Interests Should Be Organized. All real and vital interests of life should be deliberately made to conform to the requirements of the common good.[26]

The Characteristics of Social Justice

Knowing the "laws" of social justice as articulated by Ferree, we can now move to the six characteristics of social justice:

I. Only By Members of Groups. Social justice cannot be performed by individuals as individuals, but only by individuals as members of groups.[27]

---

[22] *Ibid.*, 36-37.
[23] *Ibid.*, 38.
[24] *Ibid.*, 38-39.
[25] *Ibid.*, 39-41.
[26] *Ibid.*, 41-42.

That is extremely important, because virtually everyone misunderstands it. The "efficient cause" (the "actor" or "agent" who carries out the act) of *all* social virtue is the individual as a member of a group, *not* an individual on his own ticket.

This is *not* collectivism, nor is it an individual act of virtue carried out with a vague intention to benefit the common good indirectly. It is what Aristotle called *political*: individual acts within a justly structured social order directed to the common, not the individual good..

II. It Takes Time. Social justice moves slowly and gradually. It requires organization, consensus building, more organization, solidarity, attention to the principle of subsidiarity — all the troublesome little details of working with actual human beings rather than abstract concepts.[28]

III. Nothing is Impossible. In social justice there is *never any such thing as helplessness*. As Ferree stated, "No problem is ever too big or too complex, no field is ever too vast, for the methods of this social justice. Problems that were agonizing in the past and were simply dodged, even by serious and virtuous people, can now be solved with ease by any school child."[29]

IV. Eternal Vigilance. The work of social justice is *never* finished. This is not the same as saying that social justice takes a long time! It refers to what Pius XI called "the radical instability of society." This means that human beings change, conditions change, and our institutions — our human response to the task of being what Aristotle called "political animals" — must be restructured and reformed to meet the new conditions. This change is *always* happening, therefore the work of social justice is continuous.[30]

V. Effectiveness. Work for the common good — the material cause of social justice — must be effective. You cannot just do something and hope it works, or go about chanting that it *would* work if only people were not human. A mere

---

[27] *Ibid.*, 43-46.
[28] *Ibid.*, 46-47.
[29] *Ibid.*, 47-49.
[30] *Ibid.*, 49-51.

"good intention" that the common good be benefited is simply not good enough.[31]

VI. You Cannot "Take it or Leave It Alone". As Ferree explained, "Another corollary of this characteristic of social justice (that it is never finished) is that it embraces a *rigid obligation.*" That means that each of us is directly and individually responsible for the common good — and we must organize with others for the common good.[32]

Social justice is thus not a sterile thing or a subject of mere academic interest. It is the guide or rulebook of how the human person behaves in a socially virtuous manner, but without losing his individuality. Thus, the proper working of social justice ensures (or at least optimizes the possibility) that the individual becomes more truly him- or herself and realizes his or her fullest human potential, both as an individual *as an individual*, and an individual *as a member of a social order*.

A Blueprint for Participatory, Sustainable, and Just Development

Ownership of landed capital was a key component of the Home Rule movement from the very beginning. Even before Isaac Butt began organizing, the Great Hunger had turned land into a Nationalist symbol and an integral part of the cause of Irish sovereignty.[33] True, Butt had the erroneous Hobbesian idea that the right to private property in land comes from the State rather than being inherent in every child, woman, and man,[34] but that takes nothing away from his conviction that people should be secure in their ownership of landed capital against other private individuals and groups.

The Money Question

As we noted previously, however, throughout the nineteenth century (and continuing at an accelerating pace to-

---

[31] *Ibid.*, 51-52.
[32] *Ibid.*, 52.
[33] David Thornley, *Isaac Butt and Home Rule*. London: MacGibbon & Kee, 1964, 13-14.
[34] Isaac Butt, *The Irish People and the Irish Land*. Dublin, Éire: John Falconer, 1867, 31; cf. Thomas Hobbes, "Of Those Things That Weaken or Tend to the Dissolution of a Common-Wealth," *Leviathan* (1651), II.xxix.

day), advancing technology was replacing both land and labor as the predominant factor of production. Where once ownership of labor or land alone was sufficient to ensure an adequate and secure income, ownership of technology now became essential in order to become a direct producer of marketable goods and services instead of just a supplier of labor or a recipient of welfare.

The problem is how to make every child, woman, and man an owner of productive capital, but without taking anything from anyone else. We find the solution in a new understanding of money itself.

First, however, we have to ask, Why produce? Adam Smith (1723-1790) gave the answer: "Consumption is the sole end and purpose of all production."[35]

We produce in order to consume. It necessarily follows — all other things being equal — we cannot consume unless we produce. We must either produce for our own consumption, or to exchange the products of our labor, land, and other capital for what others have produced with their labor, land, and other capital.

The "medium" by means of which we exchange our productions for those of others is called "money," regardless of the actual form it takes. That is why money is called "the medium of exchange."

To put it in legal terms, money is anything that can be accepted in settlement of a debt; "all things transferred in commerce." Thus, all money is a contract and, in a sense, all contracts — bargains and promises involving something of value — are money. Something is money when it consists of *offer*, *acceptance*, and *consideration*, for these are the "elements" of all contracts. ("Consideration" is the "inducement to enter into a contract," that is, the thing of value being exchanged.)

Given this understanding of money, it is obvious that anybody who is competent to enter into a contract can participate in money creation. No one can create money acting alone, of course. Given the natural right of free association (liberty/contract), no one, as a rule, can be forced to enter in-

---

[35] Adam Smith, *The Wealth of Nations* (1776), III.viii.

to a contract, that is, make or accept an offer against his or her will — everything else being equal, of course.

To be able to enter into a contract, however, we must have something to induce others to accept the consideration we offer. That means we must be able to produce marketable goods and services, whether with our labor, land, or other capital.[36]

This is "Say's Law of Markets," from Jean-Baptiste Say (1767-1832). Say did not develop this "law," but gave it its clearest expression.[37] Summarizing the argument, Say's Law can be stated somewhat simplistically as "Production equals income, therefore, supply (production) generates its own demand (income), and demand, its own supply."

Restoring Say's Law

Authorities like Karl Marx (1818-1883) and John Maynard Keynes (1883-1946) rejected Say's Law, claiming that it did not work. (They also had a much more limited understanding of money than Smith and Say.) Kelso pointed out that Marx and Keynes assumed — erroneously — that labor is the sole factor of production, whereas Smith and Say took into account labor, land, and other capital.

Obviously, if something other than labor is productive, thinking only labor is productive will distort the picture. There will be production (and thus income) for which you can't account. Further, if you withhold production from consumption ("save") in order to finance new capital to create jobs and stimulate economic growth, you also distort matters by reducing demand, and thus the need to produce and create new jobs, putting a brake on economic growth.

Marx claimed the production Smith and Say attributed to land and other capital was really surplus value stolen from workers and consumers. Keynes didn't really try to explain it, but advocated government creation of money backed by its

---

[36] Obviously we're ignoring for the sake of the argument obtaining marketable goods or services by gift or inheritance. These are equally valid, of course, but the rule is that in order to have something, you must produce it or the thing you exchanged for it.

[37] Jean-Baptiste Say, *Letters to Mister Malthus on Several Subjects of Political Economy*. London: Sherwood, Neely, and Jones, 1821, 2-3.

own debt to increase demand artificially, presumably clearing the excess production allegedly essential to generate savings. This was something that Say specifically warned could not work, and which has resulted in the vast increase in national debt throughout the world since the nearly universal adoption of Keynesian theory.

Kelso explained that if we want Say's Law to work, we must make every child, woman, and man into a capital owner as well as an owner of labor. Butt and many others in the Home Rule movement (notably Parnell) had the right of it, although they limited their understanding of productive capital to land: people must become capital owners if society is to be stable. The question is, where are people to obtain the purchase money?

Financing Expanded Ownership

Nor was the idea of worker ownership original with Kelso. The English Radical William Cobbett (1763-1835) was a strong proponent of expanded ownership of land,[38] while in his 1854 *Essay on the Relations Between Labour and Capital*, the investment banker Charles Morrison insisted that workers must become owners if they were to enjoy adequate income.[39] William Thomas Thornton, whose *A Plea for Peasant Proprietors* (1848) had set forth a reasonable plan to deal with the Great Hunger, also advocated worker ownership as essential to a just and stable society.[40]

The problem was that all these and more also insisted that the only way to finance new capital formation is to consume less than you produce . . . which tends to obviate the whole reason for producing something in the first place! As Dr. Harold G. Moulton summed up this "economic dilemma," "In order to accumulate money savings, we must decrease our expenditures for consumption; but in order to expand capital

---

[38] William Cobbett, *A History of the Protestant Reformation in England and Ireland* (1827).
[39] Charles Morrison, *An Essay on the Relations Between Labour and Capital*. London: Longman, Green, Brown, and Longmans, 1854.
[40] William Thomas Thornton, *On Labour, Its Wrongful Claims and Rightful Dues, Its Actual Present and Possible Future*. London: Macmillan and Co., 1870, 363-499.

goods *profitably,* we must increase our expenditures for consumption."[41]

Relying on Moulton's work, Kelso rediscovered the Banking Principle that Sir Robert Peel had replaced with the Currency Principle with the passage of the Bank Charter Act of 1844. The Currency Principle is based in part on the assumption that the only way to finance new capital formation for the future is to cut consumption in the past.

The Banking Principle is based in part on the realization that financing for new capital formation to produce in the future can (and should) come from turning those same future increases in production into money by entering into contracts — agreements — to repay the financing once the new capital becomes productive. Consistent with Say's Law, the proper use of past savings is to purchase goods and services that have already been produced and that thereby generated the income to purchase them. The proper use of future savings is to finance future production.

In other words, it is possible to finance new capital with future increases in production instead of past reductions in consumption. Kelso called this a shift from "past savings" to "future savings."

Reforming National Monetary Policy

It is a little misleading to say "the first step" in a program of reform, as all of the steps should be done concurrently. We must start somewhere, however, and monetary reform is key to the Just Third Way.

It is certainly possible for an economy to run without "currency," a standard way to measure money. Ancient Egypt attained a very high degree of civilization just by having people create money as they needed it by entering into contracts — that's why they needed so many scribes.

It is much better, however, for a government to decide on a standard unit of measure for contracts, and for people to organize and establish institutions to deal in contracts. The standard unit is called the unit of currency (from "current money"), and the institution is called a "bank."

---

[41] Harold G. Moulton, *The Formation of Capital*. Washington, DC: The Brookings Institution, 1935, 28.

The job of a commercial or mercantile bank is to accept contracts offered by people who have a capital project they want to finance. Since most people's word or "creditworthiness" is not generally recognized outside a small circle, and each one differs from all the others, they are willing to pay a fee to an institution (a bank) that has a good reputation for creditworthiness, substituting the bank's contract for their own.

Further, since each bank's creditworthiness differs from all other banks, a "bank for banks" — a central bank — is essential to establish and maintain a uniform and stable currency. Thus, where a single commercial or mercantile bank provides a uniform and stable currency among all its customers, a central bank does the same thing for all of its customers: the member banks.

Note that there is nothing in this description of central banking about financing government. It is an accident of history that central banks got into financing government operations and started backing their contracts (banknotes and demand deposits) with government debt instead of private sector productive assets. The organizers of the Bank of England, the first true central bank, had gold and silver that King William III wanted, so he demanded that they turn it over to him as a condition of getting a bank charter, replacing it with "government stock" that relied on the faith and credit of the State instead of the productive capacity of privately owned capital.

The first step in a program of monetary reform, therefore, is to stop central bank financing of government, and restrict all new money creation to purposes of new capital formation.

Through Just Third Way reforms, economic growth would be freed from the slavery of past savings ("old money"), while creating a domestic source of new asset-backed, interest-free (but not cost free) money and expanded bank credit to finance new capital repayable out of future savings. To ensure that ownership of future private sector growth and newly created wealth is universally accessible to every citizen, such newly created money and credit would only be available through economic democratization vehicles, administered through the competitive member banks of a well-regulated central banking system.

The creation of new money and credit would be non-inflationary and would simultaneously broaden purchasing power throughout the economy. To accomplish this, a key reform is a two-tiered interest policy by the central bank that would distinguish between productive and non-productive uses of credit.

Under the first tier, future increases in the money supply ("new money") would be linked to actual growth of the economy's productive assets, creating new owners of new capital through widespread access to interest-free capital credit repayable with future profits. The central bank would create (*i.e.*, "monetize") interest-free credit, with lenders adding their normal markup as service fees above the cost of money. This would establish an unsubsidized minimal rate for financing technological growth. This would provide the public with a currency backed by increasingly more efficient instruments of production, real wealth-producing capital assets, rather than unsustainable government debt.

The second tier would allow substantially higher, market-determined interest rates for non-productive purposes, for which "past savings" would remain available. The central bank would be restrained from future monetization of national deficits or encouraging other forms of non-productive uses of credit, causing upper-tier credit to seek out already accumulated savings at market rates.

The Just Third Way would also provide through capital credit insurance a rational way to deal with risk, as well as an additional check on the quality of loans being supported by the central bank. Capital credit insurance and reinsurance policies would offset the risk that the enterprises issuing new shares on credit might fail to repay the loans. Such capital credit default insurance would substitute for collateral demanded by most lenders to cover the risk of non-payment, thus enabling the poor and others with few assets to overcome the collateralization barrier that excludes poor people from access to productive credit.

Simplifying the National Tax System

The paradox of modern monetary and fiscal policy is that central banks, which were intended to provide a uniform, stable, asset-backed, and "elastic" currency[42] for private sector economic development, have been almost exclusively devoted to financing government operations. At the same time, modern tax systems, intended to provide the funds to run government, have been distorted to the point of utter incomprehensibility by using them for "social engineering" and make it easier for the rich to save money for new capital formation.

A more realistic and just tax would be a single rate imposed on all directly earned and so-called "unearned" incomes above a reasonable level needed to meet all one's basic living needs. There would also be a tax-deferral on all income used to make debt-service payments on productive capital.

In this way the cost of government would be spread proportionately among all taxpayers earning more than the exemption levels. A single tax rate would be administratively more efficient than a progressive or graduated tax. Ideally, a single-rate tax on individuals would cover all government expenditures each year, including welfare, defense, interest on the national debt, social welfare and pension obligations, unemployment, and all other current spending not covered by user fees. Income exempted from taxes could also cover the cost of private sector health insurance premiums under universal comprehensive health care coverage. Health vouchers would be supported through general revenues to enable the poor to choose among private sector providers under a single rate tax system.

This would help make government more accountable and transparent to the electorate. Each year's single direct tax rate could be adjusted up or down to provide sufficient revenues to avoid budget deficits and pay off government debt over time.

Taxes on property and capital improvements — the equivalent of raising the rent on a tenant who makes improvements — would be discouraged as impediments to development. Inheritance, gift and wealth taxes would be redesigned to encourage broad-based ownership of large aggregates of ex-

---

[42] An "elastic" currency is one that expands and contracts directly with the needs of the economy, avoiding both inflation and deflation.

isting wealth, rather than passing monopolistic accumulations of wealth and economic power from one generation to the next.

Under a national ownership strategy, inheritance policy should be restructured to discourage excessive concentrations of wealth and, in order to promote individual initiative and capital self-sufficiency, to encourage the broadest possible distribution of income-producing assets. Rather than gift and other death taxes on the estate, taxation on generational wealth transfers should be based on a one-time levy on the size of the recipient's total accumulations after receiving the gift or bequest.

Expanded Capital Ownership

A primary goal of a Just Third Way national economic policy would be universal participation in the ownership of capital resources, along with full employment of labor resources. These two goals would be the twin pillars of our economy. Monetary and tax policymakers and all public sector economic institutions would be encouraged to upgrade their programs to maximize ownership opportunities for all citizens by:

- Restructuring central bank policy and national tax policy to favor ownershipexpanding productive credit over non-productive and speculative credit;
- Unharnessing the private sector to turn underutilized and wasted human and technological potential into feasible economic growth and renewable climate-protecting energy technologies;
- Spurring the economy to new heights by increasing entrepreneurial innovations and productive private sector jobs to compete with monopolistic enterprises;
- Providing a long-term solution to unsustainable government and private debt; and
- Radically reducing the growing costs and dependency of citizens on government-created jobs and welfare.

These measures would leave more money in people's pockets so that they can meet their own needs without recourse to State aid or private charity as a result of taxing away the income people need to survive. Obviously we are not in a position even to suggest the amount of new capital formation that needs to take place in Ireland. Estimates for the United States, however, suggest that within two generations it should be possible for every child, woman, and man to have accumulated sufficient capital to provide an adequate and secure income for all family needs by means of capital ownership supplemented with labor income, rather than labor income supplemented with redistribution. There will always be the unfortunate and needy, of course, but these will be the exception rather than the rule.

Health Care, Income Maintenance, and Retirement Security

Just Third Way tax and monetary reforms would effectively address economic defects in the currently fragmented and costly health care system, and would enable all citizens to receive the care they need with minimal public sector and bureaucratic control. A family could afford to pay premiums for nationally standardized, comprehensive health care coverage offered by the private sector, with no exclusions. Needy families would receive a health voucher to pay for the same coverage. Capital credit would also be provided to health delivery systems and mutual health insurance companies owned and governed jointly by health care providers and subscribers.

The basic elements of a Just Third Way universal health coverage system would include:

- Pooling of risk. This is a basic principle of insurance: Spread out risk by pooling the entire population in the entire annual cost of health care, to determine the *per capita* cost for every individual.
- Health care coverage borne by the individual rather than the employer.
- Universal coverage with no exclusions.
- Standardized minimum insurance package.
- Required level of coverage.
- The means for citizens to choose and pay for their own health care providers through personal exemptions, de-

ductions, and deferrals to allow citizens to accumulate a viable estate of income-generating capital assets.
- Payment of all entitlements and other government spending at present levels from general revenues. This plan would eliminate any payroll tax on workers and employers, make dividends deductible to corporations, and balance the budget by substituting a single rate tax on non-exempt personal incomes from all sources.
- Government subsidies for researchers developing advances in medicine, with royalty-free licenses for companies producing and marketing future medical advances produced with taxpayer funds.

Vehicles for Changing the System

A number of private sector vehicles have been developed for implementing the transformation to a more just economy. These are based on the principles of binary economics and the free market. These include such innovations as Personal Ownership Accounts, Employee Stock Ownership Plans ("ESOPs"), Citizens Land and Natural Resource Banks, Homeowners' Equity Corporations, and Ownership Unions.

Personal Ownership Accounts (POAs)

In the United States we call these proposed tax-deferred accumulation vehicles, "Capital Homestead Accounts." In other proposals for countries where the homesteading concept is not part of the culture we call them "Economic Democracy Accounts."

The name doesn't really matter. What matters is that the concept of a personal tax deferred vehicle was developed to channel capital credit to citizens for private sector economic growth and to create private property stakes and ownership incomes for every person.

Each citizen could establish from the time of birth a tax-deferred account to provide him or her a dividend income for supplementing income from other sources and to provide for retirement. The tax system would also eliminate the traditional double taxation of corporate profits for companies paying out all future profits to their shareholders. This would maximize greater savings and private sector investments in new plant, equipment, infrastructure, rentable space and other income-generating capital assets and would remove other features that now discourage widespread ownership.

The discount window of the central bank would create new money and authorize the extension of interest-free capital credit, including only transaction costs and risk premiums. Member banks would serve as "capital credit irrigators" for financing faster rates of sustainable private sector growth. The new money would be asset-backed and channeled through bank-administered capital accumulation accounts to enable every citizen to receive equal quarterly or annual allotments to purchase new full-dividend payout shares issued to finance the economic growth. The loans would be privately insured by the pooling of risk premiums and repaid wholly out of pre-tax profits distributed on the new shares.

Employee Stock Ownership Plans (ESOPs)

Leveraged Employee Stock Ownership Plans (ESOPs) have changed the culture of many businesses around the world, turning over 10 million US workers into shareholders of 10,000 companies. ESOPs channel money power to corporate workers through self-liquidating capital credit, secured and repayable with the future profits that these worker-owners help generate. Lower-cost credit through capital accumulation accounts for workers and all members of their families would encourage more companies to add ESOPs to finance their acquisitions and growth in national and global markets.

The ESOP has been enacted into over twenty U.S. laws and is being used by over 10,000 companies in the United States, and increasingly in the United Kingdom and a growing number of other countries. What makes it different from other ways for workers to purchase ownership shares is that the ESOP enables many workers with little or no assets to gain an equity stake and share profits in the company in which they work — the workers pay for their shares out of future corporate profits, not by reducing their take-home incomes.

Citizens Land and Natural Resource Banks (CLNRBs)

For-profit Citizens Land and Natural Resource Banks would provide every citizen a single, lifetime, voting and income-earning ownership share in all land and other natural resources, as well as infrastructure. This would offer a Just

Third Way for planning and building new communities, or redeveloping low-income communities, under professional management. It would also give access to interest-free (but not cost-free) central bank financing for developing infrastructure and mining improvements.

The CLNRB is designed as a private-sector economic empowerment vehicle for all citizens who are permanent residents in a defined area of any size. It would replace typical land development corporations whose "urban removal" schemes often force out low-income residents unable to afford rising real estate costs associated with higher land values.

As a tax-deferred vehicle (similar to a leveraged Employee Stock Ownership Plan), the CLNRB would be able to receive interest-free money through the central banking system. This would enable the CLNRB to purchase land and other natural resources and build infrastructure, with the loans repaid by its land development and rental/user fee profits.

Every local citizen would automatically be a voting shareholder in this for-profit land development corporation and would share in ownership incomes from land rentals, natural resource extraction fees, and infrastructure user fees. Land now owned by government could be transferred free to its citizens through their CLNRBs. This would shift governance of natural resources from government to "We, the People."

The CLNRB can also link citizens as owners to the land and natural resources on a regional, national, and (eventually) even on a global basis. The CLNRB would have a representative board elected by citizen-shareholders for approving, financing and maintaining infrastructure projects, approving construction contracts under competitive bidding, and marketing to attract feasible new investment to the region. The CLNRB could also serve to build direct ownership and future development profits from natural resources into every citizen.

Homeowners' Equity Corporations (HECs)

A bold strategy developed to solve the home mortgage crisis — a crisis with serious repercussions throughout the world — is an innovative "rent to own" vehicle called the "Homeowners' Equity Corporation" or "HEC."

A HEC is a for-profit stock corporation whose shareholders would be homeowners in danger of foreclosure. HECs — and there should be many, to provide redundancy, lower risk, and ensure competition in a community — would purchase distressed properties at the current market value. HECs would obtain acquisition loans from commercial banks, which in turn would discount the loans at the central bank at a rate reflecting transaction costs and a revised risk premium. The homes could then be leased at a realistic market rate to their former owners or new tenants.

The tenant would earn shares in the HEC as lease payments were made, sufficient to cover debt service, maintenance, and taxes. When the loan principal on the acquisition loan for a particular property was fully paid, the tenant could exchange his or her HEC shares for title, or continue as a tenant/shareholder at a reduced lease payment, sufficient to cover maintenance and property taxes. Financing the purchase of properties through the central bank would cost taxpayers nothing and would be the first step in restoring a currency backed by hard assets instead of government debt. This pioneering alternative may require some enabling legislation to give it powers similar to those currently enjoyed by leveraged ESOPs.

Ownership Unions

An important goal of the Just Third Way is the transformation of Labor Unions into Ownership Unions. This would expand the mission of unions to reach out to and represent all new and future shareholders, including worker-owners. An Ownership Union is designed to work collaboratively with management to secure financing of advanced technologies and other new capital investments through capital accumulation accounts for all citizens. It is intended to represent a growing constituency of worker- and citizen-owners on governance rights issues as well as to help lower all barriers to accelerated and sustainable rates of green growth in a more democratically accountable corporate and financial sectors.

Ultimately, Ownership Unions will shift the source of worker incomes from inflation-inducing wage and benefit increases, to widespread distribution of growing profit and equity incomes to worker- and citizen-owners. This will enable companies to become more cost-competitive in global markets and to reduce the outsourcing of jobs to workers willing or forced to take lower wages.

Justice-Based Management (JBM)

Because of global and technological change, companies are recognizing that their survival and success will require changes in the way they do business. Increasingly, they are seeking new, more flexible ways of rewarding and motivating their workers while controlling costs and delivering ever-higher levels of value to their customers.

They are also realizing that these objectives are impeded by the adversarial nature of the surrounding economic and cultural environment. This is a byproduct of the inherent instability of the wage system and a corporate ownership system that is increasingly monopolized by a few. Businesses are coming to see that what is needed is a new way of thinking.

This new way of thinking would not reject the critical role of systems, but would redesign systems to put people first. It would create a new management approach that re-humanizes the workplace. It would shift power, responsibility and control over modern tools, advanced organizational systems, and enterprises from the few to every person affected by the process.

The new system would combine principles of equity (justice and ownership) with principles of efficiency, to raise the performance of an enterprise and its workers to their highest potential, in order to better serve their customers and other stakeholders. Instead of tapping into the wisdom, knowledge and creativity of only a few, the new system would recognize the advantages of drawing out and combining the wisdom, knowledge and creativity of every worker.

Some of the most progressive private sector firms have begun to implement successful new approaches for motivating workers, improving productivity and quality, facilitating change and maintaining continuity in their organization's culture. One comprehensive approach, developed by the Center for Economic and Social Justice (CESJ, is called "Justice-Based Management" or "JBM."

Justice-Based Management introduces within the workplace a microeconomic application of the Just Third Way.

Justice-Based Management (JBM) is a systems approach for creating sustainable cultures of ownership within all economic enterprises and institutions. JBM was developed to bring synergy where there is now conflict in productive enterprises facing global competition.

Justice-Based Management was conceived by ESOP pioneers to address the shortcomings in most worker-owned companies in America, where the rights, powers, and benefits of ownership remain concentrated in a small non-accountable *élite* controlling corporate and financial governance. JBM aims at substituting the conventional autocratic leadership philosophy with a servant leadership philosophy and a management system organized in accordance with the free market logic of binary economics and the universal principles of economic and social justice.

The ultimate purpose of JBM is to empower each person economically as a worker and as an owner, and to inspire all workers to work together to serve and maximize value to their customers. JBM embodies two precepts of equity: (1) that people are entitled to a proportionate share of what they helped to produce, both with their labor and their productive assets; and (2) that all people are entitled to live in a culture that offers them equality of dignity and opportunity, with equal access to the means of acquiring property and power to secure their fundamental rights.

Components of JBM

Justice-Based Management combines the quality, educational and participation aspects of Total Quality Management and Open Book Management, with the equity and ownership concepts underlying ESOPs. JBM provides a system of participatory structures and processes for diffusing power down to the level of each person in the company. JBM also offers workers an opportunity to participate as first-class shareholders in the company's governance, equity growth, and in monthly and annual profits on a profit center basis.

Under present expanded ownership laws, a JBM system incorporates an employee stock ownership plan (ESOP), individual and team performance feedback (*e.g.*, frequent and formula-based cash profit sharing), ownership education and sharing of financial information, and structured participatory management (including the right to vote one's shares to elect representatives to the company's board of directors). JBM also reinforces within ongoing information, communications, and education programs, a broad understanding by all worker-shareholders of the interdependency among every person, department, and profit center in serving the customer and competing in the marketplace.

Experience has shown that within a true culture of ownership, workers become empowered to make better decisions, discipline their own behavior, and work together more effectively as a team. Because each person contributes, risks and shares as an owner, as well as a worker, JBM helps unite everyone's self interest around the company's bottom line and shared vision and values. As such democratically owned and organized enterprises begin to multiply (encouraged by an institutional environment that universalizes access to credit for capital ownership), a more free and just market system can take root and thrive for the benefit of every child, woman, and man in Ireland, and serve as a model for people throughout the world who desire economic and social as well as political freedom.

Bibliography

Buro Staire Mileata 1913-21
Statements By Witnesses (Document Number)

Berkeley, George F. H. [Fitz-Hardinge], (971, 994)
Caldwell, Patrick (638)
Cosgrave, Liam T. (268)
Dalton, Charles (434)
De Róiste, Liam (1698)
Henderson, Ruaidhri (1686)
Hughes, Julia (880)
Ingoldsby, William (582)
Joyce, Colonel J[ohn] V. (1,762)
Kearns, Daniel (1,124)
Little, Patrick J. (1,769)
Lynch, Diarmuid (120)
Lynch, Judge Fionán (192)
Mac Diarmada, Séamus (768)
Neligan, David (380)
Noyk, Michael (707)
O'Brien, Nora Connolly (286)
O'Brien, William (1,766)
O'Duffy, Francis (654)
O'Doherty, Kitty (355)
O'Donoghue, Michael V. (1,741)
O'Farrell, Senator Séamus (193)
O'Kelly J[ohn] J[oseph] "Sceilg" (384)
O'Reilly, Bridie (454)
Robinson, Séumas (156)
Shouldice, John F. (162)
Wyse-Power, Dr. Nancy (587)

Newspapers, Journals, and Periodicals

The Age (Melbourne)
American Whig Review
Belfast News-Letter
Boston Evening Transcript
Bridgeport Morning News
The Century
Cork Examiner
Daily Advertiser (London, Ontario)
The Day (New London, CT)
Deseret News (Salt Lake City)
Examiner (Charlottetown, Prince Edward Island)
Glasgow Herald
The Gleaner (Northumberland and Kent)
Harper's New Monthly Magazine
Meriden Morning Record (Meriden, CT)
Milwaukee Journal
Milwaukee Sentinel
Montreal Daily Mail
Montreal Gazette
Montreal Herald
New Era (Montreal)
The Newfoundlander
New York Times
Ottawa Citizen
Pittsburg Press (PA)
Quebec Daily Telegraph
Quebec Saturday Budget
Reading Eagle (PA)
St. John Daily Sun (New Brunswick)
Sarnia Observer (Ontario)

Newspapers, etc., cont.

The Head Quarters (Fredericton, New Brunswick)
Huron Expositor (Seaforth, Ontario)
Irish Canadian (Toronto)
Irish Independent
Irish News
Irish Times
Lewiston Daily Sun (ME)
The Living Age
The London Times
Mackenzie's British, Irish, and Canadian Gazette (NY)
Sydney Mail
Sydney Morning Herald
Spectator
Toledo Blade
Toronto Daily Mail
Toronto World
True Witness and Catholic Chronicle (Montreal)
Votes for Women
Wall Street Journal
Washington Post

General

Articles, Pamphlets, Miscellaneous

Merwin, Henry Childs, "The Irish in American Life," *The Atlantic Monthly*, March 1896, 289-301.

Redmond, John E., "Ireland Since '98," *The North American Review*, April 1898, 385-397.

Books

Butt, Isaac, *The Problem of Irish Education: An Attempt at Its Solution*. London: Longmans, Green, and Co., 1875.

Cronin, Mike, *Irish History for Dummies*. Chichester, West Sussex, U.K., 2006.

Ellis, Peter Berresford, *Eyewitness to Irish History*. Hoboken, New Jersey: John Wiley & Sons, Inc., 2004.

FitzGerald, Redmond, *Cry Blood, Cry Erin*. New York: Clarkson N. Potter, Inc., Publisher, 1966.

Lyons, F[rancis] S[tewart] L[eland], *Ireland Since the Famine*. London: Fontana Paperbacks, 1973.

Kee, Robert, *Ireland: A History*. Boston, Massachusetts: Little, Brown and Company, 1982.

MacManus, Seamus, *The Story of the Irish Race: A Popular History of Ireland*. Old Greenwich, Connecticut: Devin-Adair, 1921.

Moody, T.W., and Martin, F.X., editors, *The Course of Irish History*. Boulder, Colorado: Roberts Rinehart Publishers, 1994.

Ó Faoláin, Seán, *The Story of the Irish People*. New York: Avenel Books, 1982.

Sullivan, A[lexander] M[artin], *The Story of Ireland for Young and Old, Illustrated*. New York: Henry McIlroy, 1883.

Tansill, Charles Callan, *America and the Fight for Irish Freedom 1866-1922, An Old Story Based Upon New Data*. New York: The Devin-Adair Co., 1957.

Easter Rising and Civil War

Articles, Pamphlets, Miscellaneous

Sheehy-Skeffington, F[rancis]., *A Forgotten Small Nationality: Ireland and the War*. New York: The Donnelly Press (1916).

Sheehy-Skeffington, Hanna, *British Imperialism as I Have Known It*. New York: The Donnelly Press (No Date).

Stephens, James, *The Insurrection in Dublin* (1916).

Stokes, Lillian, *The Personal Experience of Miss L. Stokes During the Sinn Féin Rebellion of 1916*. Trinity College Library, IE TCD MS 11507.

Books

Caulfield, Max, *The Easter Rebellion: Dublin 1916*. Boulder, Colorado: Roberts Reinhart Publishers, 1995.

Chesterton, Gilbert Keith, *Irish Impressions*. New York: John Lane Company, 1920.

Coogan, Tim Pat, *1916, The Easter Rising*. London: Phoenix, 2005.

Dangerfield, George, *The Damnable Question: A Study in Anglo-Irish Relations*. Boston, Massachusetts: Little, Brown and Company, 1976.

De Rosa, Peter, *Rebels: The Irish Rising of 1916*. New York: Ballantine Books, 1990.

Duff, Charles, *Six Days to Shake an Empire*. New York: A.S. Barnes and Co., Inc., 1966.

Fitzgerald, Redmond, *Cry Blood, Cry Erin*. New York: Clarkson Potter, 1966.

Irish Times, *Sinn Féin Rebellion Handbook, Easter 1916*. London: G.W. Bacon and Co., Ltd., 1917.

Sean O'Casey, *Autobiography, Volume 3, Drums Under the Windows*. London: Pan Books, Ltd., 1972.

Severn, Bill, Irish *Statesman and Rebel: The Two Lives of Eamon de Valera*. New York: Ives Washburn, Inc., 1970.

Tansill, Charles Callan, *America and the Fight for Irish Freedom, 1866-1922*. New York: Devin-Adair Co., 1957.

Townshend, Charles, *Easter 1916 — The Irish Rebellion*. London: Penguin Books, Ltd., 2006.

Vane, Sir Francis Fletcher, *Agin the Governments: Memories and Adventures of Sir Francis Fletcher Vane, BT*. London: Sampson Low, Marston and Co. (1929).

Ward, Alan J., *The Easter Rising: Revolution and Irish Nationalism*. Arlington Heights, Illinois: Harlan Davidson, Inc., 1980.

Younger, Calton, *Ireland's Civil War*. Glasgow, UK: William Collins & Sons, Ltd., 1979.

Union and Emancipation

Geoghegan, Patrick M., *King Dan: The Rise of Daniel O'Connell, 1775-1829*. Dublin, Éire: Gill and Macmillan, 2010.

Gwynn, Denis, *Daniel O'Connell, Revised Centenary Edition*. Oxford, UK: Cork University Press, 1938.

Luby, T[homas] C[larke], *The Life and Times of Daniel O'Connell*. London: R. &. T. Washbourne, Ltd., *cir.* 1870.

MacDonagh, Michael, *The Home Rule Movement*. Dublin, Éire: The Talbot Press, 1920.

MacDonagh, Oliver, *O'Connell: The Life of Daniel O'Connell 1775-1847*. (Omnibus volume based on *The Hereditary Bondsman* and *The Emancipist*.) London: Weidenfeld and Nicolson, 1991.

MacDonagh, Oliver, *The Emancipist: Daniel O'Connell, 1830-1847*. London: Weidenfeld and Nicolson, 1989.

MacDonagh, Oliver, *The Hereditary Bondsman: Daniel O'Connell, 1775-1829*. New York: St. Martin's Press, 1987.

Ó Faoláin, Seán, *King of the Beggars*. Dublin, Éire: Poolbeg Press, Ltd., 1980.

O'Ferrall, Fergus, *Gill's Irish Lives: Daniel O'Connell*. Dublin, Éire: Gill and Macmillan, 1981.

An Gorta Mór

Articles, Pamphlets, Miscellaneous

Anonymous, "British Policy Here and There: Who Feed England?" *The American Whig Review*, December 1850, 633-656.

Anonymous, "Foreign Immigration: Its Natural and Extraordinary Causes; Its Connection with the Famine in Ireland, and Scarcity in Other Countries," *The American Whig Review*, April 1848, 419-431.

Thanet, Octave, "An Irish Gentlewoman in the Famine Time," *The Century*, January 1891, 338-349.

Books

Gallagher, Thomas, *Paddy's Lament, Ireland 1846-1847: Prelude to Hatred*. New York: Harcourt Brace Jovanovich, Publishers, 1982.

Kinealy, Christine, *This Great Calamity: The Irish Famine, 1845-1852*. Dublin: Gill and Macmillan, 1995.

Woodham-Smith, Cecil, *The Great Hunger* New York: Harper & Row, Publishers, 1962

Young Ireland and the Fenians

Articles, Pamphlets, Miscellaneous

Anonymous, "A Vision of Repeal," *The Living Age*, April 5, 1845.

Anonymous, "Correspondence," *The Living Age*, October 19, 1844.

Anonymous, "Young Ireland — The Nation," *The Living Age*, August 10, 1844.

Anonymous, "Too Modest by Half," *The Living Age*, May 23, 1846.

Cobb, Frances Power, "The Fenian 'Idea'," *The Atlantic Monthly*, May 1866, 572-577.

Mitchel, John, "Old Ireland and Young Ireland," *The United States Democratic Review*. August 1848, 149-158.

Books

Duffy, Charles Gavan, *Young Ireland, A Fragment of Irish History, 1840-1850*. CreateSpace Independent Publishing Platform, 2014.

Eagleton, Terry, *Scholars and Rebels in Nineteenth-Century Ireland*. Oxford, UK: Blackwell Publishers, Ltd., 1999.

Gwynn, Denis Rolleston, *Young Ireland and 1848*. Oxford, U.K.: Cork University Press, 1949.

O'Hegarty, P.S., *John Mitchel: An Appreciation with Some Account of Young Ireland*. Dublin, Éire: Maunsel and Company, Limited, 1917.

Quinn, James, *Young Ireland and the Writing of Irish History*. Dublin, Éire: University College Dublin Press, 2015.

The Land War

Articles, Pamphlets, Miscellaneous

Adams, Henry Carter, "The Irish Land Question," *The New Englander and Yale Review*, January 1881, 68-85.

Balfour, Arthur James, "The New House of Commons and the Irish Question," *The North American Review*, December 1892, 641-651.

Butt, Isaac, *The Irish Querist: A Series of Questions Proposed for the Consideration of All Who Desire to Solve the Problem of Ireland's Social Condition*. Dublin, Éire: John Falconer, 1867.

Corrigan, Michael A., *Private Record of the Case of Rev. Edward McGlynn*, ms. cir. 1898, Seton Hall University Archives.

Davitt, Michael, *The Land League Proposal: A Statement for Honest and Thoughtful Men*. Glasgow, Scotland: Cameron and Ferguson, 1882.

George, Henry, *The Irish Land Question: What It Involves and How It Can Be Solved, An Appeal to the Land Leagues* (1881), a.k.a., *The Land Question: Viewpoint and Counter Viewpoint on the Need for Land Reform*.

George, Henry, "England and Ireland," *The North American Review*, February 1886, 185-193.

George, Henry, *The Condition of Labor, An Open Letter to Pope Leo XIII* (1891).

Leo XIII, *Saepe Nos* ("On Boycotting in Ireland"), 1888.

McQuaid, Bernard John, Correspondence of Bishop Bernard John McQuaid, University of Notre Dame Archives.

O'Reilly, John Boyle, "At Last!" *The North American Review*, January 1886, 104-110.

Parnell, Charles Stewart, "Mr. Balfour's Land Bill," *The North American Review*, June, 1890, 665-670.

Parnell, Charles Stewart, "The Irish Land Question," *The North American Review*, April, 1880, 388-406.

Plunkett, Horace, "The Irish Land Question in a New Light," *The North American Review*, January 1898, 107-120.

Turner, Frederick Jackson, "The Significance of the Frontier in American History," *Annual Report of the American Historical Association for the Year 1893*. Washington, DC: Government Printing Office, 1894.

Books

Bew, Paul, *Gill's Irish Lives: C.S. Parnell*. Dublin, Éire: Gill and Macmillan, 1980.

Burton, David H., *Holmes-Sheehan Correspondence: The Letters of Justice Oliver Wendell Holmes and Canon Patrick Augustine Sheehan*. Port Washington, New York: Kennikat Press, 1976.

Butt, Isaac, *The Irish People and the Irish Land: A Letter to Lord Lifford*. Dublin: John Falconer, 1867.

Butt, Isaac, *The Poor-Law Bill for Ireland Examined*. London: B. Fellowes, 1837.

Desmond, A.J., "America's Land Question," *The North American Review*. February 1886, 153-158.

George, Henry, *Progress and Poverty* (1879).

Heuser, Herman J., *Canon Sheehan of Doneraile: The Story of an Irish Parish Priest as Told Chiefly by Himself in Books Personal Memoirs and Letters*. London: Longmans, Green and Co., 1917.

Linehan, M. P., *Canon Sheehan of Doneraile, Priest, Novelist, Man of Letters*. Dublin, Éire: The Talbot Press, Limited, 1952.

Lyons, F[rancis] S[tewart] L[eland], *Charles Stewart Parnell*. New York: Oxford University Press, 1977.

O'Brien, Conor Cruise, *Parnell and His Party, 1880-1890*. London: Oxford University Press, 1957.

O'Brien, Richard Barry, *The Life of Charles Stewart Parnell* (Volumes I and II). New York: Greenwood Press, Publishers, 1969.

Thornton, William Thomas, *Over-Population and Its Remedy*. London: Longman, Brown, Green, and Longmans, 1846.

Home Rule

Articles, Pamphlets, Miscellaneous

Argyll, Duke of, "English Elections and Home Rule," *The North American Review*, August 1892, 129-135.

Brown, Edward, "The Irish Party," *Harper's New Monthly Magazine*, August 1887, 421-429.

Clarke, William, "Charles Stewart Parnell," *The New England Magazine*, October 1889, 190-200.

Donoughmore, Earl of, "The House of Lords and the Home Rule Bill," *The North American Review*, September 1893, 298-306.

Gladstone, W. E., "A Vindication of Home Rule. A Reply to the Duke of Argyll," *The North American Review*, October 1892, 385-394.

Hewitt, H., "Irish Home Rule Agitation: Its History and Issues," *The Bay State Monthly*, February 1886, 157-168.

Knox, Rev. Ronald A., *Reunion All Round, or Jael's Hammer Laid Aside, and the Milk of Human Kindness Beaten Up Into Butter and Served in a Lordly Dish, Being a Plea for the Inclusion within the Church of England of all Mahometans, Jews, Buddhists, Brahmins, Papists and Atheists, submitted to the consideration of the British Public* (1914).

Lecky, W[illiam]. E[dward]. H[artpole]., "Why Home Rule is Undesirable," *The North American Review*, March 1891, 349-370.

M'Carthy [McCarthy], Justin, "New Parties in Parliament," *The North American Review*. April 1894, 401-411.

McCarthy, Justin, "The Home Rulers in the English Parliament," *The Galaxy*, February 1876, 164-171.

McDonnell, Michael F.J., *Ireland and the Home Rule Movement*. Dublin, Ireland: Maunsel, 1908.

Parnell, Charles Stewart, *Manifesto to the Irish in Britain*. November 21, 1885.

Pierrepont, Edwards, "Lord Beaconsfield and the Irish Question," *The North American Review*. December 1888, 669-679.

Russell, T[homas] W[allace], "Root Difficulties of Irish Government," *The North American Review*, January 1897, 50-65.

St. Loe Strachey, [John], "Ulster and Home Rule," *The Living Age*, July 23, 1892, reprinted from *The Nineteenth Century*.

Sullivan, Alexander [Martin], "Parnell as a Leader," *The North American Review*, June 1887, 609-624.

Sullivan, Margaret F., "Home Rule and Culture," *The Century*, December 1888, 317-318.

Wheatley, Richard, "Home Rule in the Isle of Man," *Harper's New Monthly Magazine*, September 1887, 513-520.

Books

Butt, Isaac, *Home Government for Ireland: Irish Federalism! Its Meaning, Its Objects, and Its Hopes*. Dublin, Éire, John Falconer, 1871.

Dicey, Albert Venn, *A Fool's Paradise: Being a Constitutionalist's Criticism of the Home Rule Bill of 1912*. London: John Murray, 1913.

Dicey, Albert Venn, *A Leap in the Dark: A Criticism of the Principles of Home Rule as Illustrated by the Bill of 1893*. London: John Murray, 1911.

Dicey, Albert Venn, *Why England Maintains the Union: A Popular Rendering of England's Case Against Home Rule*. London: John Murray, 1887.

Hammond, J.L, and Foot, M.R.D., *Gladstone and Liberalism*. New York: Collier Books, 1966.

Hammond, J.L., Gladstone and the Irish Nation. London: Frank Cass and Co., Ltd., 1964.

Jackson, Alvin, *Home Rule: An Irish History, 1800-2000*. Oxford, U.K.: Oxford University Press, 2003.

Lecky, William Edward Hartpole, *Historical and Political Essays*. London: Longmans, Green, and Co., 1908.

Loughlin, James, *Gladstone: Home Rule and the Ulster Question, 1882-93*. Dublin, Éire: Gill and Macmillan, Ltd., 1986.

MacManus, Seamus, *Ireland's Case*. New York: The Irish Publishing Co., 1919.

St. Loe Strachey, John, *The Adventure of Living: A Subjective Autobiography*. New York: G.P. Putnam, 1922.

Thornley, David, *Isaac Butt and Home Rule*. London: MacGibbon & Kee, 1964.

The Just Third Way

Articles, Pamphlets, Miscellaneous

Ferree, Rev. William J., S.M., Ph.D., *Introduction to Social Justice*. New York: Paulist Press, 1948.

Greaney, Michael D. (2015), "The Business Cycle: A Kelsonian Analysis," *American Journal of Economics and Sociology*, 74: 379–418.

Greaney, Michael D., "Pope Francis and the Just Third Way," *Homiletic and Pastoral Review*, June 2015.

Kelso, Louis O., "Karl Marx: The Almost Capitalist," *American Bar Association Journal*, March 1957.

Kurland, Norman G., "A New Look at Prices and Money: A Kelsonian Binary Model for Achieving Rapid Growth Without Inflation," *The Journal of Socio-Economics*, Vol.30 pgs. 495-515

Books

Ashford, Robert H.A., and Shakespeare, Rodney, *Binary Economics: The New Paradigm*. Lanham, Maryland: The University Press of America, 1999.

Crosskey, William Winslow, *Politics and the Constitution in the History of the United States*. Chicago, Illinois: University of Chicago Press, 1953.

Ferree, Rev. William J., S.M., Ph.D., *The Act of Social Justice*. Washington, DC: The Catholic University of America Press, 1943.

Kurland, Norman G., Brohawn, Dawn K., and Greaney, Michael D., *Capital Homesteading for Every Citizen: A Just Free Market Solution for Saving Social Security*. Arlington, Virginia: Economic Justice Media, 2004.

Miller, Rev. John H., *Curing World Poverty: The New Role of Property*. St. Louis, Missouri: Social Justice Review, 1994.

Habiger, Matthew, O.S.B., Ph.D., *Papal Teachings on Private Property, 1891-1981*. Lanham, Maryland: University Press of America, 1990.

Kelso, Louis O., and Adler, Mortimer J., *The Capitalist Manifesto*. New York: Random House, 1958.

Kelso, Louis O., and Adler, Mortimer J., *The New Capitalists: A Proposal to Free Economic Growth from the Slavery of Savings*. New York: Random House, 1961.

Index

Act of Union, 3, 90, 92, 101, 102, 111, 114, 121, 139, 141, 171
Adler, Mortimer J., 220, 221
American Irish Historical Society, 72
Ancient Order of Hibernians, 5
Asgard, 10
Ashbourne Act, 172, 173, 178, 183
Asquith, Herbert Henry (Prime Minister), 3, 8, 11, 59, 70, 71, 189
Aud, 18, 19, 20, 22, 23, 35
Auxiliary Division ("Auxies"), 76, 77, 78
Bachelor's Walk killings, 11
Bagehot, Walter, 106, 154, 173
Balfour, Arthur James, 175-189
Balfour, Gerald William, 187
Bank Charter Act of 1844, 107, 121, 154, 230
Bank of England, 85, 107, 231
Banking Principle, 230
banks, banking, 26, 34, 44, 85, 91, 106, 107, 121, 154, 230-239
Battle of Fishguard ("Last Invasion of Britain"), 83, 84, 89
Biggar, Joseph Gillis, 140, 141, 143
Birrell, Augustine, 13, 14, 187
Black and Tans, 76, 77
Blavatsky, Helena Petrovna, 16, 168
Bloody Sunday, 77, 78, 213

Bowen-Colthurst, Cpt. John Colthurst, 37-42, 53, 58-62, 66-73
boycotting, 76, 146, 175-176
British Empire, 2, 3, 23, 53, 75, 79, 106, 119, 154
Brugha, Cathal, 33, 49, 207
Butt, Isaac, 124, 136-142, 226, 229
capital credit insurance, 232
Carson, Sir Edward Henry, 4-17, 21, 54, 75, 79, 175, 189
Casement, Sir Roger David, 5, 18, 20, 35, 55
Catholic Church, 6, 28, 95, 97, 104, 122, 127, 131, 163, 165, 178-181
Catholic Defense Association, 128
Catholic Defense League, 127
Catholic Emancipation, 87, 88, 89, 91, 92, 95, 96-101, 102, 104, 111
Catholic hierarchy, 57, 95, 97, 127, 131, 139, 146, 151, 163, 165, 173, 176, 178, 179, 183, 184
Ceannt, Éamonn, 21, 25, 33
Celtic Revival/Twilight, 128, 169-170, 185
Childers, Robert Erskine, 10
Citizens Land and Natural Resource Banks (CLNRB), 236, 237-238

Clan na Gael, 6, 142-143, 167
Clarke, Thomas, 6, 16, 17, 21, 25, 53, 55, 74, 143, 167, 196, 199, 200
Coade, James J., 38, 68
Cobbett, William, 98, 99, 229
Coercion Bills and Acts, 105, 116, 147, 149, 151, 156, 157, 161, 162, 182
Collins, Michael, 47, 77, 79, 80, 200, 204, 205, 208, 214
common good, 1, 30, 117, 123, 171, 221, 222-226
Connolly, James, 7, 14, 15, 16, 17, 21, 25, 26, 27, 28, 47, 48, 55, 74, 198
Corrigan, Michael A, Archbishop, 177, 178, 179
Cosgrave, William Thomas, 71
Craig, James, 4, 189
Croke Park ("Bloody Sunday"), 77, 213
Croke, Thomas William, Archbishop, 152, 157
Cumann na mBan, 30, 198
Curragh "Mutiny", 8-11, 74, 217
Currency Principle, 107, 230
Dáil Éireann, 58, 75, 79, 80, 209
Daly, Edward, 26, 27, 33, 43, 47, 48, 59, 64, 65
Daly, John, 6
Davis, Thomas, 112, 113, 123

Davitt, Michael, 144-166, 179, 185, 218
Deasy, Thomas, 133
Devoy, John, 6, 131, 132, 143, 144, 145, 148
Dicey, Albert Venn, 173-174
Dillon, John, 142, 146, 148-151, 159-161, 175, 177, 185, 187
Dillon, John Blake, 112, 113, 124, 125
Disraeli, Benjamin (Prime Minister), 112, 135, 140, 146
Duffy, Charles Gavan, 112, 113, 123, 124, 127, 129
Easter Proclamation, 2, 8, 16, 27-30, 58, 75, 218
Easter Rising, 1-81, 83, 93, 94, 123, 134, 143, 167, 186, 190, 194, 196, 217, 218, 221
Emmet, Robert, 92-94
Employee Stock Ownership Plans (ESOPs), 236, 237, 239, 241
Established Church, 12, 89, 90, 104, 105
Famine, Great (An Gorta Mór), 114-153, 217, 226, 229
Fenian Rising (1867), 6, 132-133, 135, 142, 156
Fenians, 6, 38, 128-134, 135-146, 156, 164-167, 177
Ferree, Rev. William J., 217, 221, 222, 223, 224, 225, 226
Fitzgerald, Lord Edward, 89, 187
Forster, William Edward, 147, 148, 160

Four Courts, 26, 27, 33, 34, 43, 45-46, 47, 48, 49, 59-66
Four Pillars, 218, 219
Friend, Major-General Sir Lovick Bransby, 13, 14
Gaelic League, 5, 15, 192, 205
General Post Office (GPO), 2, 4, 23, 27, 30, 31, 32, 33, 34, 43, 47, 48, 191, 196, 197, 198, 199
George, Henry, 159, 160, 161-166, 169, 177-181, 217
Germany, 9, 10, 12, 18, 19, 55
Gladstone, William Ewart (Prime Minister), 134-137, 139-150, 151, 153,-155, 156, 160, 161, 170-174, 175, 181, 183-185, 187
Grattan, Henry, 87, 96, 97
Griffith, Arthur, 39, 74, 79, 80
Home Rule, 2-12, 15, 16, 17, 27, 54, 74, 75, 78, 126, 128, 134, 136-142, 145, 149, 153, 158, 159-190, 226, 229
Home Rule League, 139-142
Homeowners Equity Corporation (HEC), 238, 239
hostage taking, 38, 39, 46, 62, 64, 70, 77, 96, 125
Igoe Gang, 78, 215
institutions, 1, 111, 116, 117, 136, 150, 155, 171, 220, 221, 222, 224, 225, 230, 234, 241

Intelligence Squad ("The Squad"), 77, 208-210, 215
Ireland, 132
Irish Citizen Army (ICA), 2, 7, 14-17, 21, 23, 25-27, 31, 175
Irish National Federation, 185
Irish National Land League, 127, 145-166
Irish National League, 166, 172, 182-185
Irish Question, 3, 114, 135-158, 160, 167, 171, 182, 218
Irish Republican Army (IRA), 58, 75, 77, 79, 80, 191, 205, 206, 212, 213, 216
Irish Republican Brotherhood (IRB), 6, 13-19, 28, 31, 93, 128, 129, 141, 143, 167, 191, 205-207
Irish Transport and General Workers Union (ITGWU), 7
Irish Volunteers, 2, 5-35, 43-53, 56, 58, 62,-65, 71, 73, 78, 79, 87, 103, 175, 191, 192, 197, 199, 200, 204, 206, 207
Irish Volunteers, Ascendency, 87
Irish Women's Franchise League (IWFL), 3, 37
Just Third Way, 218, 230-240
justice, distributive, 220, 221
justice, economic, 220
justice, participative, 220, 221
justice, social, 1, 29, 30, 81, 103, 105, 111, 117, 136-138, 150, 177, 217, 218, 221-226, 241

Index

Justice-Based Management (JBM), 240-242
Kelly, Thomas J., 132
Kelso, Louis O., 220, 221, 228, 229, 230, 251
Kent, Thomas, 50
Keogh, William, 128
Kickham, Charles, 130, 131
Kilmainham Jail, 94, 156, 157, 159, 161
Kilmainham Treaty, 157-161, 166
Kitchener, Horatio Herbert, 12, 70
Lalor, James Fintan, 99, 121-123, 126, 128, 143, 144
Land Bills, 147, 151, 153, 155, 158
Land Question, 137, 144, 158
Land Wars, 145
Larkin, James, 7
Law, Andrew Bonar, 5, 9, 189
Liberty Hall, 7, 27, 32, 195
Lloyd George, 78, 79
Lowe, Major-General William Henry Muir, 48, 49, 61, 65
Luby, Thomas Clarke, 126, 129-131
MacBride, John, 55
MacCurtain, Tomás, 19, 22, 23
MacDermott, Seán, 21, 25, 193, 194, 200, 205
MacDiarmada, Seán, 55
MacDonagh, Thomas, 17, 21, 25, 33
MacNeill, Eoin, 5, 6, 13, 15-17, 21-23, 33, 56
MacSwiney, Terence, 19, 20, 22, 23
Malthus, Rev. Thomas, 117-120
Malthusian theory, 119
Manchester Martyrs, 133, 141
Markievicz, Constance Georgine Gore-Booth, Countess, 32, 56
Maxwell, Gen. Sir John Grenfell, 44-45, 50, 54-66, 70-73, 217
McGlynn, Rev. Edward, 178-181
McLoughlin, John, 47, 48, 65, 199
McQuaid, Bernard John, Bishop, 177, 179
Meagher, Thomas Francis, 114, 124
Mitchel, John, 116, 123, 124, 126, 128
modernism, 168
Monteith, Robert, 18, 20
Morrison, Charles, 154, 229
Moulton, Harold G., 229, 230
Nathan, Sir Matthew, 13, 14
Nationalists, 3, 5, 8, 9, 11, 12, 38, 39, 57, 68, 73-76, 109, 115, 124, 128, 134, 135, 139, 141, 142, 151, 155, 169, 170, 173, 183, 185, 188, 226
New Departure, 142, 144, 145, 149, 157
Newman, John Henry, Cardinal, 105
No Rent Manifesto, 157, 175
North King Street, 43, 45-46, 47, 48, 49, 53, 58, 59-66, 67, 71, 73
Nulty, Thomas, Bishop, 162-165, 179
O'Brien, Conor Cruise, 157, 185
O'Donovan Rossa, Jeremiah, 129, 131
O'Brien, James, Police Officer, 26
O'Brien, William, 155, 157, 161, 171, 175, 177, 180, 181
O'Casey, Seán, 2, 23
O'Connell, Daniel, 102
O'Connell, Daniel ("The Emancipator"), 95-143, 154, 217
O'Dwyer, Bishop Edward Thomas, 57, 64
O'Farrell, Elizabeth (Nurse), 37, 48, 49
O'Leary, John, 130, 131, 143
O'Loughlin, Rev. Francis E., 69
O'Rahilly, Michael Joseph, "The O'Rahilly", 47
O'Shea, Cpt. William Henry, 161, 184
O'Shea, Katharine, 157, 160, 184
Orange Order, Lodges, 5, 75, 88, 109, 167, 188
ownership, 29, 99, 114, 118, 121, 136, 144, 145, 153-157, 159, 162, 165, 185, 187, 188, 218-220, 226-242
Ownership Unions, 236, 239
Oxford Movement, 105
Parliament, British, 2, 3, 4, 8, 15, 26, 74, 78, 79, 87, 90, 94, 98, 100, 101, 104, 106, 108, 127, 135-138, 140-142, 144, 146-147, 149-151, 155, 174, 182, 184, 189
Parliament, Irish, 3, 75, 87, 90, 91, 96, 137, 138, 188, 189
Parnell, Charles Stewart, 126, 141-219, 229

Parnellites, 147-149, 151, 152, 185, 187
Pearse, Pádraic (Patrick) Henry, 15-17, 21-32, 47-50, 53, 54, 58, 64-66, 74, 196, 198, 199
Pearse, William, 198, 199
Pearse, William, 55
Peel, Sir Robert, 8, 97, 101, 102, 107-110, 116, 121, 154, 230
Personal Ownership Accounts, 236
Phoenix Park, 33, 130, 160, 208
Phoenix Society, 129, 130
Pitt, Sir William ("the Younger"), 85, 88, 90-92, 95
Plan of Campaign, 174-177, 180-183
Plunkett, Joseph, 17, 18, 21, 25, 55, 200
Pope Leo XIII, 136, 163-165, 176-178, 219
Pope Pius XI, 136, 138, 177, 225
Power, John O'Connor, 141, 143
principles of economic justice, 218, 220
property, 26, 28, 86, 101, 114, 121-123, 162-165, 171, 173, 218-220, 226, 233, 236, 239, 241
Quakers, 117
Redmond, John Edward, 6, 11-13, 15, 17, 74, 78, 185, 187, 189, 192
Repeal movement, 92, 97, 101-110, 111-114, 123-139, 143, 154, 247
Rerum Novarum, 153, 164, 165, 177, 179, 181, 219

Roosevelt, Theodore, 72, 178
Royal Irish Constabulary (RIC), 8, 14, 20, 35, 43, 44, 48, 50, 75, 76, 77, 105, 125
Saepe Nos, 176, 185
Say's Law, 228-230
Sheehan, Canon, 132, 177
Sheehy-Skeffington, Francis, 3, 11, 22, 36-40, 58, 67
Sheehy-Skeffington, Hanna, 3, 4, 36, 67-72
Shouldice, Frank, 44
Shouldice, John (Seán), 27, 44, 65
Simon Commission, 73
Sinn Féin, 2, 3, 20, 21, 39, 42, 74-77, 213
Smith O'Brien, William, 113, 123-128, 137
socialism, 15, 17, 28, 29, 57, 74, 113, 122, 128, 131, 144, 162-178, 186, 221
socialism, Fabian, 16, 17, 74, 113, 169, 186
Stephens, James (Fenian), 128, 129, 130, 131, 132
Stephens, James (Poet), 16, 47, 53, 67
subsidiarity, 1, 225
Tammany Hall, 143, 178
theosophy, New Age, 16, 113, 128, 131, 167-169, 185
Thornton, William Thomas, 119-121, 229
Tone, Wolfe, 83, 90
Tudor, Major-General Henry Hugh, 77-78, 211-215
Ulster, 4-12, 75-88, 189

Ulster Volunteer Force (UVF), 4-12, 17, 21, 75
Unionists, 3-12, 38, 39, 54, 74-76, 174, 175, 187-189
United Irishmen, 83, 87-89, 93, 94
United Kingdom, 2, 3, 91, 98, 111, 187, 237
United Nations Universal Declaration of Human Rights, 219
United States of America, 6, 18, 20, 54, 55, 71, 87, 94, 105, 108, 124, 129-132, 138, 142-146, 149, 153-156, 165, 166, 173, 174, 235-237
Valera, Éamon de ("Dev"), 28, 32-34, 42, 47-50, 55, 56, 59, 64, 65, 73, 74, 79, 80, 141
Vane, Sir Francis Fletcher, 8, 40, 41, 62, 67-72
Virginia Declaration of Rights, 28, 218
Volunteers, National, 13
Wellington, Arthur Wellesley, Duke of, 95, 100, 101
Whigs, 104, 105, 108, 127
Wimborne, Lord, Ivor Churchill Guest, 13, 14
Wyndham, George, 95, 187
Year of the French (1798), 87-99, 113, 156
Yeats, William Butler, 32, 34
Young Ireland, 111-114, 121-126, 136, 137, 169, 185
Young Ireland movement, 129

About the Author

Michael D. Greaney is Director of Research for the interfaith Center for Economic and Social Justice (CESJ) in Arlington, Virginia, U.S.A., and a Certified Public Accountant. A graduate of the University of Notre Dame, Mr. Greaney is a member of the Ancient Order of Hibernians, Colonel John Fitzgerald Division No. 1 in Arlington, and of American Mensa, Ltd.

Mr. Greaney's articles have appeared in *Homiletic and Pastoral Review*, *Social Justice Review*, *The American Journal of Economics and Sociology*, *Military History*, *Military Heritage*, and *Learning Through History*. He also contributed a number of articles to ABC-CLIO's *The Great Depression and the New Deal* (2009) and SAGE Publications' *Encyclopedia of Politics in the American West* (2013). He won the Numismatic Literary Guild's award for best series of articles in 2002 for his history of Irish coinage during the Wars of the Roses that appeared in *World Coin News*. In 1997 he contributed a weekly column on economic and social justice for *Últimas Noticias*, the largest daily newspaper in Uruguay. His daily blog, "The Just Third Way," is read in more than fifty countries.

His published works include *In Defense of Human Dignity* (2008), *Supporting Life: The Case for a Pro-Life Economic Agenda* (2010), *The Restoration of Property* (2012), and *The Political Animal* (2014). He has also published *So Much Generosity* (2013), a compendium of essays on the fiction of Nicholas Cardinal Wiseman, John Henry Cardinal Newman, and Msgr. Robert Hugh Benson.

An alumnus of the Notre Dame Glee Club, Mr. Greaney lives in Falls Church, Virginia, where he is a member of the Washington Men's Camerata and sings with the St. Thomas More Cathedral Choir.

Advertisement
A CESJ Economic Justice Classic

A PLEA *for* Peasant Proprietors

With the Outlines of a Plan for Their Establishment in Ireland

By William Thomas Thornton, C.B.
Foreword by Michael D. Greaney, CPA, MBA

During the Great Famine in Ireland (1846-1852), William Thornton proposed that unused land be purchased by the government and leased or sold on credit to families that would put it into production. In this way funds spent on famine relief would be turned from an expenditure into an investment, jobs would be created, and the benefits of widespread capital ownership would accrue to individuals, families, and the nation.

Originally published in 1848, this newly annotated and indexed edition of *A Plea for Peasant Proprietors* was prepared from Thornton's 1874 revision includes a foreword that examines a new framework for solving the global financial crisis, financing economic growth, and enabling every child, woman, and man to become an owner of productive capital, as well as appendices explaining topical references and the political and economic environment within which Thornton worked.

Paperback • 364 pages • ISBN 978-0-944997-10-9
Economic Justice Media

$25.00 (U.S.)   £20.00 (U.K.)

Advertisement
Just Third Way Edition

FREEDOM UNDER GOD

By Fulton J. Sheen
PH.D., D.D., LITT.D., LL.D.

In 1940, on the eve of the United States entry into World War II, the late Fulton J. Sheen (1895-1979) published *Freedom Under God*. This new, annotated "Just Third Way Edition" of a neglected classic includes an in-depth foreword, as well as a bibliography and index not included in the original.

While *Freedom Under God* addresses the loss of true freedom throughout the world, Sheen's special concern was freedom of religion. This is under increasing attack today. Individual life as well as marriage and the family are also in grave danger as the State continues to expand its power to fill the vacuum left by the growing powerlessness of ordinary people.

Speaking to people of all faiths and philosophies, albeit from a "Catholic" perspective, then-Monsignor Sheen traced the rise of totalitarian State power in the first half of the 20th century to the fact that fewer and fewer people in America and throughout the world owned capital — what Sheen called "creative wealth." As Sheen argued, only widespread private property in capital has the capacity to restore the foundation of true freedom.

The world needs the wisdom of Fulton Sheen now more than ever.

Paperback • 264 pages • ISBN 978-0-944997-11-6
Economic Justice Media

$20.00 (U.S.) £14.00 (U.K.)

Other Just Third Way Publications from
Economic Justice Media

Norman G. Kurland, *et al.*, ***Capital Homesteading for Every Citizen*** (2004). A "policy manual" for politicians and civic leaders interested in the essential natural law principles for establishing and maintaining a just economic and political order. 231 pp. ISBN 978-0-944997-00-0, **$18.00**.

Michael D. Greaney, ***In Defense of Human Dignity*** (2008). A collection of articles first published in *Social Justice Review*, the official journal of the Central Bureau of the Catholic Central Union of America, this book helps us understand why so much of what is proposed as remedies for today's social, political, and economic crises cannot work. 303 pp. ISBN 978-0-94499-70-2, **$20.00**.

Michael D. Greaney, ***Supporting Life: The Case for a Pro-Life Economic Agenda*** (2010). Is there a common ground on which pro-life and pro-choice can meet? Yes — an economic proposal that has the potential to deliver a good life for everyone. 116 pp. ISBN 978-0-944997-05-5, **$10.00**.

Michael D. Greaney, ***The Restoration of Property: A Reexamination of a Natural Right*** (2011). Can we supplement or replace wages and welfare with ownership income? This book suggests abandoning dependence on Keynesian past savings and adopting a Kelsonian "pure credit" system, using future savings to finance widespread ownership of new capital without inflation or redistribution of existing wealth. 132 pp. ISBN 978-0-944997-07-9, **$10.00**.

Harold G. Moulton, ***The Formation of Capital*** (2010). Originally published in 1935 to present an alternative to the Keynesian New Deal, Moulton's book shows how a program of widespread capital ownership could be financed without reducing consumption or cutting pay. 232 pp. ISBN 978-0-944997-08-6, **$20.00**.

William Cobbett, ***The Emigrant's Guide*** (2008). In 1829, William Cobbett wrote a series of pamphlets to give advice to help people relocate to the "Land of Opportunity," where anyone could become an owner of income-generating productive capital. 240 pp. ISBN 978-0-944997-01-7, **$20.00**.

www.ingramcontent.com/pod-product-compliance
Lightning Source LLC
Chambersburg PA
CBHW021146160426
43194CB00007B/706